SPRING

Also Available in the
Spiritual Biography of the Season
Series

Edited by Gary Schmidt and Susan M. Felch

Summer: A Spiritual Biography of the Season
Illustrations by Barry Moser

Autumn: A Spiritual Biography of the Season
Illustrations by Mary Azarian

Winter: A Spiritual Biography of the Season
Illustrations by Barry Moser

Spring

A SPIRITUAL BIOGRAPHY
OF THE SEASON

EDITED BY GARY SCHMIDT
AND SUSAN M. FELCH

ILLUSTRATIONS BY MARY AZARIAN

Walking Together, Finding the Way
SKYLIGHT PATHS®
PUBLISHING
Woodstock, Vermont

HUNTINGTON CITY-TOWNSHIP
PUBLIC LIBRARY
200 W. Market Street
Huntington, IN 46750

Spring:
A Spiritual Biography of the Season

2006 First Printing
Text © 2006 by Gary Schmidt and Susan M. Felch
Illustrations © 2005 by Mary Azarian

All rights reserved. No part of this book may be reproduced or reprinted in any form or by any means, electronic or mechanical, including photocopying, recording, or by any information storage and retrieval system, without permission in writing from the publisher.

For information regarding permission to reprint material from this book, please write or fax your request to Skylight Paths Publishing, Permissions Department, at the address / fax number listed below, or e-mail your request to permissions@skylightpaths.com.

Pages 313–317 constitute a continuation of this copyright page.

Library of Congress Cataloging-in-Publication Data
Spring : a spiritual biography of the season / edited by Gary Schmidt and Susan M. Felch ; Illustrations by Mary Azarian.
p. cm.
Includes bibliographical references.
ISBN 1-59473-114-4
1. Spring—Religious aspects. 2. Seasons—Religious aspects. I. Schmidt, Gary D. II. Felch, Susan M., 1951–III. Azarian, Mary.

BL590.S67 2006
261.5'5—dc22
2005032993

10   9   8   7   6   5   4   3   2   1

Manufactured in the United States of America

Jacket Design: Tim Holtz

SkyLight Paths is creating a place where people of different spiritual traditions come together for challenge and inspiration, a place where we can help each other understand the mystery that lies at the heart of our existence.

SkyLight Paths sees both believers and seekers as a community that increasingly transcends traditional boundaries of religion and denomination—people wanting to learn from each other, walking together, finding the way.

Skylight Paths, "Walking Together, Finding the Way" and colophon are trademarks of LongHill Partners, Inc., registered in the U.S. Patent and Trademark Office.
Walking Together, Finding the Way
Published by SkyLight Paths Publishing
A Division of LongHill Partners, Inc.
Sunset Farm Offices, Route 4, P.O. Box 237
Woodstock, VT 05091
Tel (802) 457-4000   Fax (802) 457-4004
www.skylightpaths.com

For John Blake Schmidt,
awakening to the eternal resurrections of spring
—G. S.

For John Foos,
who first awakened me to words and
the world
—S. M. F.

SPRING

The faint silvery warblings heard over the partially bare and moist fields from the bluebird, the song sparrow, and the red-wing, as if the last flakes of winter tinkled as they fell.

Henry David Thoreau

CONTENTS

Contents

PREFACE

Writing at age eight while living in Concord, Massachusetts, Louisa May Alcott gave over her first crafted poem to the season of spring. It was called "To the First Robin," and perhaps does not bear very strong evidence of the skills Alcott would later acquire.

> *Welcome, welcome, little stranger,*
> *Fear no harm, and fear no danger;*
> *We are glad to see you here,*
> *For you sing "Sweet Spring is near."*
>
> *Now the white snow melts away;*
> *Now the flowers blossom gay:*
> *Come dear bird and build your nest,*
> *For we love our robin best.*

The images of the poem are rather familiar and expected—and perhaps no season conjures up the clichéd image as spring does. The snow melting away, the new flowers, the appearance of the robin, the building of nests—they are all here, just as we might expect. And everything is set in a secure world, where winter snows have ended: "Fear no harm, and fear no danger."

It is tempting and lovely and winsome and charming to see spring in this guise. Winter frosts are gone; everything is green and yellow; butterflies are flying; robins with their red breasts have returned with the warm spring rains; and everywhere there are crocuses and daffodils and tulips.

Spring is the season of returning light and life, and perhaps therein lies cause for much of the hope and confidence that it suggests. And so it is not surprising to find this season associated with gladness of heart, with joy.

> *My beloved spake, and said unto me, Rise up my*
> *love, my fair one, and come away.*
> *For, lo, the winter is past, the rain is over and gone;*
> *The flowers appear on the earth; the time of the*
> *singing of birds is come, and the voice of the tur-*
> *tle is heard in our land;*
> *The fig tree putteth forth her green figs, and the vines*
> *with the tender grape give a good smell. Arise,*
> *my love, my fair one, and come away.*

These words from the Song of Solomon suggest the rising up of new love. The following passage, written by the journalist Henry Timrod while surveying the destruction in Columbia, South Carolina, immediately following the Civil War, suggests the rising up of new hope and determination.

> [Spring] covers our devastated courts with images of renovation in the shape of flowers; she hangs once more in our blasted gardens the Jessamine; in the streets, she kindles the maple like a beacon announcing peace; and from amidst the charred and blackened ruins of once happy home, she pours through the mouth of her favorite musician, the mocking-bird, a song of hope and joy. What is the lesson which she designs by these means to convey? It may be summed in a single sentence—forgetfulness of the past, effort in the present, and trust for the future!

This hope comes from a man who had fiercely espoused a cause now lost, who had to hide in Charleston during Sherman's occupation, since his fiery editorials had made him a danger to the Union cause. But in the new season, everything seems to change.

The season of spring evokes, perhaps more than any other season, a sense of movement and of change. When Samuel Johnson in his *Dictionary of the English Language* (1755) came to define *spring*, he began with "the vernal season," though even in this he suggested movement: "the season of the year when plants begin to vegetate and rise." All of the other nuanced meanings that he supplied for the noun form of *spring* also involve movement: an elastic body or force, an active power, a leap or bound, a leak or start of a plank, an issue of water as in a fountain, a source by which something is supplied, a rise or beginning, a cause or origin. Is it too much of a pun to imagine that when Johnson's friend Alexander Pope wrote "Hope springs eternal in the human breast" he meant to convey a whisper of the season in the verb form?

The movement from the white frosts of winter to the green risings of spring has served as a powerful metaphor for physical and spiritual renewal. In this sense, it is truly the season for joy and hope, for the movements that it involves are so all-encompassing and pervasive. It suggests the stirring and waking of lethargic and hibernating souls. It suggests outward growth in its vernal risings and inner growth in its renewals. It recalls the human social activities of pilgrimage and dance with its predictable patterning and rhythms. It leads us to celebration in its fecund and fertile energy. "What is all this juice and all this joy," asks Gerard Manley Hopkins in his "Spring"; whatever it is, he concludes, it is "Most, O maid's child, thy choice and worthy the winning."

But in her "Spring," the Victorian poet Christina Rossetti suggests that harm and danger have not passed with the coming of spring, as Alcott suggests, but are, in fact, implicit in the season. The "tips of tender green," which are sprouting now, she writes, remind us "of the hidden life" that is "nursed in its grave by Death"—this is the opening of the poem. For a few lines, Rossetti lapses into Alcott's sweet world. "Blows the thaw-wind pleasantly," she writes, and there is "young grass" and "young leaves" and "curled-headed ferns" and singing and pairing birds. "There is no time like Spring, / When life's alive in everything," she claims, seeming to be thoroughly filled with the joys of the season until she repeats, but with a variation, the same line in the final stanza: "There is no time like Spring, / Like Spring that passes by." The life alive in everything, she notes, will again pierce the sod, though in decay. All that is now newly born, is "now / hastening to die." This is the final word of the robin—quite a distinction from Alcott's poem.

Rossetti's is an adult poem, with an adult sensibility that has learned through experience that spring does indeed bring with it renewal, growth, rebirth, and resurrection—all the sweet images that so quickly come to mind. But the season also initiates a cycle that inevitably brings us back to winter, where what has been born and reborn will hasten to die.

Hopkins, too, senses this pattern of spring; death is necessary, and it will come and bring with it darkness and cold. "Have, get, before it cloy, / Before it cloud," the poet advises us about spring—"before it sour with sinning." It will, it must, sour. But unlike Rossetti, Hopkins will not give that knowledge the last word. Instead, the season—and all that it entails—is held up for the winning of God. Spring calls us to recognize the value, authenticity, and precious worth of life itself.

The season of spring thus couches the resurrection from the dead that lies at the center of Easter, the escape from disaster into new life that is implicit in Purim, and the prayers of the Vedas for fertility and peace.

> May there be peace in the higher regions; may there be peace in the firmament; may there be peace on earth. May the waters flow peacefully; may the herbs and plants grow peacefully; may all the divine powers bring us peace. The supreme Lord is peace. Shanti—Shanti—Shanti!

In these spring celebrations, ceremonies, and prayers, the newly born life is closely associated with the divine. It is appropriate, then, that one fifteenth-century Indian prayer from the Hindu poet Sur-das uses a striking spring image to suggest the loving relationship between humanity and God: "As the cow keeps by her calf, so art Thou ever with Thine own."

It may be that spring reminds us that life emerges from death and must one day descend back into the earth. But it also reminds us that life is resilient, that life is precious, that though we are needy and frail creatures, we are loved, and our needs are constantly being filled in graceful ways. Though we rush from renewal to cloying loss and sin, we can at least live deliberately in contexts of joy and hope.

The Shaker tradition captures this sense of celebration, gratitude, and awareness in its hymnody. Coming from a close connection between work, land, and spirit, late nineteenth-century Shaker hymns suggest the ways in which the Shaker community endeavored to create a unity in its life—a fact suggested even by the pronouns used in these hymns, which are always plural and communal. In these hymns, spring is celebrated for its annual return: "Our God whose wisdom made the earth, / Guides the rolling year" and "The seasons in their order come and go." This faithful and repeated pattern leads to a certainty in the beneficence of God and spirit: Because the seasons run in their order, we can look toward the fulfillment of our planning; there will be a harvest. This, in turn, suggests the metaphoric quality of spring. Even as we plant and await the promised "fruitage," we can toil with love for God and expect that work and truth "to the spirit will return again."

These assertions of spiritual certitude are couched in expressions of real joy at the physical beauty of the returning springtime. Bud, blossom, light, flower, merry birds, and rippling streams all strike the eye and lead, in the Shaker vision, quite directly to joy. And so each hymn is sung to a quick rhythm—with more sixteenth notes than one might find in many religious traditions—with one exception: the words "happy springtime" in the refrain for "Spring is Coming" are sung during rests in the musical accompaniment. It is as though the hymn writer wanted the singers to pay attention during the busy-ness of the melody, during the busy-ness of their lives.

Spring is the season that simultaneously calls us to celebration and to a sober sense of gratitude for the time that we have been given. The grace of renewal should lead to gratitude for the newness, and it should lead to an acute awareness of our need for renewal.

PART ONE

Stirrings

INTRODUCTION

After a time of winter—after a time of grief, of discontent, of mourning, of darkness that is emotional or physical—after such a time, spring comes. It tends to come upon us slowly, subtly, as if it had sent out spies beforehand. You are mourning a loved one who has meant more to you than the moon, and your days are counted by sorrows; then one afternoon, who knows how, you realize suddenly that for a moment, you have been happy; maybe you have even awakened that morning and sorrow was not the first thing to fill your mind. You are a cancer patient and have battled the effects of chemotherapy for a year; then one morning you wake up and realize, with a start, that you feel well, that, in fact, for several days now, wellness has been stealing upon you. Or you have struggled with unhappiness that has tinged all the elements of your life, but suddenly a moment comes in—only a moment, but still a moment—that gives you a glimpse of a different country, and you can imagine being happy again.

Spring begins not with a kettledrum, but with the small notes of the piccolo. It whispers itself into our awareness, as we begin to notice that it hasn't snowed for a time, that the days seem a little longer, that there is the occasional blue sky. We find ourselves thinking about the garden, and wondering whether the bulbs will emerge again. We decide not to take the crosstown bus today, because it's just warm enough for a good walk to work where, that afternoon, we will crack open the window to finally let in some fresh air. We notice the first crocus in the park and the red breast of the first robin.

There is no doubt that the life of the spirit can have its sudden and powerful moments—its great joys and calamities, its ecstasies and darknesses. But we do not live on the peaks of ecstasies or in the caverns of calamities; we are more like Peter, Susan, and Lucy in *The Lion, the Witch, and the Wardrobe,* who, when the White Witch's eternal winter is ended by the coming of Aslan, mark the signs of the coming spring, and then end the day "feeling very dreamy and quiet inside as one does when one is coming to the end of a long day in the open." Changes are often quiet, like spring, beginning deep down, as small stirrings toward something new.

In her enormously popular gardening book, *Wood and Garden* (1899), the Edwardian writer Gertrude Jekyll brought her observant eye to the description of a formal garden in March—the time when a garden is just beginning to stir.

> A kind of sullen dullness pervades all plant life. Sweet-scented shrubs do not give off their fragrance; even the woodland moss and earth and dead leaves withhold their sweet, nutty scent. The surface of the earth has an arid, infertile look; a slight haze of an ugly grey takes the colour out of objects in middle distance, and seems to rob the flowers of theirs, or to put them out of harmony with all things around. But a day comes, or, perhaps, a warmer night, when the wind, now breathing gently from the south-west, puts new life into all growing things.

This passage begins in a garden still subdued by winter; it ends with the first stirrings of spring when the growing things—which are already there—are given "new life." We are reminded that spring does not so much create as re-create. Spring insists that we begin with life.

But where do we end? Spring is that time when perennial gardens begin to emerge, and we watch the first shoots and see in our imaginations the full plants. But will they flourish? Will we have time to keep the weeds at bay? Will they have to be divided? The vegetable gardener setting out seeds and young plants imagines a fertile and well-ordered vegetable garden, yielding so much produce that she'll have to fob off the zucchini onto neighbors. But will the garden match those expectations?

The stirrings of spring prompt expectations and hopes, but also a measure of humility because who can know what lies in front of us? Uncertainty is part of being human, finite and mortal as we are, and we cannot know all the ways that spring's renewal will lead us. Jim Heynen, in *The One-Room Schoolhouse: Stories About the Boys* (1994), pictures the coming of spring to the youngest of the boys in a Midwest farm family.

> But for the youngest boy spring really started in the air, com-ing to him not as clean, fresh-air smells but as thick, rich smells that were neither sweet nor foul. Breathing the full odors of spring left the boy teetering, unsure of where he was in the picture he saw around him. It was like a big body close to him, sweating, but he couldn't see or touch it. Something more is coming, he felt, something more than I am ready for or know what to do with.

The stirrings of spring, its enlivening of what has lain dormant, is exciting and thrilling in its renewals, and perhaps also frightening in its implications.

But perhaps we hardly pay attention to those implications, though they lurk only slightly beneath the surface. We are creatures made for joy, and the rhythm of our lives suggests that joy follows sadness: "Weeping may endure for a night, but joy cometh in the morning," promises the Psalmist, and "they that sow in tears shall reap in joy." We are creatures made for joy, and spring reminds us of that inheritance.

"Spring is coming," the Shaker hymn reminds us, and with that announcement, renewal and all of its joys are promised. Writers such as Jane Kenyon, Molly Wolf, and Harry Thurston point to spring's reminder that we begin with stirrings only; there is still mud to deal with and the ice hasn't fully broken away. But Nathaniel Hawthorne points to the buds; Thomas Wentworth Higginson calls to mind the warming days of April; Allen Young evokes the first sounds of spring, the spring peepers; Lucy Larcom looks to the early flowers; and Nancy Stringfellow reminds us that "the tansy is shouting hallelujias of joy / For Easter coming."

On the first warm Saturday in Boston, it seems that everyone in the city pours out onto the Common. Setters sprint after Frisbees, their red coats against the green of the grass and the yellow of the daffodils. Skateboarders weave back and forth between cones that someone has set up to follow the slant of Beacon Hill. The Frog Pond is clear of ice, and some children dabble at the clear water. The Swan Boats are being painted. The first tennis players are out, their strokes rusty from winter disuse. The breeze is warm, and it carries the songs of birds newly back from the south. The chimes of Park Street Church sound.

The stirrings of spring are the stirrings of the heart and soul toward joy.

A Shaker Hymn

"SPRING IS COMING"

Oh, list to the jubilant music,
That cometh from mountain and plain,
And this the sweet song that is ringing—
The springtime is coming again.

Refrain:
The springtime, happy springtime is coming again,
We've caught the joyous refrain;
We'll sing with its myriad voices—
The Springtime is coming again.

The hum of the stream from the hillside,
That's broken its cold icy chain,
Is murmuring the anthem of gladness—
The springtime is coming again.

Our hearts would be glad with the springtime,
And banish life's sorrow and pain,
And join with the chorus of voices—
The springtime is coming again.

7

For sure as the May opes the blossom,
And sunshine succeedeth the rain,
Hope singeth this glad song of promise—
Life's springtime will flower again.

Jane Kenyon

"Mud Season"

*J*ane *Kenyon's poems often record the seasonal changes at Eagle Pond Farm, where she lived for the last twenty years of her life. "Mud Season" invokes the earliest stirrings of spring during the cold, damp March days that are beginning their escape from winter's grasp. The migratory and hibernating animals quietly return to the land-scape; birds resume their natural diet; flower stalks, not yet in bloom, push through the snow. Such stirrings, for Kenyon, take the form of an ascent: the aspara-gus pushes up through the mud,*

> *The migratory and hibernating animals quietly return to the landscape; birds resume their natural diet; flower stalks, not yet in bloom, push through the snow.*

the crocus lifts up its still-green head, and the soul takes its first shaky steps onto Mount Purgatory—eyes and hope fixed upon the "exaltation of pur-ple" that the resurrection promises.

Mud Season

Here in purgatory bare ground
is visible, except in shady places
where snow prevails.

Still, each day sees
the restoration of another animal:
a sparrow, just now a sleepy wasp;
and, at twilight, the skunk
pokes out of the den,
anxious for mates and meals....

On the floor of the woodshed
the coldest imaginable ooze,
and soon the first shoots
of asparagus will rise,
the fingers of Lazarus....

Earth's open wounds—where the plow
gouged the ground last November—
must be smoothed; some sown
with seed, and all forgotten.

Now the nuthatch spurns the suet,
resuming its diet of flies, and the mesh
bag, limp and greasy, might be taken
down.

Beside the porch step
the crocus prepares an exaltation
of purple, but for the moment
holds its tongue....

Molly Wolf

FROM *WHITE CHINA:* FINDING THE DIVINE IN THE EVERYDAY

In White China, *Molly Wolf sets about the task of trying to perceive the holy within the mundane. This is no easy task during mud season, a season that Wolf locates in Ontario, but which is familiar to most regions. It is a time of transition, when the skies are bleak and the ground just a mess with the remnants of winter, without the hardy solidity of high summer. It is too late to shovel anymore; the snow comes down as slush, and the frost melts quickly. But it is too early to plant, because the ground is too wet. Spring is the season between seasons, Wolf suggests, and we are impatient for it to be over.*

> *We* can have hope, we can heal, and we can grow, because time does move on. That is the lesson of spring.

Therein lies the spiritual value of the season—because mud season and springtime do come to an end, and summer appears. In the mud and the bleakness lie buried the fact that time does move on; if it seems too slow, or if the season seems hopeless, then we must look not to the large and glorious things around us—the skies, the trees—but instead, beneath our feet, where the new season is already stirring with weeds and grasses. We can have hope, we can heal, and we can grow, because time does move on. That is the lesson of spring.

FROM *WHITE CHINA: FINDING THE DIVINE IN THE EVERYDAY*

Where I live, in southeastern Ontario, we have not one season but at least six and possibly seven, to wit: spring, summer, fall, mud season, winter (high and low), and mud season redux. The two mud seasons are preparatory inter-seasons, times when the landscape cools down for winter or begins, with what feels like infinite slowness, to warm up for spring.

Mud season actually only lasts for six to eight weeks, but it can feel endless—particularly spring mud season, because by that time we're all so totally fed up after winter. It can also be terribly hard on the soul, since the landscape is dun and gray and the weather tends to be overcast but uneventful.

But I have long since realized that mud season, properly considered, does have its virtues. Sometimes we need to be held in a space of quietness and non-event, a time of preparation. Mud season is a substantial vote against the "fun right now!" values shouted by the media and popular culture. It is a witness to slowness, groundedness, and living with the moment, however unlovely the moment may seem. It begs for patience, a virtue most of us need to cultivate anyway, and for a richer understanding of how this earth really works. So I've learned to treasure mud season—at least occasionally. When I get fed up with it, I find there's usually some God-Stuff lurking under last fall's leaves, if I'm willing to look.

I am sure that somewhere, possibly in the Smithsonian or some other highly respected institution, there resides a clock that ticks the days precisely, each second exactly measured and tabulated. To this clock each second is exactly the length of that second, each day's count of seconds and minutes and hours duly recorded, with allowances being made for slight natural irregularities in the turn of the Earth or her orbit around the Sun. Time, to this clock, is a steady procession, as well defined and amenable to measure as a finely chiseled chunk of granite, as definite as diamond.

But to the soul, time doesn't work like that. It's not definite and adamantine; it's more like yarn, or perhaps even Silly Putty, stretching out or contracting depending on what's going on. In spring mud season, for example, time stretches out in a sagging wobbly loop, stretches almost to breaking point sometimes. Each hour seems day-long; each day seems to go on for a week. This is because we are all fed up to the hind teeth with Canadian winter and we want spring and we want it *now*. But it isn't now. It isn't for at least a couple-three more weeks, with any luck. Until then, it's mud season.

I wonder if it felt thus to Jesus in the desert—that each day of hunger and loneliness, each night of cold, seemed endlessly extended, time stretching out until it sagged. I'd like to believe he was too close to God to notice, that instead of time dragging along it whipped by as he walked in companionship with his Abba. I know how time can stop altogether at rare moments, and then you know that you are with your Creator and wish only to be there for eternity. I imagine this is what Jesus experienced. I wish I could be that way too—so wrapped up in my Creator that such irritants as cold rain and whippy winds are irrelevant, or at least tolerable in the certainty of glory. But that's not where I am right now. So time stretches, and the mud season days feel long.

But looking back, I find a pattern that is profoundly comforting. I can remember any number of mud seasons; we have two a year after all, and they add up. I can remember any number of periods of suffering, if I flip back through the calendar. I know now that with healing I can revisit how I felt in those fits of anger or suffering or grief. But although I can remember in full detail, with the color of recollected emotion, I find I can't really revisit those times in any immediate sense. They used to own me; now they don't. I can't (and wouldn't want to if I could) re-enter the experience and *be* there. With real healing, suffering, like mud season, finally gets left behind.

What I can remember with immediacy and vividness are other moments, moments of blessedness. I can remember moments that, as I was in them, I wrapped carefully in memory and stowed away, like wrapping something in amber, so that I could pick them up and return to them fully whenever I wanted. Sitting with my first baby in the Public Gardens in Halifax; walking through the woods in the mountains I loved; standing in the kitchen being jumped by joy for no reason whatsoever. In these moments, time didn't stretch; it stopped altogether. A very different matter.

You can't arrange these moments; they simply arrive when it's possible to experience them, if you're willing to stop for them. There are times when, for whatever reason, they aren't on the possibility list. Too much stress, I find, and I'm going to do mud season-type time-stretching, not those flickers of pure eternity. Not because God isn't out there waiting to connect, but because I'm in no condition to entertain him.

Mud season is something that a person has to get through without whining too much, knowing that each day will end, and each day does bring you a little closer to spring, although it doesn't feel that way. It's easier to believe this about the season itself, because the calendar is reassuring and experience says that it really is only a matter of time.

It's harder to believe that the soul's mud season will end in time, and that joy does wait, especially if mud season has been going on for far too long. But as I tell myself over and over, it's only a matter of doing the work of healing and giving it time. Time may seem to stretch to threadlike extensibility in mud season, but it does pass. Time only stands still in joy.

Barbara Hurd

"MARGINALIA" FROM
STIRRING THE MUD

For Barbara Hurd, the stirrings of spring begin in Finzel Swamp, a hidden space in the Appalachian Mountains still marked by retreating glaciers and the frozen wastes of the Arctic Circle. It is precisely this March coldness, this desolate northern-ness that makes her think of the swamp as the "marginalia of some creator who mused for a while on the edge of the page, then dropped the pen and headed north."

Finzel Swamp invites meditation on the meaning of such edges, the blurry boundaries that divide—and unite—swamp and forest, dry land and bog. In the natural world, such marginal places teem with life, the vegetation a complex mixture of trees and water lilies, although their very indistinctness makes human beings uneasy and nervous. We like our surroundings, and our lives, to be more orderly, more rational, more under our own control.

Margins are a good place to doodle, to relax our logical minds and let the tendrils of imagination run rampant.

But margins are a good place to doodle, to relax our logical minds and let the tendrils of imagination run rampant. Perhaps, Hurd suggests, margins have much to teach us. Perhaps we see more clearly when we look obliquely, sideways, from the edge. Perhaps our soul is best stirred in the spring by the swamp.

"MARGINALIA"

I love a broad margin to my life.... Sometimes I sat from sunrise til noon ... in undisturbed solitude and stillness.... I grew in those seasons like corn in the night.
—Henry David Thoreau

It is March and I have left the tidy community of Finzel perched on the ridge of Little Savage Mountain, left its black roads, its tavern, the Community Fire Hall, and small, dark houses, each with its plume of smoke rising into the winter air, turned east and dropped into the white valley of Finzel Swamp. I have walked out of order and certainty and into the margins of a land still shadowed by the Arctic.

Finzel Swamp is a relict community, formed thousands of years ago when the icy tongues of glaciers pushed Canadian flora and fauna south for hundreds of miles. When the glaciers receded some ten thousand years ago, most of the boreal plants and animals migrated slowly back with them. But not here. Here they stayed, the tamaracks and black calla, in a poorly drained bowl perched high in the Maryland Appalachians, protected by the even higher ridges on either side. Here in this frozen valley, now owned by the Nature Conservancy, there is no asphalt, no stop sign, no sidewalk, just the wide, white space, pathless, interrupted only by the frozen etchings of alder and black spruce, the scribbled, heart-shaped tracks of deer, the marginalia of some creator who mused for a while on the edge of the page, then dropped the pen and headed north, leaving us to decipher the notations.

I am standing on the frozen surface of the swamp, surrounded by the just-emerging tips of skunk cabbage, a plant that can work on March snows the same way my mug of hot tea does if I set it down on a snow-covered log. The frozen hoods of the skunk cabbage spathe locked in ice just a few inches below the surface begin to breathe in midwinter, and the heat produced by this respiration can actually melt the surrounding snow. Though they say its temperature can be twenty degrees higher than the surrounding air, I have never tried warming my hands over that thick nub of a plant shouldering through the surface. I am too plagued by the memory of my father's decree that we children should weed every last leaf of it out of the streambed that bordered our yard. I hated everything about this chore—wading among fleshy, purple-splotched spathes that rose like hooded bruises, wrapping my small hands around a clump of leaves, large as elephant ears, the fetid smell of mangled green. I know that skunk cabbage has its benign moments—it shelters the nests of warblers, soothes toothaches and whooping cough, and calms the seizures of epileptics, has even, some say, graced dining room tables—but I cannot rid myself of the image of its thick root, like a pale arm plunged into the wet ground, the fist on the buried end tightening its clench around some iron bar of survival each time we tugged. I cannot forget the banks heaped with its yanked and withered leaves, the streambed tidy at last. Or that blurry sense of loss.

Tracks in the untidy edges offer hope, the promise that the page might yield something beyond its justified margins. All my life I have been stumbling over asterisks embedded in texts, slipping out of paragraphs and searching for the footnote, combing the margins for some small note of explanation, the next clue in the treasure hunt, the translation of a word I didn't understand. Always there is the invitation to lift our eyes from the tidy print of our lives and look to the bottom of the page, the end of the chapter, for the source of some idea, for the elaboration of a theory too hastily mentioned. Always there is the chance to trace the path of a creature like the star-nosed mole with its twenty-two pink fingerlike projections blooming on the end of its nose. Crammed with nerves and blood vessels, these extremely sensitive tentacles probe and shimmy through the muck, foraging like an asterisk.

When the German poet Rilke tells us to leave our houses and enter the enormous space outside, surely what he means is to follow the asterisk to the bottom of the page, to drop to our knees in algae, push hands into the fringed and seepy edges into which pieces of our lives have sunk, places where year after year the crust grows thin, too thin, finally, to mask the sense that underneath this unkempt border something else is breathing: the origins of our words, wiser afterthoughts, the whispered asides of the spirit. Viewed with suspicion and dread by many cultures for thousands of years, wetlands are habitats where the water table has bulged up close to the surface of the land or where poor drainage allows shallow water to linger for months or decades or hundreds of years. Technically, Finzel Swamp is a palustrine wetland—meaning marshy, but not associated with a river or lake. The presence of woody vegetation—trees and shrubs— makes Finzel a swamp. Not far from here, at the other end of the county, lies Cranesville Swamp, also palustrine, but more truly a bog, characterized by evergreen trees and a bog mat of sphagnum moss.

After weeks of cold, Finzel and Cranesville Swamps are both frozen. My boots crunch in the mud as I step between skunk cabbage tips and set off in a northeast direction, where the swamp is bordered by wooded hills. Whether bog or swamp, all wetlands have edges, rich strips where two hands clasp. On the edge, vegetation is always more varied, a mix of mature trees and grassland, or bog mat and shrubs, water lilies and spruce saplings. Browsing creatures and wind-carried seed cross over from one biotic community to another. The young are often raised along these edge zones where, for example, the forest on one side offers shelter and the open fields on the other offer food. These margins are places of transitions and diversity and abundance, one of the most highly trafficked places in the natural world. They are visited not only by creatures who normally inhabit one community or the other and occasionally cross over, but also by creatures known as "edge species," who have specifically adapted to spending their lives in this strip between two communities, which winds, wrinkled and bunched, like the imperfect and wavy seam at the waist of a full-skirted dress.

Humans don't seem to be this kind of edge species, and mostly we're not comfortable here. This margin is, after all, not the continental margin as we know it on summer beaches, where land and sea, in decent intervals, take turns on a tidal edge. Here there is only a constant and languid saturation. It looks as if someone has snapped a photo of a shallow lake and then another of a shrubby, welted, plant-tangled valley and forgotten to advance the film between shots. What you get is a double exposure. You stare at it, trying to separate one photo from the other, assigning this pool of water to the first photo, that clump of grass to the second. Everything is a tad blurry, including yourself as you crawl through both pictures at once.

Maybe our discomfort has something to do with the vulnerability of having an internal skeleton or with our deeply folded brain's hunger for tidy categories. I happened upon an article once by William Hammitt, a professor of wildland recreation, that describes researchers' attempts to figure out how to design boardwalks and trails in wetland areas. They wanted to know what would most appeal to visitors and so they measured their visual reactions to bogs. Either before or after a guided hike through a bog, visitors studied photographs of various bog scenes and then indicated how much they liked the scene in the photograph. What interests me most about this study is the comparatively low ratings visitors gave to photographs of the edges of bogs. Ecologically rich and diverse, that overlap of bog and forest habitats did not appeal to visitors, who found them "unreadable," having no focus and little coherence. This uneasiness is partly about lack of definition. It reminds me of creative writing students whose first drafts of poems are scribbled messes. "I don't know where this is going; nothing hangs together," they wail, and I urge them to slow down and stay where they're uncomfortable. I tell them "being on edge" is partly what good writing, especially poetry, is all about and I hope they never get used to it. I want them to move out of the places where they feel safe and secure, out of the centers of attention or power or knowledge, out of the center of an ideology, a class. I want them to creep to the edge, nervous and uneasy, to sit as long as they can in that margin between the known and the unknown.

According to Hammitt's research, the least preferred bog scene is the one depicting the open bog mat. In these photos, the bog mat looks like an ordinary field where you might find cows grazing, a couple of deer switching their tails as they raise their heads and watch you, an ordinary field ringed, in the distance, by low hills and dark forest. Yet the people rating the appeal of this scene knew all about deception. They knew any cow who ventured into the mat would sink to its knees, that what is most disorienting about a bog is not only its lack of ground but also its indistinct edges, which make it difficult to find the exact point where you left the forest and sloshed into its quaking belly, the point that, heading home now, you might want to aim for. Hammitt's researchers note this dilemma is easily solved: at the edge of the forest where you enter the bog, you tie a handkerchief. It's an agreement you make with yourself, that no matter how much wandering in tundralike habitat, no matter how disoriented you get keeping your eyes on your boots, making sure they emerge from the muck still laced to your feet, when you're ready to head home, you agree to recognize the bit of cloth you fastened on some spruce branch several hours ago.

It's an agreement you should think twice about, if only because handkerchiefs carry too much history of deception and forgetfulness. Think of Othello, spying Desdemona's handkerchief in Cassio's possession, agreeing yes, this is hers and therefore she must have been with him, her dying, innocent, in his murderous arms. Or Aegeus, waiting on the cliffs to see if the cloth tied to the top of Theseus's mast would be white, signaling his son's safe return from slaying the Minotaur, or black, signaling his death. Theseus, caught up in the revelry of triumphant homecoming, forgot to lower the black flag and haul up the white one, and his father, spying the dark flutter, hurled himself off the cliff. Whole families have been haunted by murder and suicide caused by putting too much significance on the location and color of a bit of cloth. You'd be better off forgetting about fabric. Things in the margins, including humans who wander there, are often on the brink of becoming something else, or someone else, whose memory may not include the significance of old markers.

Under a maple tree where the snow hasn't accumulated, a small hole, maybe two inches across, a tidy entrance. Chipmunk, I think. I picture them down there, half dozing in winter torpor, in their maze of underground tunnels, chambers for napping and eating, and wonder whether they raise their sleepy, tawny heads at the pound of my boots on their ceiling. What goes on in the margins is not always visible. Sometimes, of course, that's because the edges are teeming with what the center does not want to see—the homeless, the abused, the disenfranchised, whatever does not fit the current definitions of normal. We love high drama in this country, mountain peaks and soap operas. They offer us something to tilt our lives toward—that triumph of ascent, that heart-pounding eye-to-eye intensity, that feeling of being wildly alive. Our nature aesthetics sound like movie reviews: We thrill to the surprising twist in the road that reveals the vast panorama, the unexpected waterfall. We canonize beauty that can be framed on the walls, in the camera, or on the postcard.

To love a swamp, however, is to love what is muted and marginal, what exists in the shadows, what shoulders its way out of mud and scurries along the damp edges of what is most commonly praised. And sometimes its invisibility is a blessing. Swamps and bogs are places of transition and wild growth, breeding grounds, experimental labs where organisms and ideas have the luxury of being out of the spotlight, where the imagination can mutate and mate, send tendrils into and out of the water. It should come as no surprise that the most common carnivorous plants are found in wetlands. Here there is room for the thought not fully formed to stretch, roll over, poke its eyes above water. Here is the valley of split-pea soup where what floats like a chunk of ham might lift its meaty head out of the muck and haul itself onto the log next to you, blinking in the sunshine.

Away from the rigor of scrutiny and definition, the need for distinction falls away. Drifting deepens into reverie. You lie half asleep at four A.M. while your life as you know it unravels, plays footsie with some other life. You slip toward the borders of yourself, toward the obscure blooming in the creases, into the forgotten pockets against whose seams your fingers have fretted and chafed until threads finally thin and your fingers plunge into dark, invisible territory of thigh-skin. You drift in a bog as you do in those moments just after sex, everything matted and moist, when you don't know if you and your partner are one body or two. Hours later you crawl out of bed and examine your feet, searching for mud, some smudgy evidence of having traipsed through a place where there is no such thing as ground, where sphagnum moss, curly and limp, holds the lingering twilight the way it holds water. You recall a line of poetry and you know why poets love that white space at the end of a line, how that space invites you to forgo the usual eye-dropping to the left and down to the next line. How it invites you, instead, to launch yourself into that white margin of imagination, where the countryside lies uncharted, wild habitat at the edge of civilized thinking, where the mind is rampant with phrases *(the opposite of stones, the sound of emerald green)* and you feel a certain exhilaration in the tangle and thicket of plant and word, image and water, the mind curling and leaping at the far edge of itself, tiny tendrils of imagination twining their way down stems of waterweeds, cartwheeling across cranberry mats and sundew, never minding the here-and-there unexpected plunge into tea-colored water. At the edge, an open mind leans out so far it brushes the landscape, like the hand of a blind person exploring a patch of grass. This is the edge of a mind foraging through the edge of a landscape. Daddy long-legs and salamanders clamber between your fingers; lichen-covered rocks settle into the folds of your mind.

The paradox is that to see clearly, you must learn to see obliquely. You must look ahead and, at the same time, widen your peripheral vision so that it extends not just in great arcs around your head, but over the edge, into the margins where the visible and invisible, dreams and reality, land and water, emptiness and profusion mingle.

The sublime is like poetry; it will not be caught or chased down. It exists at the edge of things, in the vast margins, like a wild animal. The trick is to learn how to wander there without intention, to float eye-to-eye with fringed orchids, to make yourself available to what lives there, whether it is the rare bittern or a poem or the whole damp and water-lilied world.

The imagination loves freedom first, and then form. And there is an odd kind of freedom in the fringes that comes, in part, from jettisoning our love of function. For centuries, so much in a swamp seemed useless—all this muck and dead trees and algae—and lack of function in our culture means lack of value. *What's it for?* we want to know. *What does it do?* One of the reasons we are now beginning to preserve wetlands, such as Finzel, has, of course, to do with learning their function. We can tick off their benefits on our fingers: they help control flooding or they filter toxic waste, both of which have to do with our physical and economic health.

But what kind of cultural enlightenment will it take for us to freely say that we value this or that because it is beautiful, because it nourishes the imagination, because it is good for the soul? How much longer until we grant ourselves carte blanche to move beyond the neatly printed page into the margins strewn with skunk cabbage, the twilight world of dozing she-bears, to drift in the liminal space between what is and what could be? And after that, what kind of handkerchief knotted at the edge of the familiar could possibly lead you back the same way you came in?

Lucy Larcom

A GATHERING OF POEMS

*B*orn *in Beverly, Massachusetts, in 1824, Lucy Larcom began her life in somewhat dire circumstances. She was the eighth of nine children, and at the death of her father, her mother moved to the newly built manufacturing town of Lowell, where Lucy went to work at the looms. It was, by her own account, an entrance into her vocation as a writer. She began to write for the* Lowell Offering, *the journal of the mill girls. During the Civil War she continued to write poetry for weekly papers, and soon afterward became the editor for* Our Young Folks, *a children's periodical. The fame associated with this successful magazine helped her to publish a series of very popular collections of her poems, with* Wild Roses of Cape Ann *capturing most perfectly her ability to render her surroundings in poetic form.*

In her eyes, the natural world is very much alive in the Emersonian sense, sending rich and thick messages to us through its beauty.

In her day, Larcom was considered one of the Fireside Poets whose works were memorized and recited in so many New England schoolrooms and at town orations. Her work carries the sentimentality and overt didacticism that have made those poets unfashionable today, and some of her imagery is predictable and almost clichéd by contemporary standards. Still, Larcom used the remarkable precision of her eye for the natural world to convey powerfully a scene out of the New England countryside, her personal sense of piety and devotion endowing scenes with rich spiritual connotations. In her eyes, the natural world is very much alive in the Emersonian sense, sending rich and thick messages to us through its beauty.

Between Winter and Spring

*That weary time that comes between
The last snow and the earliest green!
One barren clod the wide fields lie,
And all our comfort is the sky.*

*We know the sap is in the tree,—
That life at buried roots must be;
Yet dreary is the earth we tread,
As if her very soul were dead.*

*Before the dawn the darkest hour,
The blank and chill before the flower!
Beauty prepares this background gray
Whereon her loveliest tints to lay.*

*Ah, patience! ere we dream of it,
Spring's fair new gospel will be writ.
Look up! good only can befall,
While heaven is at the heart of all!*

Entangled

Birds among the budding trees,
  Blossoms on the ringing ground:
Light from those? or song from these?
  Can the tangle be unwound?

For the bluebird's warbled note,
  Violet-odors hither flung;
And the violet curved her throat,
  Just as if she sat and sung.

Dandelions dressed in gold,
  Give out echoes clear and loud,
To the oriole's story, told
  With gay poise and gesture proud.

And the swaying yellow-bird,
  Trilling, thrills their hollow stems,
Until every root is stirred,
  Under their dropped diadems.

Swallows thicken through the air,—
  Curve and drift of plumy brown,—
Wafting, showering everywhere,
  Melody's light seed-notes down.

Beauty, music on the earth;
  Music, beauty in the sky;
Guess the mystery of their birth!
  All the haunting what and why.

Nature weaves a marvellous braid:
    Tints and tones how deftly blent!
Who unwinds the web she made?
    Thou, who wearest her wise content.

Wrapped within her beauty's fold,
    Of her song thyself a part,
Plainly are her secrets told
    Unto thee, O pure of heart!

Apple-Blossoms

Apple-blossoms, budding, blowing,
    In the soft May air:
Cups with sunshine overflowing,—
Flakes of fragrance, drifting, snowing,
    Showering everywhere!

Fairy promises, outgushing
    From the happy trees!
White souls into love-light blushing,—
Heavenly thoughts to utterance rushing,—
    Are ye not like these?

Such an overflow of sweetness
    Needs the heart of spring;
In her wealth of bloom is meetness,
Though to the ripe fruit's completeness
    All she may not bring.

Words are more than idle seeming;
    Blossoms of good-will.
What she would do, Love is dreaming;
What she can, ashamed of scheming,
    Cramped and stinted still.

Apple-blossoms, billowy brightness
    On the tide of May,
Oh, to wear your rose-touched whiteness!
Flushing into bloom, with lightness
    To give life away!

Would You?

Could you keep the tints of spring
    On the woods in the misty brightness,—
Keep the half-veiled boughs a-swing
    To the linnet's flitting lightness,—
Through the birch leaves' rippling green
    Hold the maple-keys from dropping,—
On the sward with May-showers clean,
    Cheat the violets into stopping;

Could you make the rosebud's lips
    Vow to be a bud forever,—
From the sedges' wavering tips
    Bid the dewy pearl drop never;
Could you make the sunrise hour
    For a lifetime overbrood you;
Could you change the year's full dower
    For its first faint promise—would you?

Though a bubbling quaff,
    Fresh from sunny mounts of morning.
When the world is all a laugh,
    And a welcome without warning;—
At life's Cana-feast, the guest,
    Lingering on, with thirst unsated,
Finds a later draught the best:
    Miracles,—when thou hast waited!

Thought must shade and sun the soul
    With its glorious mutations;
Every life-song is a whole
    Sweeter for its variations.
Wherefore with your bliss at strife?
    'T was an angel that withstood you!
Could you change your perfect life
    For a dream of living—would you?

Harry Thurston

"MARCH: THE DAY THE ICE GOES OUT" FROM *A PLACE BETWEEN THE TIDES*

*L*iving on the tidal flats along the Tidnish River in Nova Scotia, Harry Thurston records the vast changes he sees as each season comes to eastern Canada. In this selection, set in March, he begins with Henry David Thoreau's observations about ice, the breakup of which Thoreau used as a metaphor for the breakup of prejudices and inhibitions in the human soul. Thurston, however, does not use the ice's breakup metaphorically. He is instead fascinated by the cyclical movements of the year that the breakup represents.

> *I*t is the springtime breakup of the ice that inaugurates the cycle anew.

What comes across in Thurston's observations is a strong sense of the interconnectedness of all things, and how that interconnectedness is manifested in nature's cyclical movements. As he watches the return of the foxes, seals, birds, and otters that comes with each spring, he recalls the larger cycles too: the return of the nesting eagles to Nova Scotia and even his own return to the salt marshes of his youth. It is the springtime breakup of the ice that inaugurates the cycle anew, and Thurston finds that not only are his senses exhilarated, but his solitude is allayed.

"MARCH: THE DAY THE ICE GOES OUT"

Now that there is more light in the evenings, my neighbor Charles and I meet casually in our adjoining backyards after supper. Like most Maritimers, Charles is an inveterate weather watcher. "Baie Verte was black today," he says, casting a wary glance toward the glowering sky above the marsh. "You can always tell we're in for dirt when it's black like that." His augury of the landscape, born of a lifetime's accumulation of local knowledge, proves true. Winter blusters back with a vengeance in the following days. Snow and ice again blanket the marsh and the river, after a premature breakup in mid-March.

That breakup had been dramatic and telling of the perils of living on a river floodplain. It had begun overnight with twelve hours of torrential rain. By morning the river was in spate, higher than I had ever seen it before. Most of the dyke was underwater, and there was a strong flow through the marsh itself, a steel gray sheet of menacing force pushing toward the sea. The ice had broken into large pans under the pressure of the rising river, and I worried that they would jam, causing catastrophic flooding. The water was already well up on the lawn and continued to rise all morning, even though the tide was ebbing. I feared the wind would back into the northeast, holding the rising tide against the land. I called Sherman for his historical perspective.

"Oh yes, I've seen the river this high before," he said. "One time there was a river running right overtop the ice. This year, of course, there's been no frost, so the ice isn't hard against the shore. They say it's that El Neen-yo or whatever they call it, I don't know. But it has been a strange winter. It was warmer here than in Florida the other day.

"The temperature's going down, that's the good thing. The river won't come up with the temperature dropping. They say it's going down to minus eighteen tonight. Of course, I don't know, we have to take their word for it. That's the difference between us and them, I guess, Harry, they get paid for telling lies."

During the day, a bald eagle perched in a tree on Lucius's Marsh, across the road from Sherman's, like us, seemingly mesmerized by the river's rise. The marsh was now a lake, lapping the tree line. I was worried not only for our home but also for the foxes' den, as the icy waters were backed up against their front entry. Next door, the river was seeping into Charles's basement woodworking shop. At midnight, under a hazy full moon, I was still monitoring the rogue river. I had noted during the daylight that the river appeared only to flow one way, out to sea. The normal rhythm of the tide had been obscured by the great rush of fresh water. The incoming tide must have flowed invisibly under the layer of fresh water. As the weatherman said, it had turned bitterly cold. Outside, I could hear the ice—broken in a day—grinding and shifting ominously in the dark. By morning, however, as Sherman had predicted, the river had dropped with the dipping mercury and had backed off the lawn. The marsh was again frozen, and only patches of open water appeared in the river ice.

No event is more keenly anticipated along the river than ice-out, and this is as true for wildlife as it is for us winter-bound river people. When that longed-for day will occur is anybody's guess and, I'm told, was once the source of a lottery in the community. In my experience it varies, depending upon the severity of the freeze-up, from early March until late April.

I look for the first signs of the ice going out 3 kilometers (about 2 miles) upriver from my house at a bend known as the Wabash. This is the head of the tide, 7 kilometers (about 4 miles) from the coast, and open water occurs here first. Within a week the ice along the length of the river begins to rot under the longer hours of sunlight and, further weakened by the twice-daily tidal action, starts to move seaward in great rafts that batter and ram each other like warring navies.

It would be misleading, however, to give the impression that this transition to open water is a linear process; it is anything but. Spring in Maritime Canada is a painfully fickle season of brief promise and lengthy reversals, a meteorological two-step: one step forward, two steps back; two forward, one back.

Pack ice covers much of the Gulf of St. Lawrence in winter. This is the breeding and pupping platform for tens of thousands of gray and harp seals. Pupping begins in late February and continues until mid-March, but it occurs far offshore, near the Magdalen Islands and in the Northumberland Strait, and therefore out of sight. When I travel to the country store, to replenish our staples of bread, milk, eggs, and cheese, I keep an eye out for the state of the ice in Baie Verte, or Green Bay, so called for the fringe of rich salt marsh that transforms its border into a sea of green grasses in summer. Some days the bay is white, icebound: on others, black waters are visible, depending on the direction of the wind. Northeast winds—the storm winds of winter—push the ice onshore, while southwest winds—the predominant winds of summer—move the ice seaward. This seesaw movement of wind and ice may continue into late April, before the last pans dissolve into the warming waters of the strait and the gulf.

The tardy progress of spring relates directly to the slow warming of the waters. The sea heats up more slowly than the land, and its cold breath hovers over the region much longer than most of us would like.

Late-winter storms are common in March and may be dangerous for some marine creatures. Several years ago, following a late-winter snowstorm, a harbor seal—probably the young of the previous year—was found stranded by the side of the road in the Tyndal Woods, halfway between the Bay of Fundy and the Northumberland Strait. Had it originated in the bay or the strait? Either way, it was hopelessly lost and disoriented. Ice was still fast on the lakes and rivers, so it had crawled overland on its belly, some 10 to 20 kilometers (6 to 12 miles), seeking open water. I heard the story at the country store from John, one of a number of men who spend their free time there, trading local gossip and exchanging heated opinions about national and international affairs. He last saw the young seal waddling through the woods, turning downriver toward the sea. "No doubt," he declared with grim certainty, "it was a coyote's breakfast in a couple of hours." This harsh judgment of the young seal's fate might very well have been true, and for the coyote, at least, good news.

Over a week in late March, I watch as a pair of foxes acts out escapades of caching and pilfering. White Face, identified by a particularly white brow, excavates a small hole in the snow near the den entrance and drops a large food item into this deep freeze. The next day she returns to check on the contents of the cache, tasting it before heading downriver. Not long after, I observe another, much darker fox making off with the cached animal—either a chicken or a hare, I can't tell. This fox also runs downriver before heading into the woods. Then, at suppertime, White Face returns, this time carrying a rat in her mouth, which she deposits in the cache.

Are these pilfering raids? It seems so; later in the week, I watch as the dark fox, much muddied from the rains, raids the food cache, making off with a muskrat stored there. A few minutes later, it returns and removes another partially thawed muskrat, which dangles limply from its mouth in a most unappetizing manner. The fox goes only 20 meters (22 yards) or so into the woods and returns yet a third time. Finding the larder bare, it disappears into the woods, but this time in the opposite direction from its newly created cache of ill-gotten gains. What is this all about? Are these two animals really competitors, or are they mates with a different concept of housekeeping? It is yet another example of how our glimpses into the lives of wild animals are usually so brief and fragmented that it is often impossible to piece together a coherent plot of their lives and motivations, however vigilant we might be. We see what we can see—we observe their actions—but we cannot always intuit their meaning for the simple reason that we do not think, as the poet said, in the language of the wild, as foxes do.

Although my neighbors and I may not be able to call the date the ice will leave the river, the birds know the instant there is open water. Common mergansers make a beeline upriver and appear at the Wabash seemingly the moment it opens. The belted kingfisher, that halcyon bird, materializes above a narrow patch of black water, dives like a circus daredevil into a bathtub-sized hole in the ice, and to my surprise comes up with a silvery fish twitching in its oversize beak. Other feathered and furred fishers will follow the lead as more of the river shakes off its icy mantle, until one day it is ice free. One morning I wake and blink in the familiar but seemingly fresh vista; the dark aqueous eye of the river stares back, its cataract of winter removed.

The biological implications of this event are profound. The light that all winter has been blocked by ice and snow cover floods into the water column, fueling the exponential growth of phyto-plankton. This proliferation of microscopic plant life feeds a host of marine organisms—from the tiniest zooplankton, such as copepods, mysids, amphipods, and rotifers, to the larvae of larger marine organisms such as crabs, snails, clams, worms, and starfish. These small animals, in turn, feed larval fishes that develop in the nurseries of marsh creeks, estuaries, and shallow bays.

Dead plant material, so-called detritus, is perhaps the most important food source in the salt marsh ecosystem. The ice that has ridden up on the marsh, settling there for the winter, has sheared off the plant tops and, like natural grist stones, has ground the bases of the marsh grasses into meal. As the ice backs out to the sea, it takes with it some of this pulverized plant material, and what remains behind is flushed out by the large spring tides. It is fed upon by a hardy group of small organisms known as detritus eaters, bottom-dwelling invertebrates that are capable of digesting the coarse plant matter. If they cannot, bacteria and fungi break down the tough cellulose for them. The bottom dwellers then ingest the bacteria and

HUNTINGTON CITY-TOWNSHIP
PUBLIC LIBRARY
200 W. Market Street
Huntington, IN 46750

fungi. One way or another, the great store of energy produced by the tidally nourished plants the year before is given back to the sea, where it is entrained and exchanged in a complex marine food web.

Ice-out releases food, sound, smell, and sight, enlivening the senses. Life quickens on the Old Marsh with the return of migrants, exiled for long months by the ice and snow.

Most are fishers of one kind or another. As the kingfisher demonstrates, minnows are emerging from their winter homes in the mud; in the estuary there is a mustering of schools of smelt, readying themselves for their spawning run into fresh water once the water reaches the optimum temperature. Winter flounder, which have bred in the inshore waters during the winter, are moving offshore, to be replaced by summer flounder migrating landward from the ocean depths, in a piscatorial changing of the guard.

The common mergansers fly ramrod straight, bill, head, body, and tail on the same horizontal axis, their wings seemingly rotating on this axis like those on a whirligig. Their flight appears programmed, as they follow the lifeline of the river precisely, unwavering in their sense of purpose. When I see a flock pass, it's as if I am watching a squadron perform a synchronized air show, without the hellish noise of jet engines thundering over-head. Male mergansers, with their iridescent green heads and white bodies, seem as crisply turned out as sailors. Handsome as they are, I await, impatiently, the return of their diminutive cousins, the hooded mergansers, which follow only, it seems, when the river has completely cleared of ice.

For the naturalist who puts down roots as I have, there are two distinct kinds of pleasures that derive from being in one place over time and tracking the rounds of the seasons. The first relates to the expected, the ability to predict what will happen at certain times of the year—when the spring and fall migrants will appear and disappear, when the fish will make their spawning runs, when the birds will begin nesting or the first fox kits emerge from their den by the white birches, or even when I might expect to see the first deer cropping marsh grass. Then there is the unexpected: the first and only time you might spy a rare species, or the infrequent visits from a little-seen animal or bird. It is difficult to choose between the two, the satisfaction of one being equal to the excitement of the other.

March seems to deliver both the comfort of the familiar and the exhilaration of surprise. One day at the end of March, I arrive home midday to see a great bull gray seal making its lugubrious way upriver, against the ebbing tide. It moves slowly, ponderously, sometimes arching its back to dive, but mostly sculling along with its head out of water, like a gentleman in a straw boater from an unhurried, bygone era. Such a great head—which has earned it the sobriquet "horse head," and its scientific name *Halichoerus grypus,* Latin for "hook-nosed pig of the sea." Spiky whiskers bristle its fleshy snout and shine in the sun like fiber optics, receiving bytes of sensory information I cannot begin to decipher. But it is by this prominent Roman nose, which is convex, rather than concave, that I can distinguish a gray seal from its smaller relative, the harbor seal. Also, its great size—up to 300 kilograms (660 pounds) for a male like this one—leaves little doubt of its identity. It has come in from the strait, where it has bred on the ice, probably lured inland by fish moving upriver from the estuary. Or perhaps it is merely exploring—its manner seems so casual. At the bend above our house, where the river elbows, it treads water, then sinks, its telltale head slowly submerging. To the impressionable, such an outsize, even monstrous, head might inspire stories of Nessie and the like.

Other aquatic furbearers make their appearance before March is out, now that the river highway is again open.

The phone rings; it's Charles: "Did you see that otter? He's just below us, he's eating some kind of fish."

"I'll take a look and give you a call back." I run into the living room to have a look through the scope. The otter—the first one I've seen since moving here—has come up in a lead in the ice and is trying to finish off the head of the fish. It looks like a salmon head, being too big, I think, even for one of the sea trout that run upriver in spring. I doubt my diagnosis, as there are very few Atlantic salmon left in the river since its spawning grounds have become laden with silt as a result of clear-cutting in the headwaters. Whatever it is eating, I am impressed by the mechanics of the otter's teeth; its great molars seem to crush the fish head with the same ease with which I eat an apple.

I call Charles back: "I don't know what it was eating. It looked like a salmon, but then it might have only been a big sucker. I couldn't see it clearly enough. It's great to see them, eh?"

"I know. Years ago, Sherman used to trap them upriver," Charles says. "I hadn't seen otters down here before."

The increased activity of late March is not confined to the water but surges onto the land and into the air.

Two hunchbacked forms skulking across Lucius's Marsh prove to be raccoons. With the ice gone, they have ventured onto the marsh in broad daylight to see what winter leftovers they might scavenge. How devious they look, even at a distance, as if they were up to no good. It is not only their masks—and their audacious-ness—that give them their reputation as bandits, but I now see it is their posture, too. They are hunched, as if they are hiding their heads under turned-up collars, like suspicious characters on a shady street. Skunks, too, have come out of semi hibernation; later, when the frost is gone, they will drill my lawn at night for grubs, leaving their telltale holes. Now, it is only their scent that lingers in the night air. It is like the smell of the marsh itself, pungent, mephitic, as marsh gases bubble to the surface with the warming temperatures. Skunk smell is a heartening odor; it announces spring and wakens the somnolent senses like a blast of smelling salts. For me it is also a nostalgic smell. I remember how welcome that commingling of odors from the marsh and iodine from the sea was when I crossed the Tantramar Marsh into Nova Scotia after a two-year absence in Central Canada. Smelling it, I knew I was home; smelling skunk, I know it is spring at last.

Land birds are also returning—robins and grackles in the van-guard—probing the lawn for food but also working the newly exposed marsh. And my family of crows is doing its spring cleaning on the marsh, carrying out its yeoman environmental function. I compare crows to the bottle pickers that appear along Maritime roads this time of year. We pass them with a sense of pity, that they must pick bottles from the ditch for pennies, but we should praise them for this seasonal work that keeps us from drowning in an accumulation of our own careless acts.

We have all heard the old saw "Nature abhors a vacuum," and year after year I observe practical demonstrations of this principle that apply to the marsh habitat. Open river, mergansers. Open marsh, harrier. Open marsh pools, black ducks. A day doesn't pass between the availability of a niche and the arrival of its rightful exploiter.

The skies, too, are opening, though you might argue they are always so. Warmer air rising from the land provides a new ladder for soaring birds, primary among them the resident bald eagles. All winter, eagles have passed by on their excursions from their upriver roosting sites to the coast and back again in the evening, occasionally stopping by to perch atop a black spruce, their piebald heads occulting like lighthouse lanterns as they scan the landscape, or to hunch on the marsh, Atlas-like, seeming to shoulder the sky itself. Now, as the late-March sun sends up thermals, the eagles circle the marsh in ever-mounting spirals.

Now, too, I see them not only singly, enjoying their powers of flight, but soaring together, a courtship behavior that helps to renew their bonds—which may be lifelong. Sometimes the breeding birds will lock talons and cartwheel toward the earth.

Twice every month the tides are especially high. We call them spring tides, from the Anglo-Saxon word *springen,* "to leap up." These high tides occur at the full and the new moons, when the sun and the moon are in alignment with the Earth and therefore, together, exert greater gravitational pull on the ocean's waters. The spring tides tend to be especially high in the spring and the fall, during the equinoxes, because of the declination of the moon and the sun with respect to the Earth's equator. The factors influencing tides—some two hundred of them—can amplify or minimize tidal range, but suffice it to say that March is often a time of unusually high tides. These particular spring tides have an important function in opening up the ecosystem.

The highest tides entirely flood the marsh, bursting through the derelict *aboiteau,* until only the top of the dyke pokes above the sepia-colored waters like a battlement. When one of these spring tides recedes, I can see, for the first time in months, islands of bare marsh. With each succeeding spring tide, these islands grow in size and coalesce until nearly the whole marsh is ice free. The brittle, brown stalks of seaside goldenrod wave in the wind, a harrier flies low on its stiff wings over its newly exposed hunting ground, and a killdeer's harsh call rings out.

Sound, other than the mechanics of ice, again begins to define my world. It is not only as if bandages have been taken from my eyes but also as if cotton has been removed from my ears. Still, the senses seem rusty, out of practice, somehow. So it takes me a few seconds to connect a faintly familiar sound to its maker. The clangor sounds like old ox bells echoing in a distant field. Then the auditory memory directs my eyes upward, where I see a flock of geese—perhaps a hundred strong—wedging their way north.

Their calls are the most potent sign of imminent spring for us northerners, and their arrival is intimately related to the clearing of the ice from the marsh. While the uplands may still be covered with snow and ice, the salt marsh is cleared early by the high spring tides. Moving north cautiously, egged on by southerly winds and forced to retreat by northerlies—two steps forward, one back—the geese converge on these ice-free marshes to feed. They strip what vegetation the ice has left standing, excavate for roots, and glean what little new growth has begun to push its way toward the sun. When food is available nowhere else, it is there for the taking on the marsh and critical to the geese's successful migration north to the breeding grounds.

With the ice gone for good, spring leapfrogs forward. The marsh poises for a greening that will support a legion of new life. As Thoreau said, the breaking up of ice from rivers and ponds "is particularly interesting to us who live in a climate of so great extremes." To northern marsh dwellers like me, there is no more exhilarating event in the round of seasons than the day the ice goes out. It promises the return of the many migrants and marsh breeders that give meaning to my days, engaging my senses, allaying my solitude. One by one the long-absent feathered, furred, and scaled creatures of the marsh make their appearance on land and in the water and skies.

Allen M. Young

"SPRING PEEPERS" FROM SMALL CREATURES AND ORDINARY PLACES

It is likely that few of us would claim to have a favorite frog, particularly one barely half an inch long; but Allen Young, curator of zoology at the Milwaukee Public Museum, has been stalking spring peepers for forty years.

These tiny creatures appear at the first thaw before much of the spring wildlife awakes from its winter dormancy. Belonging, as they do, to the ecosystem of temporary ponds, they live a haphazard and dangerous life: their eggs and tadpoles are food for larger animals; their home is dependent on winter snows and summer suns—and the goodwill of humans who refuse to drain muddy pools and level the landscape.

> *Their very presence reminds us that spring has returned again, stirred into life by forces we can neither predict nor control.*

Spring peepers are both ubiquitous and vulnerable, especially in the suburbs. Their very presence reminds us that spring has returned again, stirred into life by forces we can neither predict nor control. And yet their continued existence depends upon our ability to see and hear them, to be called to attention by the least of these, God's creatures.

"Spring Peepers"

Even after many years of studying nature, I am still amazed at how clear particular first experiences remain in the recesses of my mind. Part of this, I am sure, has to do with the many reminders of them I've since encountered. Take, for example, spring peepers, a quasi-tree frog about half an inch long that is widely distributed throughout much of eastern North America. The spring peeper *(Pseudacris [Hyla] crucifer)* is without question one of my favorite frogs.

I remember cold spring late afternoons 40 years ago, crawling on my belly toward a golf course drainage ditch swelled almost to overflow by a thaw. From the low, matted dead brush sticking up through the slow-moving flowage came the soft purr of the peepers. Their endearing persistent chirping filled the dusk spring air long before many songbirds and the calling insects appeared on the scene. My goal was always to catch some for a closer look, but usually I failed. Many times I came very close to a spot along the ditch where I thought a spring peeper might be, only to discover that the frog's call had played tricks on me.

One thing I have come to appreciate over the years is that seemingly sloppy and haphazard pools of standing water created by spring thaws are in fact key natural features of our landscape, whether located in forest or on old farmland, and they support an amazingly diverse array of life. The temporary pool's recurrent wet and dry phases within each year, together with its tendency to appear every year in the same place, gives it some semblance of seasonally interrupted permanency, and the unpredictable beginnings and endings of its wet phases establishes a habitat that can only be occupied by certain creatures.

First and foremost, the animals that live in spring pools must have the means of dealing with their ephemeral condition. Creatures that cannot migrate when the water dissipates have to burrow into the mud and survive for a long time, even when the mud becomes hard-baked by summer's heat. Whether mature or not, these animals have to stay inactive until the following spring when the pools fill up again. This obviously is quite chancy. A winter with light snowfall means a shallow pool or even no pool at all. Other animals, unable to withstand staying inactive down in the hard earth through summer, have the choice of migrating to more permanent bodies of water by the time the pools dry up. Either way, creatures that live in these pools must synchronize their life cycles so that the appropriate phase or phases are completed before dryness sets in.

For two spring seasons many years ago, when I was a graduate student in zoology at the University of Chicago, my thesis research advisor, Thomas Park, took us to temporary pond sites in suburban Chicago as part of his field zoology course. As we waded through the frigid water in hip boots, seining for creatures in the deep brown water, I was impressed by just how many kinds of animals appeared in the samples. We found small snails, chironomid midge larvae, water boatmen, diving beetle larvae, damselfly larvae, various crustaceans, and bright red aquatic mites. Very quickly I realized that these ponds, which became bone-dry by early summer, nurtured a lot of life in a relatively short breeding period. They also hosted very high numbers of some species and very low ones of others. Researchers have found that even among species able to breed in more permanent water, those who choose to do so in the temporary pools—where certain predators are absent—reach greater numbers even when the time period for breeding is quite compressed.

While spring peepers and other amphibians make their way from the surrounding land into woodland temporary pools to breed, other colonist species, in the form of insect eggs adhering to the feet of passing water-fowl, drop into the pool from the sky, while still others awaken from the softening mud below. This rich influx of life establishes an ecological battlefield within the little pool, a network of interconnecting creatures competing for limited resources and contending with short breeding times and carnivory.

All these biotic interplays help enrich the decaying leaf mulch that slips into the pool as it forms with the thaw. What happens is that a miniature ecosystem of sorts develops in the water, complex enough in its own organization and design, but not disconnected from the surrounding landscape and sky. Spring rains add more to the pools. Sunshine first helps fill and then drain them. Spring peepers simply enter into this arthropod-dominated domain, their eggs and tad-poles becoming food for larger animals looking for an early meal. Many frog eggs may go into these pools; later, far fewer adult frogs are matured from them.

The life challenges of spring peepers offer important lessons to humanity, I believe. When resources are unpredictable from one year to the next and fleeting at best, the creatures exploiting them are rushed to breed and leave. Temporary pools, then, despite their humble appearance, are critical. Rich in rotting mulch and small lifeforms, they are key entities in the long-term success and well-being of forests, and thus cannot be dismissed lightly. They support the existence of not only midges, bugs, beetles, and frogs, but that of many larger creatures as well. What many of the approximately 200 species of returning songbirds often need the most in late spring are large stores of insects on which to nourish themselves and feed to their fledglings. Temporary pools, with the capacity to warm up faster than deep-water permanent ponds and lakes and thereby to produce populations of springtime flying insects quickly, are vital links in the sustenance of these bird populations. The adult insects fly off attempting to reach other bodies of water and fall victim to songbirds returning to these parts on the northward migration.

When I listen to courting spring peepers in the forest, I worry that we're ignoring this lesson. Many common human activities—filling in drainage ditches, shaving earth off the land and changing its natural contours, and emptying wetlands—destroy temporary pools and threaten the frail network of creatures that need them. In the spring peeper, a small and easily dismissed creature to many, I see a symbol of the need to conserve the pools, to reaffirm their vital role in the cycles of life that define a healthy northern woodland

and old field. Both peepers and pools play crucial roles in the great recycling project that is nature. Thawing snow and ice first creates a broth or brew of rotting plant and animal matter, which in turn supports legions of mold, bacteria, algal plants, and eventually animals. The spring peeper, in one sense at least, is the recycled detritus and scum of this place; later on the fledgling jays, mice, and dragonflies will become part of the reworked nutrient profile of spring peepers.

I find great joy in walking the woods in spring, just when life is awakening after the long cold, and often come here again and again. At first there appears to be nothing afoot and stirring. Then suddenly the air is filled with a symphony of peeper song and its hopeful message that life has survived winter. These descendants of past growing seasons sing of life's renewal, a continuance of the species beyond now. The spring peeper's music coats the surface of what is happening in these woods; otherwise, except for the patter of rain, the whoosh of a breeze, or the scurrying of a squirrel, all is very silent. If the peeper music ever stops, fades away in spring seasons yet to come, the earth is in big trouble.

So I take this opportunity to enjoy the sounds of the spring peeper where and when I can, one spring to the next. Sometimes when winter has been slow in coming, fooling the frogs into a false sense of spring so that they breed early, I might even hear them in the fall. In summer, when their songs are drowned in the cacophony emerging from many other small creatures, I must simply trust that the peepers will come again with spring. But the seasons are fickle here in the north. Like much of nature, they steadily ask us to bend, to pause, to pay attention to the minutia we're free to ignore elsewhere. They remind us that we can't predict the return of the peepers by the calendar or the almanac or any of our other tools; we have to watch the weather and simply come here, again and again, listening until we hear the fleeting melodies of frog song. They, along with the rest of the life sounds in the forests and fields, right now are setting the mood, tone, and tempo of an unfolding acoustical drama. We are called first to attention by the spring peepers, whose impending silence welcomes warmer days; then, as summer arrives, the repertory of returning songbirds and frogs from permanent water will sound. Much later the insect musicians will enter, and although by this time the peepers' melodies will have faded, nature remembers them and keeps their promise alive: after winter comes the spring.

Nathaniel Hawthorne

"BUDS AND BIRD-VOICES"

*I*n the summer of 1842, Nathaniel Hawthorne moved to the Old Manse in Concord, Massachusetts, with his new wife, Sophia Peabody. The house, located on the Concord River next to the North Bridge, had been built by Reverend William Emerson, grandfather of Ralph Waldo Emerson, in 1770. Hawthorne settled into the second-floor study, writing tales, sketches, and other short essays, many of which were later collected in Mosses from an Old Manse, *first published in 1846.*

What spring offers is not a magical dismissal of old sorrows but rather a "periodical infusion of the primal spirit," a beauty that is not delusional, and the promise that, once again, all things can be made new.

In this piece, Hawthorne begins with a familiar lament: it has been a long winter and many times it seemed as if spring would never arrive. Yet the lingering cold and the snow that stayed too long now serve as counterpoint, a basso continuo, to the emerging season. And although he rejoices in the new sprigs of grass, the chorus of bird voices, and even the returning clouds of insects, Hawthorne also notices the untidiness of spring. As the forgiving snow melts away, we are confronted with dead branches and withered asparagus stalks and ruined birds' nests, an accumula-

tion of decay we would rather not face, as, indeed, we would prefer to turn away from the debris of our own lives.

What spring offers is not a magical dismissal of old sorrows but rather a "periodical infusion of the primal spirit," a beauty that is not delusional, and the promise that, once again, all things can be made new.

"BUDS AND BIRD-VOICES"

Balmy Spring—weeks later than we expected, and months later than we longed for her—comes at last to revive the moss on the roof and walls of our old mansion. She peeps brightly into my study window, inviting me to throw it open and create a summer atmosphere by the intermixture of her genial breath with the black and cheerless comfort of the stove. As the casement ascends, forth into infinite space fly the innumerable forms of thought or fancy that have kept me company in the retirement of this little chamber during the sluggish lapse of wintry weather; visions, gay, grotesque and sad; pictures of real life, tinted with Nature's homely gray and russet; scenes in dreamland bedizened with rainbow hues which faded before they were well laid on,—all these may vanish now, and leave me to mold a fresh existence out of sunshine. Brooding Meditation may flap her dusky wings and take her owl-like flight, blinking amid the cheerfulness of noontide. Such companions befit the season of frosted window panes and crackling fires, when the blast howls through the black-ash trees of our avenue, and the drifting snow-storm chokes up the wood-paths and fills the highway from stone-wall to stone-wall. In the spring and summer time all somber thoughts should follow the winter northward with the somber and thoughtful crows. The old paradisiacal economy of life is again in force: we live, not to think nor to labor, but for the simple end of being happy; nothing for the present hour is worthy of man's infinite capacity save to imbibe the warm smile of heaven and sympathize with the reviving earth.

The present Spring comes onward with fleeter footsteps, because Winter lingered so unconscionably long that with her best diligence she can hardly retrieve half the allotted period of her reign. It is but a fortnight since I stood on the brink of our swollen river and beheld the accumulated ice of four frozen months go down the stream. Except in streaks here and there upon the hillsides, the whole visible universe was then covered with deep snow, the nethermost layer of which had been deposited by an early December storm. It was a sight to make the beholder torpid, in the impossibility of imagining how this vast white napkin was to be removed from the face of the corpse-like world in less time than had been required to spread it there. But who can estimate the power of gentle influences, whether amid material desolation or the moral winter of man's heart? There have been no tempestuous rains, even no sultry days, but a constant breath of southern winds, with now a day of kindly sunshine, and now a no less kindly mist, or a soft descent of showers, in which a smile and a blessing seemed to have been steeped. The snow has vanished as if by magic; whatever heaps may be hidden in the woods and deep gorges of the hills, only two solitary specks remain in the landscape; and those I shall almost regret to miss when to-morrow I look for them in vain. Never before, methinks, has spring pressed so closely on the footsteps of retreating winter. Along the roadside the green blades of grass have sprouted on the very edge of the snowdrifts. The pastures and mowing fields have not yet assumed a general aspect of verdure; but neither have they the cheerless brown tint which they wear in later autumn, when vegetation has entirely ceased; there is now a faint shadow of life, gradually brightening into the warm reality. Some tracts in a happy exposure,—as, for instance, yonder southwestern slope of an orchard, in front of that old red farmhouse beyond the river,— such patches of land already wear a beautiful and tender green to which no future luxuriance can add a charm. It looks unreal; a prophecy, a hope, a transitory effect of some peculiar light, which will vanish with the slightest motion of the eye. But beauty is never a delusion; not these verdant tracts but the dark and barren landscape all around them is a shadow and a dream. Each moment wins some portion of the earth from death to life; a sudden gleam of verdure brightens along the sunny slope of a bank which an instant ago was brown and bare. You look again, and, behold an apparition of green grass!

One of the first things that strikes the attention when the white sheet of winter is withdrawn is the neglect and disarray that lay hidden beneath it. Nature is not cleanly, according to our prejudices. The beauty of preceding years, now transformed to brown and blighted deformity, obstructs the brightening loveliness of the present hour. Our avenue is strewn with the whole crop of autumn's withered leaves. There are quantities of decayed branches which one tempest after another has flung down, black and rotten, and one or two with the ruin of a bird's nest clinging to them. In the garden are the dried bean-vines, the brown stalks of the asparagus bed, and melancholy old cabbages which were frozen into the soil before · their unthrifty cultivator could find time to gather them. How invariably, throughout all the forms of life do we find these intermingled memorials of death! On the soil of thought and in the garden of the heart, as well as in the sensual world, lie withered leaves—the ideas and feelings that we have done with. There is no wind strong enough to sweep them away; infinite space will not garner them from our sight. What mean they? Why may we not be permitted to live and enjoy as if this were the first life and our own the primal enjoyment, instead of treading always on these dry bones and mouldering relics from the aged accumulation of which springs all that now appears so young and new? Sweet must have been the springtime of Eden, when no earlier year had strewn its decay upon the virgin turf, and no former experience had ripened into summer and faded into autumn in the hearts of its inhabitants! That was a world worth living in. Oh, thou murmurer, it is out of the very wantonness of such a life that thou feignest these idle lamentations. There is no decay. Each human soul is the first created inhabitant of its own Eden. We dwell in an old moss-covered mansion and tread in the worn footprints of the past and have a gray clergyman's ghost for our daily and nightly inmate; yet all these outward circumstances are made less than visionary by the renewing power of the spirit. Should the spirit ever lose this power,—should the withered leaves, and the rotten branches, and the moss-covered house, and the ghost of the gray past ever become its realities, and the verdure and the freshness merely its faint dream,—then let it pray to be released from earth. It will need the air of heaven to revive its pristine energies.

What an unlooked-for flight was this from our shadowy avenue of black-ash and balm of Gilead trees into the infinite! Now we have our feet again upon the turf. Nowhere does the grass spring up so industriously as in this homely yard, along the base of the stone wall and in the sheltered nooks of the buildings, and especially around the southern doorstep—a locality which seems particularly favorable to its growth, for it is already tall enough to bend over and wave in the wind. I observe that several weeds—and most frequently a plant that stains the fingers with its yellow juice—have survived and retained their freshness and sap throughout the winter. One knows not how they have deserved such an exception from the common lot of their race. They are now the patriarchs of the departed year, and may preach mortality to the present generation of flowers and weeds.

Among the delights of spring, how is it possible to forget the birds? Even the crows were welcome, as the sable harbingers of a brighter and livelier race. They visited us before the snow was off, but seem mostly to have betaken themselves to remote depths of the woods, which they haunt all summer long. Many a time shall I disturb them there, and feel as if I had intruded among a company of silent worshipers as they sit in Sabbath stillness among the tree-tops. Their voices, when they speak, are in admirable accordance with the tranquil solitude of a summer afternoon; and, resounding so far above the head, their loud clamor increases the religious quiet of the scene instead of breaking it. A crow, however, has no real pretensions to religion, in spite of his gravity of mien and black attire; he is certainly a thief, and probably an infidel. The gulls are far more respectable, in a moral point of view. These denizens of sea-beaten rocks and haunters of the lonely beach come up our inland river at this season, and soar high overhead, flapping their broad wings in the upper sunshine. They are among the most picturesque of birds, because they so float and rest upon the air as to become almost stationary parts of the landscape. The imagination has time to grow acquainted with them; they have not flitted away in a moment. You go up among the clouds and greet these lofty-flighted gulls, and repose confidently with them upon the sustaining atmosphere. Ducks have their haunts along the solitary places of the river, and alight in flocks upon the broad bosom of the overflowed meadows. Their flight is too rapid and determined for the eye to catch enjoyment from it, although it never fails to stir up the heart with the sportsman's ineradicable instinct. They have now gone farther northward, but will visit us again in autumn.

The smaller birds,—the little songsters of the woods, and those that haunt man's dwellings and claim human friendship by building their nests under the sheltering eaves or among the orchard trees— these require a touch more delicate and a gentler heart than mine to do them justice. Their outburst of melody is like a brook let loose from wintry chains. We need not deem it a too high and solemn word to call it a hymn of praise to the Creator; since Nature, who pictures the reviving year in so many sights of beauty, has expressed the sentiment of renewed life in no other sound save the notes of these blessed birds. Their music, however, just now seems to be incidental, and not the result of a set purpose. They are discussing the economy of life and love and the site and architecture of their summer residences, and have no time to sit on a twig and pour forth solemn hymns or overtures, operas, symphonies, and waltzes. Anxious questions are asked; grave subjects are settled in quick and animated debate; and only by occasional accident, as from pure ecstasy, does a rich warble roll its tiny waves of golden sound through the atmosphere. Their little bodies are as busy as their voices; they are in a constant flutter and restlessness. Even when two or three retreat to a tree-top to hold council, they wag their tails and heads all the time with the irrepressible activity of their nature, which perhaps renders their brief span of life in reality as long as the patriarchal age of sluggish man.

Insects are among the earliest births of spring. Multitudes of I know not what species appeared long ago on the surface of the snow. Clouds of them almost too minute for sight hover in a beam of sunshine, and vanish as if annihilated when they pass into the shade. A mosquito has already been heard to sound the small horror of his bugle horn. Wasps infest the sunny windows of the house. A bee entered one of the chambers with a prophecy of flowers. Rare butterflies came before the snow was off, flaunting in the chill breeze, and looking forlorn and all astray in spite of the magnificence of their dark velvet cloaks with golden borders.

Thank Providence for spring! The earth—and man himself, by sympathy with his birthplace—would be far other than we find them if life toiled wearily onward without this periodical infusion of the primal spirit. Will the world ever be so decayed that spring may not renew its greenness? Can man be so dismally age-stricken that no faintest sunshine of his youth may revisit him once a year? It is impossible. The moss on our timeworn mansion brightens into beauty; the good old pastor who once dwelt here renewed his prime, regained his boyhood, in the genial breezes of his ninetieth spring. Alas for the worn and heavy soul if, whether in youth or age, it have outlived its privilege of spring-time sprightliness! From such a soul the world must hope no reformation of its evil, no sympathy with the lofty faith and gallant struggles of those who contend in its behalf. Summer works in the present, and thinks not of the future; autumn is a rich conservative; winter has utterly lost its faith, and clings tremulously to the remembrance of what has been; but spring, with its outgushing life, is the true type of the movement.

Thomas Wentworth Higginson

"APRIL DAYS"

*T*homas Wentworth Higginson is perhaps best known to us as a friend of Emily Dickinson and one of the first editors of her poems. But in his own day he was celebrated as an essayist, scholar, minister, and leader in the abolitionist movement. He served as colonel of the first black regiment in the Civil War, the First South Carolina Volunteers, and wrote of these experiences in Army Life in a Black Regiment *(1870).*

*I*f we don't always appreciate winter, particularly when the snow drags on into April, its scouring work clears the slate for the re-emergence of spring life.

In this essay, he takes on the task of celebrating April—not the April of the Carolinas, rich with the scent of dogwoods and azaleas, but the early April of Massachusetts, still emerging from its wintery cocoon. If we don't always appreciate winter, particularly when the snow drags on into April, its scouring work clears the slate for the re-emergence of spring life. Yet it is a life that we must learn to see—and here Higginson presses a theme to which he often returns: that we must slow down and train ourselves to "see that which is before our eyes."

Higginson helps us do just that, with his platoon of early blooming spring flowers—"bloodroot, cowslip, houstonia, saxifrage, dandelion, *chickweed, cinquefoil, strawberry, mouse-ear, bellwort, dogtooth violet, five species of violet proper, and two of anemone"*—and his lovingly drawn picture of life dancing on and under the water: whirlwig beetles, caddis-worms, water-skaters, water-boatmans, turtles, and tritons. He reminds us that the cold, barely stirring days of April are prophetic. They foretell *"the whole splendor of the coming summer"* even as they herald the rebirth of the year.

"April Days"

> *"Can trouble dwell with April days?"*
> —In Memoriam

In our methodical American life, we still recognize some magic in summer. Most persons at least resign themselves to being decently happy in June. They accept June. They compliment its weather. They complain of the earlier months as cold, and so spend them in the city; and they complain of the later months as hot, and so refrigerate themselves on some barren seacoast. God offers us yearly a necklace of twelve pearls; most men choose the fairest, label it June, and cast the rest away. It is time to chant a hymn of more liberal gratitude.

There are not days in the whole round year more delicious than those which often come to us in the latter half of April. On these days one goes forth in the morning, and finds an Italian warmth brooding over all the hills, taking visible shape in a glistening mist of silvered azure, with which mingles the smoke from many bonfires. The sun trembles in his own soft rays, till one understands the old English tradition, that he dances on Easter Day.

But days even earlier than these, in April, have a charm,—even days that seem raw and rainy, when the sky is dull and a bequest of March wind lingers, chasing the squirrel from the tree and the children from the meadows. There is a fascination in walking through these bare early woods,—there is a pause of preparation, winter's work is so cleanly and thoroughly done. Everything is taken down and put away; throughout the leafy arcades the branches show no remnant of last year, save a few twisted leaves of oak and beech, a few empty seed vessels of the tardy witch-hazel, and a few gnawed nutshells dropped coquettishly by the squirrels into the crevices of the bark. All else is bare, but prophetic: buds everywhere, the whole splendor of the coming summer concentrated in those hard little knobs on every bough; and clinging here and there among them a brown, papery chrysalis, from which shall yet wave the superb wings of the Luna moth. An occasional shower patters on the dry leaves, but it does not silence the robin on the outskirts of the wood. Indeed, he sings louder than ever during rain, though the song sparrow and the bluebird are silent.

Then comes the sweetness of the nights in latter April. There is as yet no evening primrose to open suddenly, no cistus to drop its petals; but the Mayflower knows the moment, and becomes more fragrant in the darkness, so that one can then often find it in the woods without aid from the eye. The pleasant night sounds are begun; the hylas are uttering their shrill *peep* from the meadows, mingled soon with hoarser toads, who take to the water at this season to deposit their spawn. The tree-toads soon join them; but one listens in vain for bull-frogs or katydids or grasshoppers or whip-poor-wills or crickets: we must wait for most of these until the nights of June.

The first wild-flower of the year is like land after sea. The two which, throughout the Northern Atlantic States, divide this interest are the *Epigæa repens* (Mayflower, ground laurel, or trailing arbutus) and the *Hepatica triloba* (liverleaf, liverwort, or blue anemone). Of these two, the latter is perhaps more immediately exciting on first discovery, because it is an annual, not a perennial, and so does not, like the epigæa, exhibit its buds all winter, but opens its blue eyes almost as soon as it emerges from the ground. Without the rich and delicious odor of its compeer, it has an inexpressibly fresh and earthy scent that seems to bring all the promise of the blessed season with it; indeed, that clod of fresh turf with the inhalation of which Lord Bacon delighted to begin the day must undoubtedly have been full of the roots of our little hepatica. Its healthy sweetness belongs to the opening year, like Chaucer's poetry; and one thinks that anything more potent and voluptuous would be less enchanting—until one turns to the Mayflower. Then comes a richer fascination for the senses. To pick the Mayflower is like following in the footsteps of some spendthrift army which has scattered the contents of its treasure chest among beds of scented moss. The fingers sink in the soft, moist verdure, and make at each instant some superb discovery unawares; again and again, straying carelessly, they clutch some new treasure; and, indeed, the plants are linked together in bright necklaces by secret threads beneath the surface, and where you grasp at one, you hold many. The hands go wandering over the moss as over the keys of a piano, and bring forth odors for melodies. The lovely creatures twine and nestle and lay their glowing faces to that very earth beneath withered leaves, and what seemed mere barrenness becomes fresh and fragrant beauty. So great is the charm of the pursuit, that the epigæa is really the wild-flower for which our country people have a hearty passion. Every village child knows its best haunts, and watches for it eagerly in the spring; boys wreathe their hats with it, girls twine it in their hair, and the cottage windows are filled with its beauty.

May Day is never allowed to pass in this community without profuse lamentations over the tardiness of our spring as compared with that of England and the poets. Yet it is easy to exaggerate this difference. Even so good an observer as Wilson Flagg is betrayed into saying that the epigæa and hepatica "seldom make their appearance until after the middle of April" in Massachusetts, and that "it is not unusual for the whole month of April to pass away without producing more than two or three species of wild-flowers." But I have formerly found the hepatica in bloom at Mount Auburn, for three successive years, on the 27th of March; and it has since been found in Worcester on the 17th, and in Danvers on the 12th. The Mayflower is usually as early, though the more gradual expansion of the buds renders it less easy to give dates. And there are nearly twenty species which I have noted, for five or six years together, as found always before May Day, and therefore properly to be assigned to April. The list includes bloodroot, cowslip, houstonia, saxifrage, dandelion, chickweed, cinquefoil, strawberry, mouse-ear, bellwort, dogtooth violet, five species of violet proper, and two of anemone.

After the epigæa and the hepatica have blossomed, there is a slight pause among the wild-flowers,—these two forming a distinct prologue for their annual drama, as the brilliant witch-hazel in October brings up its separate epilogue. The truth is, Nature attitudinizes a little, liking to make a neat finish with everything, and then to begin again with *éclat*. Flowers seem spontaneous things enough, but there is evidently a secret marshalling among them, that all may be brought out with due effect. As the country people say that so long as any snow is left on the ground more snow may be expected, for it must all vanish together at last,—so every seeker of spring flowers has observed how accurately they seem to move in platoons, with little straggling. Each species seems to burst upon us with a united impulse; you may search for it day after day in vain, but the day when you find one specimen the spell is broken and you find twenty. By the end of April all the margins of the great poem of the woods are illuminated with these exquisite vignettes.

As the spring comes on, and the changing outlines of the elm give daily a new design for a Grecian urn,—its hue first brown with blossoms, then emerald with leaves,—we appreciate the vanishing beauty of the bare boughs. In our favored temperate zone the trees denude themselves each year, like the goddesses before Paris, that we may see which unadorned loveliness is the fairest. Only the unconquerable delicacy of the beech still keeps its soft vestments about it: far into spring, when worn to thin rags and tatters, they cling there still; and when they fall, the new appear as by magic. It must be owned, however, that the beech has good reasons for this prudishness, and has hereabouts little beauty of figure; while the elms, maples, chestnuts, walnuts, and even oaks have not exhausted all their store of charms for us until we have seen them disrobed. Only yonder magnificent pine-tree,—that pitch pine, nobler when seen in perfection than white pine, or Norwegian, or Norfolk Islander,— that pitch pine, herself a grove, *una nemus,* holds her unchanging beauty throughout the year, like her half brother, the ocean, whose voice she shares; and only marks the flowing of her annual tide of life by the new verdure that yearly submerges all trace of last year's ebb.

How many lessons of faith and beauty we should lose if there were no winter in our year! Sometimes in following up a watercourse among our hills, in the early spring, one comes to a weird and desolate place, where one huge wild grapevine has wreathed its ragged arms around a whole thicket and brought it to the ground,—swarming to the tops of hemlocks, clinching a dozen young maples at once and tugging them downward, stretching its wizard black length across the underbrush, into the earth and out again, wrenching up great stones in its blind, aimless struggle. What a piece of chaos is this! Yet come here again, two months hence, and you shall find all this desolation clothed with beauty and with fragrance, one vast bower of soft green leaves and graceful tendrils, while summer birds chirp and flutter amid these sunny arches all the livelong day.

To the end of April, and often later, one still finds remains of snow-banks in sheltered woods, especially among evergreens; and this snow, like that upon high mountains, has often become hardened, by the repeated thawing and freezing of the surface, till it is more impenetrable than ice. But the snow that falls during April is usually what Vermonters call "sugar-snow,"—falling in the night and just whitening the surface for an hour or two, and taking its name, not so much from its looks as from the fact that it denotes the proper weather for "sugaring," namely, cold nights and warm days. Our saccharine associations, however, remain so obstinately tropical that it seems almost impossible for the imagination to locate sugar in New England trees, though it is known that not the maple only, but the birch and the walnut even afford it in appreciable quantities.

Along our maritime rivers the people associate April, not with "sugaring," but with "shadding." The pretty *Amelanchier Canadensis* of Gray—the *Aronia* of Whittier's song—is called Shad-bush, or Shad-blow, in Essex County, from its connection with this season; and there is a bird known as the Shad-spirit, which I take to be identical with the flicker or golden-winged woodpecker, whose note is still held to indicate the first day when the fish ascend the river. Upon such slender wings flits our New England romance!

In April the creative process described by Thales is repeated, and the world is renewed by water. The submerged creatures first feel the touch of spring, and many an equivocal career, beginning in the ponds and brooks, learns later to ignore this obscure beginning, and hops or flutters in the dusty daylight. Early in March, before the first male canker-moth appears on the elm-tree, the whirlwig beetles have begun to play round the broken edges of the ice, and the caddis-worms to crawl beneath it; and soon come the water-skater *(Gerris)* and the water-boatman *(Notonecta)*. Turtles and newts are in busy motion when the spring birds are only just arriving. Those gelatinous masses in yonder wayside pond are the spawn of water-newts or tritons: in the clear, transparent jelly are imbedded, at regular intervals, little blackish dots; these elongate rapidly, and show symptoms of head and tail curled up in a spherical cell; the jelly is gradually absorbed for their nourishment, until on some fine morning, each elongated dot gives one vigorous wriggle, and claims thenceforward all the privileges of freedom. The final privilege is often that of being suddenly snapped up by a turtle or a snake: for

Nature brings forth her creatures liberally, especially the aquatic ones, sacrifices nine tenths of them as food for their larger cousins, and reserves only a handful to propagate their race, on the same profuse scale, next season.

It is surprising, in the midst of our museums and scientific schools, how little we yet know of the common things around us. Our *savans* still confess their inability to discriminate with certainty the egg or tadpole of a frog from that of a toad; and it is strange that these hopping creatures, which seem so unlike, should coincide so nearly in their juvenile career, while the tritons and salamanders, which border so closely on each other in their maturer state as sometimes to be hardly distinguishable, yet choose different methods and different elements for laying their eggs. The eggs of our salamanders, or land lizards, are deposited beneath the moss on some damp rock, without any gelatinous envelope; they are but few in number, and the anxious mamma may sometimes be found coiled in a circle around them, like the symbolic serpent of eternity.

It is no wonder that there is so little substantial enjoyment of nature in the community, when we feed children on grammars and dictionaries only, and take no pains to train them to see that which is before their eyes. The mass of the community have "summered and wintered" the universe pretty regularly, one would think, for a good many years; and yet nine persons out of ten in the town or city, and two out of three even in the country, seriously suppose, for instance, that the buds upon trees are formed in the spring; they have had them within sight all winter, and never seen them. So people think, in good faith, that a plant grows at the base of the stem, instead of at the top: that is, if they see a young sapling in which there is a crotch at five feet from the ground, they expect to see it ten feet from the ground by and by,—confounding the growth of a tree with that of a man or animal.

But we are lingering too long, perhaps, with this sweet April of smiles and tears. It needs only to add, that all her traditions are beautiful. Ovid says well, that she was not named from *aperire,* to open, as some have thought, but from *Aphrodite,* goddess of beauty. April holds Easter-time, St. George's Day, and the Eve of St. Mark's. She has not, like her sister May in Germany, been transformed to a verb and made a synonym for joy,—*"Deine Seele maiet den trüben Herbst,"*—but April was believed in early ages to have been the birth-time of the world. According to the Venerable Bede, the point was first accurately determined at a council held at Jerusalem about A.D. 200, when, after much profound discussion, it was finally decided that the world's birthday occurred on Sunday, April 8,— that is, at the vernal equinox and the full moon. But April is certainly the birth-time of the season, at least, if not of the planet. Its festivals are older than Christianity, older than the memory of man. No sad associations cling to it, as to the month of June, in which month, says William of Malmesbury, kings are wont to go to war,— *"Quando solent reges ad arma procedure,"*—but it contains the Holy Week, and it is the Holy Month. And in April Shakespeare was born, and in April Shakespeare died.

Nancy Stringfellow

"REPORT FROM GRIMES CREEK AFTER A HARD WINTER" FROM *REPORT FROM GRIMES CREEK AFTER A HARD WINTER*

*N*ancy Stringfellow spent nearly all her life in Idaho, managing The Book Shop in Boise and living in a cabin, hand built by her husband, on Grimes Creek. She dwelt among books, the river, and her garden. Her daughter, Rosalie Sorrels, tells us that "she brought smooth river stones for a patio and planted thyme and mint and other herbs, shrubs, wild roses, lilacs, tress, until the house that once stood bare now looks like a bower and everywhere you put your foot a cloud of fragrance envelopes you. The whole place seems to have grown from the ground."

*T*he lemon thyme with its delicate, shriveled roots may not be dead, but only awaiting its awakening call. As, indeed, are we.

It is that ground, in its slow thaw, which also disgorges the hardiest herbs, those tempered by snow and ice and sorrow. But, as Stringfellow reminds us, it's early yet; the lemon thyme with its delicate, shriveled roots may not be dead, but only awaiting its awakening call. As, indeed, are we.

Report from Grimes Creek After a Hard Winter

The rue survived;
The rue and the bitter hyssop.
Remembered sorrow can survive the bitterest cold.
But the lovely lemon thyme
Lost its life in the stone-hard ground,
Its delicate roots shriveled for lack of warmth.

Some of the herbs are coming back:
Hardy horehound, lemon balm, and the astringent
Bee balm,
That western bergamot
Whose faintly medicinal fragrance
Mormon ladies used to scent their handkerchief
Boxes:
Schooled in hardship
It drove its roots deep underground
And waited out the winter.
Now toughened and durable,
It makes its way to the sun.

Stray tendrils of mint wandering far from their beds,
Battening on earthworm castings,
Smothered the sage.
Mint is fine on lamb,
But it takes the pungency of sage
To give any flavor to an Albertson turkey.

Nothing can stop the thyme. Never say that thyme
must have a stop.

The tansy is shouting hallelujas of joy
For Easter coming, and of course
Jonquils and crocuses and grape hyacinths
Never have given a damn.
Cold snow or warm rain,
Spring is spring, and
Damn the elements. Full speed ahead.
And
It's early yet.
Some roots may be still asleep
Warm and safe and lazy
Waiting for May. Or June.
Or maybe the Second Coming.

PART TWO

*A*wakenings

INTRODUCTION

In "The Inukok," the opening chapter from *The Peregrine Falcon,* Robert Murphy writes of springtime in the Great Barrens, northwest of Hudson Bay. Everything here is seen from the perspective of a single falcon, who is watching winter retreat and life begin again. For the falcon, springtime means the preservation of his own life— there is now more food to eat—as well as his participation in the larger cycles of life: he will look soon for a mate. But meanwhile, springtime awakens the landscape.

> Below him, in the reindeer moss and under the stunted willows that branched out and spread low to the ground under the constant harassment of the wind, the warmth of the sun was hurrying the low plants of the tundra back to their short summer life. They had to bloom quickly and bear their fruit before the snow covered them again, and the earliest of them, the saxifrage with its deep pink flowers, was already starring the moss with blossoms that came up at the edge of the snow. The ground squirrels emerged from hibernation and the collared lemmings that had moved about through their dark tunnels under the snow all winter crept out blinking into the sun and sat as if hypnotized in the warmth of it. The songs of snow buntings and pipits, longspurs and wheatears, came down the wind, for the birds were arriving daily on their long migrations

from the south. They were already beginning their courtships; the summer nights, so short in this latitude, would give them almost continuous daylight in which to gather food for their young and get them on the wing.

Only a short while ago, the falcon would have looked upon an utterly barren landscape. Snow would have extended over everything; but with the return of spring, there is a new light, the plants are blooming, animals are coming out of long hibernations, and birds are returning. It is a time of awakenings.

In his concluding chapter to *Walden,* entitled "Spring," Henry David Thoreau similarly evokes a scene at the pond: the hardwoods are putting out new leaves against the dark pines, the sun is shining on the hillsides, the birds have returned, and the pollen of the pitch pine is covering the shoreline. This scene sets up his conclusion to the book, a call that seems to emerge right from his evocation of spring: "Only that day dawns to which we are awake. There is more day to dawn. The sun is but a morning star."

The awakenings of spring represent an emergence into full life and consciousness. There is a sense of completeness to this particular motion of spring, a sense of wholeness. Stirrings indicate that we are beginning to move out of darkness, hibernation, and stillness, and that something more needs to happen. But awakenings indicate complete movement from sleep to wakefulness, from inattention to attention, from hibernation to participation, from darkness to light. What has been still and quiet is now fully emerged and ready to take up its role in the cycles of life. The actors have stepped onto the stage, and the great drama is about to begin.

In "The Spring," written in 1640, the poet Thomas Carew uses this sense of wakefulness playfully. Winter is gone, he writes, and "the warm sun thaws the benumbed earth, / And makes it tender ... ; wakes in hollow tree / The drowsy cuckoo and the humblebee." Everything is filled with the energy and joy of youth, and "the valleys, hills, and woods in rich array / Welcome the coming of the longed-for May." His love, however, refuses to respond to this new life, and though "all things keep / Time with the season: only she doth carry / June in her eyes, in her heart January." The humor of the poem lies in the distinction; this is spring, and everything is awake and responding to the calls of youth and love—except that his own love denies the wakefulness of springtime, and, with the cold of winter in her heart, denies her love.

Carew identifies the wakefulness of spring with youth, and certainly spring does seem to be identified with *new* growth, with beginnings. But the wakefulness to which spring calls us is not only for the young, and spring does not insist upon this designation. The falcon who sits above the Great Barrens has seen many springs come and go, and still he feels the urge to participate in the cycles that spring inaugurates—an urge that may be coupled with experience and the wisdom that experience gives. Writing in the last spring of his life, Thoreau noted, "I suppose that I have not many months to live; but of course I know nothing about it. I may add that I am enjoying existence as much as ever, and regret nothing." He died two months later, in the beginning of May.

The Shaker hymn that begins this section, "Returning Spring," speaks to this movement of waking up: "The voice of the returning spring / Bids nature wake and rise." Our proper response in a life of wakefulness, the hymn insists, is praise and thanksgiving. The pieces that follow explore the implications of the movement from slumber to wakefulness, both understood metaphorically. Certainly Abiel Abbot's sermon to mariners departing the safety of Beverly in the spring, exhorting them to see in the springtime ocean the bounties and providence of God, chimes with the words of "Returning Spring." Charles Abbott, however, uses spring to write about an interior wakefulness, as he gropes in a fog toward a "penetrative vision." Robert Finch and Annie Dillard affirm this perspective as they see spring as a time for gaining perspective upon their place in this world. Noel Perrin wants us to come with a state of surprise at the fecund bounties of the natural world—something the Shakers would have affirmed—while Rebecca Cox Jackson begins her springtime vision and Lisa Couturier ends her evocation of the outcasts of Manhattan with surprise and joy.

For these writers, springtime awakenings mean new awareness, sharper consciousness, and a more intense understanding of the edges of life against which we are being constantly rubbed. To choose not to awake is to stay in perpetual winter, to dull ourselves so that we hardly see those edges—and certainly much in North American culture urges us toward this state of spiritual dullness. Spring insists otherwise. "There is more day to dawn. The sun is but a morning star."

A Shaker Hymn

"Returning Spring"

The voice of the returning spring
Bids nature wake and rise,
And put her best new garments on,
For she has fresh supplies.

How wondrous are the ways of God!
How bountiful His hand!
We see his love in ev'ry tree,
And broadcast o'er the land.   (repeat)

Then why should we, whose lines have fallen
In such a pleasant place,
Be backward in the praise of Him,
Or e'er fall short of grace.

We ought to leap, and shout, and sing,
Till all the mountains round,
Reverberate the joyful news,
To earth's remotest bound.   (repeat)

We've all the eye of man could wish,
And fruitful is the land;
And greater than Assyrian hosts,
The angels round us stand.

And yet, to many thousands more,
We such a home could give,
If they would leave a carnal world,
And learn in Christ to live.   (repeat)

Charles C. Abbott

"A Cheerful Fog" from *In Nature's Realm*

Not many of us would think to call a fog "cheerful," but Charles Abbott knows better. In the chill of an early spring morning, he hears redbirds and field-sparrows and particularly "the little rattling frogs," all of whom pierce the damp to announce—at least to the listening human ear—the coming warmth of the April afternoon. Yet to be fully awake, Abbott reminds us, is not merely to look through the fog, but to lean into it, to feel and love the moment when we can only hear and not yet see the busy animal life around us.

If we cannot wholly shake off our ambitions and indifference, our impatience for the fog to lift, perhaps a spring morning can slow us down and help us recapture a moment of pure awareness.

Fog sharpens Abbott's perspective by removing the distractions of the big picture; unable to see the whole forest, he focuses on a single oak and finds it strangely magnified. Stripped of the comparisons that make us say "this one is smaller; this one is greater," we, too, learn to pay attention—to the distinctive call of a small bird, to a silent teenager, to an acquaintance perched on the

edge of disaster. If we cannot wholly shake off our ambitions and indiffer-
ence, our impatience for the fog to lift, perhaps a spring morning can slow us
down and help us recapture a moment of pure awareness.

"A Cheerful Fog"

No words can more aptly describe the conditions of a recent morning than that the world was wrapped in a cheerful fog. This is con-
tradictory, for fog is the embodiment of "damp and chilly," a phrase
the very mention of which suggests discomfort. Yes; it was damp
and chilly this morning, but there was compensation: the redbirds
whistled in their optimistic way and from far away in the trackless
mist came the trill of a field-sparrow, which series of sweet notes
rendered into our language means cheerfulness, an interpretation
more applicable to this little bird than to any other. But we need
not look wholly to birds of any kind for an explanation of what
nature means, and to-day there is many a croaking frog that has an
inkling of her significance and is more confident than most mortals
are that in due time this fog will roll away and the meadows bask in
sunshine.

It would be very rash and probably wide of the mark to say
that the little rattling frogs that now fill the whole air with this crisp
and snappy sound, as of intricate machinery in rapid motion, was
merely the announcement of coming sunshine and unclouded
skies. It is nothing of the kind to them, but it does mean something
of all this to us. This is an important distinction not always recognized. That which an animal does may have no reference to the
outside world, but sometimes it has been found out that certain
animal activities occur only under a given set of conditions, and,
therefore, the creatures we see or hear become proclaimers of what
obtains in their vicinity, but not necessarily prophets even of the
immediate future. Warm to-day and cold to-morrow may hold
good of all April, and when we have despaired of having spring we
find ourselves in summer. Too frequently is May intolerably hot. It
is safer to accept the incidents of each day as they come, and extract

their sweets, than attempt to generalize upon them as a whole and seek their bearing as to futurity. I know this foggy morning that the animal life of upland and meadows is all astir and do not propose to consider what many a gray-bearded man and wise old grandmother will tell you of the sunny afternoon that but a few hours will bring about. Sufficient unto the moment is the fogginess thereof.

Looking directly down I can see the well-worn narrow foot-path and know somewhat vaguely where I am going, but to step aside for a few paces is really to be lost. Groping in a fog is as uncertain as blindly feeling one's way in the dark, but there is the important difference that the sense of sight has some value in the former case, as I quickly realized as I walked slowly over the meadow. A small oak was suddenly dimly outlined before me, and how large it had grown! The tree was the same I had known for many years, yet strangely magnified. It was not a trick of the peculiar light prevailing, but was readily accounted for by the absence of other trees with which to compare it. Low hills are mountains to the level plain. When the conditions are normal we are influenced much more than we realize by the comparisons we are making all the while. No tree so tall but we look about for one that towers still higher; no flower so bright but we look for others that glow with a greater glory. Compared to myself the little oak was a giant, and except the grass at my feet, I could see no other object. What a chance to have a quiet chat with a tree, I thought, and doubtless would have stormed it with a volley of questions had not a bird suddenly appeared. I think it must have been by mere chance that it reached the tree. Why a bird should attempt flight through such a trackless mist is undeterminable. Enough for my purpose that it did so, and then, as if it had knowledge of my earlier impressions of the day, made good my assertion that the mist, if not cheerful of itself, was at least no dampener of a red-bird's spirits. Such splendid whistling! I think our Jersey cardinals are better musicians than their Southern cousins. This lone cardinal fairly made the air tremble; or was it mere coincidence that, as it sang, drops fell in vast profusion from the oak's branches. The appearance concerned me more than the probabilities of the case, and I gave the latter but a passing thought. My cardinal did not look upon me so much with suspicion as with surprise, and doubtless wondered why I was out in such a place.

What ... could a garden be without its song-sparrow? Does not its old-fashioned song attract as strongly as the old-fashioned flowers? If some one would do justice to the song of this bird, it would be the exaltation of the humble that ought long ago to have occurred,—a task worthy of any naturalist's best efforts. We are apt to speak of the bird without realizing the full significance of the name. It has, over a host of competitors, been chosen as the "song" sparrow, and right worthily does it prove equal to the expectations its name calls forth. I cannot imagine any one being disappointed in the bird.

All April, when nature saw fit to laugh at our almanacs and continue winter when and where spring had a better claim, the song-sparrow took things philosophically, and was just as ready to sing to a dismal blank of leaden sky as to the brilliant sunrise. A merit of the song not to be over-looked is that it fits words of wisdom better than any nonsense syllables one can coin. There is a sparrow in my gooseberry-hedge that all day sings, *"Cheer-cheer-cheer-cheer-cheerfulness."* Nothing else can be made of it, and who so prosy as to want it rendered otherwise? Why use nonsense in wording or phrasing a bird's song, when some expression can be used that is characteristic of the bird? I am duly thankful my Carolina wrens never did say "teakettle," but all sorts of things that suggest the bird, yet never one of the latter had gotten into the text-books. In them we find nothing but "teakettle," which, I am happy to say, I never heard and never expect to. There is nothing of the wren's excessive nervous energy in the song-sparrow's singing. The wren, I take it, wants the whole world to hear him; the song-sparrow's effort is for its own entertainment. Ambitious birds, like ambitious men, are not always pleasant company; they are apt to be tiresome, but the song-sparrow, combining cheerfulness with amiability, reassures you, if despondent, and demonstrates that pessimism is an outcome of weakness that a little faith can overcome. It is something to hear the sparrow singing before the roll of thunder has ceased, and better still to hear it when the driving storm deadens all other sounds. We are likely to remember it then, if not as one of many songs of a bright May morning.

The change for which anxious stay-at-homes looked for came at last. The dull, gray, heavy fog was slowly dissolving into a lighter, yellow mist, and the sun shone dimly through, a disc of dull gold. As if its warmth was anticipated, for I am sure it could not yet be felt, there was general rejoicing throughout the land. Not a bush without its bird, not a bird without its song; and in ever-increasing volume rose the croaking of frogs without number—in very truth a million voices exulting in the sun's victory.

It is at such a time we can realize the abundance of life, and what is of greater significance, how few of the facts concerning it have been gathered. Nature can keep a secret if man cannot and woman will not. How few have been brave enough to outweather all the year's changes, to learn at last what the busy world about us has been doing. Nature does not wear her heart upon her sleeve, but how few have that penetrative vision which sees through the coverings beneath which her real self is busy. The world is growing old. We hold ourselves as wise, but the crack o' doom will find us ignorant still. The hold of indifference is so powerful that we cannot wholly shake it off. We are all fog-bound, even when the sun shines.

Noel Perrin

"FLOW GENTLY, SWEET MAPLE," FROM *FIRST PERSON RURAL*

*I*n his poem "Sweet Afton," Robert Burns evokes a spring scene by a small Scottish brook. The birds are singing, the valley is green, and the primroses are blooming. Mary is asleep by the murmuring stream, and the poet asks the Afton to flow gently so as to "disturb not her dream." Though invoked in the title of Perrin's essay, the quiet mood and slow tones of "Sweet Afton" have little to do with the frenetic pace of work that Perrin describes during an unusual maple sugar season. His prayer to the maples is not answered; the result is a frantic splurge.

> *T*hough the nights are still freezing, the days are warmer, and the sap is enticed up into the trunk of the tree. It is one more sign that the cycle is about to begin again, one more sign that winter will not always be with us.

One of the first sure signs of spring is the running of the sap in the maple sugar trees very late February, more likely March. Though the nights are still freezing, the days are warmer, and the sap is enticed up into the trunk of the tree. It is one more sign that the cycle is about to begin again, one more sign that winter will not always be with us. It is a sign of new life.

Perrin seems intensely aware of this; he does not want to waste any of it. He fears that the sap will spoil, that it will run onto the ground, that it will be lost as it dribbles down the bark. And this is not mere economic greed; it is a deep sense that somehow this is a sign of spring, a sign of renewal. It is not to be taken lightly. It suggests something greater than itself.

"Have, get, before it cloy," says Gerard Manley Hopkins of spring, for it is "thy choice and worthy the winning."

"Flow Gently, Sweet Maple"

Last year was one of the great syrup years of this century. I have never seen maples run harder than they did on March 11th, 1977, and again on March 21st, and again on March 28th. Only once or twice have I ever known the sap as sweet. Even the poorest trees I tapped were running sweet to the taste. The best trees were behaving as if they thought they were sugarcane.

By the time the season finally ended, Vermont had produced 437,000 gallons of syrup. No other state produced even nearly as much. New York, five times as big as Vermont, came the closest to providing competition. New York produced a piddling 320,000 gallons. Many Vermont sugarers, myself included, made double what they did in 1976.

Sounds nice, doesn't it? Sounds like the kind of year you'd like to have every year. Well, it's not. I can barely stand it the one year in every ten or twelve that it does happen. Listen to the story of the wonder-year 1977, and then you'll understand why I hope we don't have another like it until about 1990 … or maybe 1995.

The season began quietly. There was no hint of the excitement to come. I started hanging buckets on March 2nd, which was a day of bright sun and cold wind after a good hard freeze. Just like normal. By March 8th, I had my whole 104 buckets up—twenty on General Miller's lawn in the village, about 50 scattered around my own land, and the rest up the hill at Alice Lacey's. The next day, which was a Sunday, I placidly made my first gallon of syrup.

At this point it still seemed a typical year. There had been a couple of pretty good days, with three or four inches of sap in good buckets. (Half an inch in bad ones.) There had also been several days when nothing ran at all. But then on March 11th there was a quantum jump. We suddenly got a day when it was probably warmer in Vermont than in Miami Beach. The temperature rose from 26 at 7 AM to 70 at noon. It clearly excited the maples. By 10 AM some spouts were actually running a tiny stream, instead of just dripping the way they are supposed to. I gathered all afternoon. By suppertime the holding tank at the sugarhouse was full, and the gathering tank on the back of my truck was nearly full. We had just one worry. The sun was so powerful that the sap in some buckets was warm to the touch, and we feared it would spoil before we could make syrup.

So I hurried. Over the next two days, boiling late after work, I made ten gallons of syrup—which in my small evaporator takes thirteen or fourteen hours. No sap spoiled, but the grade of the syrup gradually dropped from Fancy down to A, and then on the last couple of gallons on down to B. Meanwhile, the weather stayed warm. We went three nights in a row without a frost. Then it rained for two days. Practically all the snow melted, and people began to worry that the season was already over, after that one splendid run.

They needn't have. On March 20th it snowed again, and on the 21st the maples went wild. Trees that normally drip a scanty half-gallon on a good day were filling a sixteen-quart pail right up. Two hours after I got home from work I had the holding tank full, and the gathering tank full, and 30 buckets still to gather. Most of them, full to the brim, were briskly running good sap onto the ground.

To make room to empty them, we'd have to boil. My wife announced an indefinite delay in supper, and fired up. By dark she had used enough sap so that I could empty each of the last 30 buckets halfway. Then I put them back on the trees, each with two gallons of sap still in it. This is not easy even by daylight. It's downright hard when you're doing it in the dark by feel.

The next day was a Saturday, and I boiled from 7:45 AM until 6 PM, making eight and a half gallons, all Fancy. But I didn't gain an inch. The trees ran almost as hard as they had yesterday. In the afternoon, while I furiously boiled, my wife and daughters gathered for me, getting all but eight buckets they didn't know about, which are on a little hill behind the sheep pasture.

I might have tried to go on boiling by candlelight after it got dark, but just before 6 PM I ran out of wood. Don't sneer. My normal year's production is 25 gallons, and that's what I keep wood enough at the sugarhouse for, with a small margin for safety. This year I had already made 29 gallons. Instead, after dinner I went out with a flashlight to get those last eight buckets. The radio said we were going to have a blizzard with twelve to eighteen inches of snow. It would be a lot easier to climb the hill to those buckets now than tomorrow. Big wet snowflakes were coming down hard as I hurried up the hill at 9 PM with my flashlight and gathering pails. All eight buckets were running over, and I had four round trips to make, stumbling in the dark. (The flashlight helps in emptying, but you put it in your pocket when you're coming down with a full gathering pail in each hand.)

Sunday is a day of rest. For people who don't sugar, that is. Me, I got up at 6 AM to resume boiling. I noticed with joy that the blizzard hadn't come. There were barely three inches of new snow. By 6:30 I had loaded my truck with firewood from the barn (good hardwood from the house supply, not the pine slabs and spruce tops I normally use at the sugarhouse), and was off. On my way I checked a couple of roadside buckets, and my spirits immediately sank. The trees had been running all night. Both buckets were half full.

Worse news was in store at the sugarhouse. Much worse. When I ran out of wood the evening before, I had grabbed a few oak logs from the barn to finish off the last gallon I made. And being very tired, I had also failed to check the float valves when I quit boiling. One of them, I now discovered, was jammed. No sap had come into the finishing pan all night.

Normally that wouldn't have mattered; pine and spruce leave no coals, and the pans would have cooled off before any harm was done. But oak is another matter. The pans had been gently steaming all night—indeed, the sap pan still was. As for the finishing pan, it held a twisted mass of black carbon—all that was left of what would have been two gallons of Fancy syrup. It took three hours to scrape and scrub it clean. I tried to be grateful that at least I hadn't ruined the pan itself, just melted a little solder.

Meanwhile the sun came out and the maples, which had now been running 24 hours straight, picked up speed. By the time I could start boiling at 10 AM, some buckets we had emptied yesterday afternoon were two-thirds full again. Both tanks, of course, were completely full.

The next day was the low point of the season. Though it was a Monday, and though I was bone-tired, I stayed home to boil. I didn't want to keep on using dry housewood—I didn't have that much left. I took just enough down to get the fire going well, and then began feeding in some red maple I'd cut just a couple of months earlier.

The fire practically went out. I could make the pans simmer, but except when I borrowed more dry wood from the barn, I couldn't make them boil. Between 7 AM and 3 PM I managed to produce only three and a half gallons. Then I gave up, and went to the woods to cut dead elms. Standing dead elm is the only dry wood you can harvest in March. I naturally also checked a couple of buckets, and noted with sorrow that though it was a bleak windy day when by rights the trees shouldn't be running at all, they were in fact dripping briskly along. It was no hard run—but my 104 buckets would probably yield 40 or 50 gallons today, and me with no storage space, and no wood to boil with.

I took two more half-days off from work that week. Gradually I worked my tanks down, and built the supply of dead elm up. But during the enormous run on Friday, I lost every bit I had gained. Friday at dark I had 44½ gallons of syrup, full tanks, and no more elm.

Most people in town who make syrup were in a comparable plight, and at this point some of them pulled their buckets and called it a season. One of them, in fact, tried to give me three barrels of good sap he had on hand when he quit. I eagerly refused it.

I didn't pull my buckets, though. Not that I wasn't tired of sugaring (and cutting dead elms), but having tapped the maples, I felt it would be a sort of betrayal to remove the spouts and let the sap just dribble down the bark. A little as if a worker at a Red Cross blood center came up to a donor and pulled the needle out of his arm after half a pint, explaining that they'd filled the day's quota, and suggesting he just go bleed on the street. I couldn't do it. I kept boiling.

When I boiled the last time on April 6th, and closed down, I had made 57 gallons: 14 of Fancy, 23 of A, 12 of B, and 8 of C. I had prettied up something like five acres of woodland by removing all the dead elms. I still had the evaporator and all the buckets to wash. And I was so tired I slept twelve hours a night for the next three nights.

This spring I won't mind if we have a good season, but if we have another spectacular one, I shall probably quit midway and take a trip to South Carolina. Might even get a pickup while I'm there.

Robert Finch

"LONG NOOK" AND "SHADOW ON THE POND" FROM *DEATH OF A HORNET*

*D*uring winter, we tend to shield ourselves from the weather of the sea-son, as though we are cocooned, waiting to come out into warmth and light. Springtime brings that warmth and light, and we find our-selves, almost by surprise, walking once again out into the world, released, seeing what we have been hidden from.

*I*n spring, the journeys may begin with our outward motion, but inevitably those same journeys move us within.

The nature writer Robert Finch, who has lived on Cape Cod for the last thirty years, recounts such springtime walks— both after storms. In "Shadow on the Pond," Finch describes a new perspective he gains over a swampy bog, finding that he seems to leave his role as observer and enter into the spring-time world, becoming a real part of it. In "Long Nook," he again begins as the observer, recognizing the power of the natural world and its independence of humanity. At the same time, that very independence, the health of the landscape before him, fills him with joy. It is a joy, he writes, that strips away all small seductions, and brings us back to who we truly are.

In spring, the journeys may begin with our outward motion, Finch seems to suggest. But inevitably, those same journeys move us within.

"Long Nook"

I would give up much to live near Long Nook, perhaps the loveliest of Cape Cod's ocean "hollows"—those dozen or so long, glacial valleys that are truncated perpendicularly by the Cape's Atlantic cliffs from Head of the Meadow Beach in North Truro to LeCount Hollow in South Wellfleet.

Long Nook, in Truro, is one of the highest and steepest of these Outer Beach accesses. Set between high, camel-hump dunes and ridges, it drops vertically some sixty feet down an unvegetated sand slope to the beach. There are no permanent steps or trails. Instead, diagonal foot paths are made and remade throughout the year as the cliff face itself is constantly reshaped by storms.

One April morning, following an easterly blow, Kathy and I arrived at the small parking lot about 9:30. The air was sunny, calm, and full of water vapor and negative ions. We felt exhilarated even before we saw the water, which gradually appears between the steep dunes that form the sides of the hollow, as if filling up a giant, V-shaped vase. The ocean was astonishingly glorious, as it often is the day following a storm. What struck us first, even before we could see the surf, were the colors on the sea's surface: contrasting shades of opalescent greens and pale moire blues, spread out over the ocean's vast surface like some fabulous Oriental bazaar of silks blowing in the wind. The blues were of the exact hue and texture of the vapor-softened sky, so that sky and sea blended indistinguishably at the horizon, and from there to the shore islands of blue sky floated on a jade sea.

Then the surf came into view—a magnificent milky aftermath of yesterday's blow—a quarter mile of range after range of foamy, plunging breakers, blanketing the shore with a continuous, thick roar. It was nearly low tide when we arrived, so that the beach was a good seventy-five yards wide, leaving a hard, wide, nearly flat sandy highway for walking. We headed south and at first were aware only of the surf to our left. Its impending power translated irresistibly into images of assault: enormous breakers pounding ashore like waves of amphibious panzers. The lines of swells were perfectly parallel to the shore and, crashing far out in the calm air, they exploded like watery mortar bursts, sending up unchoreographed geysers of spray into the air. By the time the fury of the breakers reached the beach, it had been rendered into viscous sheets and probing fingers of foam, like scouting parties, advancing up the shallow incline twenty, thirty, fifty feet, then retreating with whatever information they had gleaned. It was D-Day on the beach that morning, but a benign invasion, a symphonic version of destruction, heavenly warfare.

At first it seemed as if the night's high-ranging tide had swept the beach clean in a shallow arc that flattened near the water. Ours were the first footprints of the morning. But a closer look revealed signatures of the deep reach and throw of yesterday's storm. It had scattered dozens of sea clam shells along the beach, including two that were still whole and alive, which we retrieved to sweeten the previous evening's oyster stew. It had torn several brightly colored lobster buoys from their moorings and tossed them along the very uppermost part of the beach, where they lay like a string of party lights. During the night the retreating tide had left a series of light overlapping arcs of rockweed down the face of the beach.

Close to the surf we came upon the washed-up, wave-battered form of a common murre, a penguin-like pelagic bird, the size of a small duck, that breeds on the rocky cliffs of Newfoundland and Labrador. Its black-and-white plumage was matted; its breast had been cleanly plucked by something in the ocean; but its light-blue eyes were still intact, and the serrated lining of its long, thin, black beak was as yellow as a child's raincoat.

At this point Kathy decided to turn back, but I continued on to the first break in the cliff, about a mile from the parking lot. From there I gained the crest and headed back along the cliff edge trail. The landscape of the crest still had a solidly wintry look: bare, blue-grey jungles of scrub oak branches with a few dangling dead brown leaves; wind-burned tufts of creeping pitch pine; bleached-straw waves of beach grass on the dune slopes, and grey rags of poverty grass lining the trail.

But as I rose and dipped across its contours, this drained and unresurgent terrain gradually dropped hints of a new season already in progress. Here, small, efflorescent, pale-green rosettes of dusty miller protruded from the sand; there, sharp-pointed, bright-green spears of new beach grass blades rose out of last year's dead collars, like souls half-emerged from their bodies. Mats of bearberry were beginning to undergo their mysterious transformation from dark wine to dark green hues; and from the thickets of bare oak branches came the clear, territorial song of the song sparrow.

At such moments we are filled with a profound satisfaction with life and with our body's own motion, with the health of the landscape before us and its existence independent of us—the wide expanse of sea and sun-washed beach, Whatever personal avulsions we carry with us, whatever nagging mental knowledge of the earth's worsening wounds that dogs our heels, stay gratefully at the edge of consciousness, and for the stretch of a morning we can assent to Thoreau's triumphant assertion that "Surely joy is the condition of life"—in all its amoral, physical totality. The flattened blossom of grey feathers I find on the path, sign of a violent and fatal encounter, are as beautiful and healthy as the forced narcissi on the breakfast table. The strong scent of skunk that filters through my nostrils is as sweet and bracing as the flowers' perfume, or the smell of a newborn's head. How lucky are we who live in proximity to such a landscape, that has such easy powers to lift us out of our narrow lives, to strip away our self-made blinders, and so seduce us into being who we really are!

As I descended the final hill to the parking lot where Kathy waited in the car, I could see a mile to the north the two white radar domes of the North Truro Air Force Station. Once a primary target for the defunct Soviet Union's ICBMs, they now appeared like twin full moons rising against the sun-bathed camel's hump of

Long Nook's dunes—as if even these reminders of the human urge to self-destruction had been transformed by the spell of the morning into a benign version of themselves—a double blessing on the earth and of all its inhabitants.

"Shadow on the Pond"

I went down to Berry's Hole this morning, taking along a notebook and binoculars, thinking I might write and record what I saw there for an hour or two. The weather was beautiful after heavy, dark rains the week before. Now it was in the mid-sixties with only a slight breeze, yet just enough to make things in the yard—leaves, birds, limbs—seem almost weightless, as objects rest lightly on the bottom of the ocean, making me aware of a physical connectedness between things through a common medium.

Chickadees, titmice, jays, and woodpeckers all sang loudly in the yard. The phoebe pair, back for several weeks now, are still flitting around the rear side of the house, making indecisive feints toward the corner under the eaves where I have built a nesting shelf for them. The grass in the yard is beginning to green, and a clump of clover has poked its way up between two of the back steps.

I walked down the toboggan run into the kettle hole, noticing how the beech buds were beginning to swell, and lifting up the small, leathery green leaves of the mayflower plants along the leaf-littered slopes to see if the first of their diminutive blossoms had opened yet.

From below I could hear the scattered, intermittent calls of the woodfrogs—wooden, explosive, arrhythmic sounds, like strings of miniature fireworks going off. As I approached the bog at the bottom of the hollow, I caught a glimpse of a black, shiny plated shell in the water—a turtle! This was the first time I had ever seen one in this small wetland, whose shallow, fluctuating waters are too inconstant to support permanent fish or other vertebrate populations. What kind of a turtle was it, and where could it have come from?

But before I could fumble my binoculars out of their case, the turtle spotted me and scuttled down out of sight into the mud. Nature watching, it seems, is largely a losing game of trying to see things before they see you.

The bog is technically a swampy marsh, or a marshy swamp, I suppose, ringed with shrubs and with a center island of small trees and more shrubs, but with good-sized patches of open water when the rains have been generous. When I reached the edge, I could see a mixed clump of a dozen or so egg masses near the shore: the smaller, clear globes of the woodfrogs and the larger, cloudier masses of the yellow-spotted salamanders. The light breezes sent the water shimmering and skittering to the far side, while water skaters and whirligigs hopped and slid across the surface. Light played with sound, as the dead oak leaves, hanging intact in dry clumps on the white branches, rustled on the hillsides.

I worked my way around to the far side of the bog where some large swamp maples loomed out over the water. I was planning to circle the entire perimeter before settling down, but, following a sudden urge, I laid my glasses case and notebook at the base of the largest maple and climbed up its trunk out onto one of the more substantial limbs that overhung the bog. I stayed up there for almost an hour.

Reaching the highest and farthest-extending branch that I thought would support my weight safely, I looked down and saw the bog in a way I never had before, from a bird's eye (or at least a squirrel's eye) view, seeing straight into its muddy mind, its murky workings. As I looked, other masses of amphibian eggs began to appear here and there in the bog; light-colored, translucent globes and opalescent strings, emerging like daytime stars against the reflected sky.

The largest clump, nearly two feet across, was directly beneath me and attached to a half-sunken limb. Others were attached to twigs near the surface, or stuck to rocks deeply embedded in the muck. Some of the clumps were already partly exposed to the air, and I knew that if in the weeks to come the level of the bog dropped further, many of the eggs would be doomed to desiccation.

On the other hand, the rains could fall in abundance, inundating the blueberry roots along the shore and flooding out some of the small pine saplings that have begun to take hold in places during the drought of the past two years. But that is nature's way. One gets nothing for effort or endurance. It is all accident, help or hurt.

Then I saw the turtle again, almost directly beneath me. This time I didn't need binoculars to see that it was a painted turtle, a large one nearly six inches long, lying just at the surface, its hind half submerged, the white scute lines and red rim around the shell showing plainly. It was drifting freely, and as the light wind blew some floating surface leaves around it, it kept its place by alternately stroking its front left foot and rear right one.

The breeze also moved the limb on which I lay, stretched out along its rough length. Slowly, almost imperceptibly, it lifted and lowered me with great restrained force and rhythm, distilling and resolving the thin dispersed wind into a more confined but authoritative movement. It was a kind of flying.

Then a second turtle appeared, a few feet away from the first, a smaller one perhaps four inches long, surfacing next to a half-submerged branch. Very gradually, like the hands of a clock, it moved out of the water and up onto the branch: first the notched blunted snout, then the slitted eyes, then a wrinkled neck veined with yellow, and red, long-nailed foreclaws—so slowly that its dark shell dried as it emerged. I lay very quiet and still in the tree above it, while the woodpeckers rattled and the chickadees threw their contrapuntal songs back and forth across the hole.

It did not seem that either of the turtles was aware of me, great red-shirted thing in the trees overhead. Perhaps they do not recognize humans in strange or unexpected locations. I have noticed, for instance, that I can sometimes swim within a few yards of shorebirds resting on the bank of a tidal creek—birds which, were I on land, would not let me approach within a hundred feet of them.

After a while the larger turtle swam off toward the center island, giving me an unusual opportunity to observe clearly the sequence of its swimming motion. It seemed basically to be one of alternate coordination: right-front and left-rear together, followed by left-front and right-rear, with the rear swipe or thrust lagging slightly behind the front each time, resulting in that characteristic side-to-side "waddle" motion of turtles. It struck me that this was exactly the movement of my daughter's plastic mechanical bathtub turtle, an unexpected bit of commercial biological accuracy.

When do these turtles *do* something? I wondered—something besides hibernate, sunbathe, or practice their side-to-side strokes? So often the animals we observe—herring gulls, frogs, seals, squirrels, snakes—do not seem to be doing much of anything at all, as though they wished to pretend in front of us that their existence is merely a matter of assent, and only we were thrown out of the Garden. In a sense this is what they are pretending in our presence, keeping their more vital activities hidden from view.

But I was not really impatient. In fact, I found myself strangely serene and unruffled, unaware of time or place. I seemed to have adapted myself to the turtles' tempo, lifted and lowered gently there in the soft April breezes above the dark bog. Not only did the turtles appear not to notice me, but shortly thereafter I also saw a cat before it saw me—an extremely rare occurrence. This was a large grey and white feral that had paraded by my house many times. Now I saw it padding down into the hole and noiselessly circling the bog, though there was no potential prey in sight. It stopped, lounging and licking itself for several minutes before it finally seemed to sense something above it. It looked up, but even then, from the strangeness of my location or my stillness, it chose to ignore me, and continued on its rounds without haste.

I had, it seemed, by assent to a series of unforeseen opportunities, inclined and climbed my way into a position of utter centrality and perspective, heretofore unattained in scores of previous trips made to this bog. I looked down again, and this time I saw reflected on the surface neither dark water and turtles and buried leaves, nor the darkened image of the overhead sky and clouds, but a pattern of shadows stretching out across the entire bog—the meshed, depthless maze of branch and limb. And there, in the center of the pattern, was my own foreshortened silhouette—hulking, looming like some huge gall-like growth out of the tree, moving only as the tree shadows themselves moved, slowly, smoothly, resolved in the wind.

For once, then, momentarily suspended ten feet above the bog, I found myself a part of this maze of intersecting patterns, accepted by it, carried along with it. Turtles, water-bugs, and unseen tadpoles swam through my image. I harbored within myself the clouded and seed-sprinkled globes of egg masses. And then, from out of my floating shadow, as though out of a cocoon, the lovely form of a mourning cloak butterfly emerged into daylight.

Tu Fu
Translated by Irving Y. Lo

"RANDOM PLEASURES: NINE QUATRAINS"

*T*u Fu, the eighth-century Confucian poet, is considered one of the greatest of the ancient Chinese writers. His life was marked by disappointment at court, civil war, and exile, but despite this instability he wrote finely crafted poems that explored both the minute details of ordinary life and the historic sweep of the Tang dynasty as it fell into decline.

In this poem, Tu Fu looks at the coming of spring with what appears, at first, to be a jaundiced eye. Spring is a wanton thief, its wind a master bully. The spring rains first swell the rivers, then trickle away to nothing. Swallows and gnats plague the scholar at his books. Tu Fu reminds us that what awakens us in the spring is not just its lovely sprightliness but also its sharp edges. Yet, amidst these aggravations—and the poem ends, as it began, with a cruel wind—there are random pleasures: fragrant petals, green moss, sleeping ducklings, white cattails, the sound of words falling exactly into place. But for the traveler far from home, such quiet happiness, however, can only be glimpsed.

> *T*u Fu reminds us that what awakens us in the spring is not just its lovely sprightliness but also its sharp edges.

Random Pleasures: Nine Quatrains

1

See a traveler in sorrow: deeper is his grief
As wanton spring steals into the river pavilion—
True, the flowers will rush to open,
Yet how the orioles will keep up their songs.

2

Those peach and plum trees planted by hand are not
*   without a master:*
The rude wall is low; still it's my home.
But 'tis just like the spring wind, that master bully:
Last night it blew so many blossomed branches down.

3

How well they know, my study's low and small—
The swallows from the riverside find reason to visit
*   me often:*
Carrying mud to spot and spoil my lute and books,
And trailing a flight of gnats that strike my face.

4

March is gone, and April's come:
Old fellow, how many more chances to welcome the
*   spring?*
Don't think of the endless affairs beyond the
*   hereafter;*
Just drain your lifetime's few allotted cups.

5

*Heartbroken—there springtime river trickles to
      its end:*
*Cane in hand, I slowly pace and stand on fragrant
      bank.*
*How impertinent the willow catkins, to run off with
      the wind;*
So fickle, the peach blossoms to drift with the stream!

6

I've grown so indolent I never leave the village;
At dusk I shout to the boy to shut the rustic gate.
Green moss, raw wine, calm in the grove;
Blue water, spring breeze, dusk on the land.

7

Path-strewn catkins spread out a white carpet;
Stream-dotting lotus leaves mound up green coins.
By the bamboo roots, a young pheasant unseen;
On the sandbank, ducklings by their mother, asleep.

8

*West of my house, young mulberry leaves are ready
      for picking;*
Along the river new wheat, so tender and soft.
*How much more is left of life when spring has turned
      to summer?*
Don't pass up good wine, sweeter than honey.

9

The willows by the gate are slender and graceful
Like the waist of a girl at fifteen.
Morning came, and who could fail to see
Mad wind had snapped the longest branch.

Abiel Abbot

From Sermons to Mariners

In the spring of 1804, Reverend Abiel Abbot, minister of the First Church in Beverly, Massachusetts—a seaport—began a series of sermons aimed particularly at sailors about to leave their homes after the winter storms to begin a new season on the sea, mostly working the great schools of fish off the Grand Banks. He maintained the series each spring for eight years, until, moved by the tremendous loss of men during that time, he published the collection so that the series and the accompanying prayers might be read aloud for the men while at sea, thus maintaining at least a tangential connection between the pastor and his flock.

The first sermon and prayer in this springtime series opens with a recognition that the imminent

> *We begin by waking up, by understanding the intimate connections between ourselves and our place and the spiritual possibilities to which those connections point.*

separation of the minister and so much of his congregation is a "solemn" moment, and so Abbot wants to give his parishioners a kind of exhortation. It turns out to be an exhortation that defies modern stereotypes of the condemning Puritan divine. He begins with a sense of the awe and majesty of creation, and then moves toward a call to live in an awareness of that creation.

If spring is a time to begin a journey, Abbot reminds us that we begin by waking up, by understanding the intimate connections between ourselves and our place and the spiritual possibilities to which those connections point.

From *Sermons to Mariners*

Sermon I

The works and wonders of God in the deep, observed and improved.

Psalm cvii, 23, 24: They that go down to the sea in ships, that do business in great waters; these see the works of the Lord, and his wonders in the deep.

We have selected a passage from the mariner's portion in this psalm to give occasion to a particular address to a considerable number in this assembly, who may soon leave us, to *do business on the mighty waters.* Several circumstances render this occasion a solemn one. It is a parting with souls, committed to my charge, if not *final,* at least for a season. Leaving us, they will be removed from the reach of admonition, which will be constantly repeated to those who remain. They will cease to have the enjoyment of many of the means of grace, and may also fall into special temptations to forget God and the great concerns of religion. The regular return of sabbath privileges, of temple worship, of social praise, of ministerial instruction, and holy ordinances, will be interrupted. Add to this, they are departing into dangers, from which they may never return. These circumstances being justly affecting both to them and their pastor, I hope they will attend to this address with great seriousness, and will indulge me with being very particular and earnest in those counsels, with which I design to occupy the greater part of this discourse.

Let us consider those *works and wonders of God in the deep,* which seafaring men constantly behold.

Says the Psalmist, *The sea is the Lord's, and he made it.* It is a world of wonders; who can look upon it without admiration bordering on terrour? When it displays to our eyes an unruffled boson, and is like a boundless sheet of glass, reflecting the image of heaven, the azure sky and sun by day, and the moon and stars by night, what an august spectacle do we contemplate! Behold it, at another time, tempest-tost, when *God commandeth and raiseth the stormy wind, which lifteth up the waves thereof.* See yonder distressed vessel; *they mount up to heaven; they go down to the depths; their soul is melted because of trouble.* How sublime and terrifick is the world of waters in this dreadful commotion! *Great and marvellous are thy works, Lord God Almighty.*

These are views of the ocean, often presented to the mariner, which the dullest spectator cannot behold uninterested. Yet the surface, however varied by calm or storm, shows not half so many wonders, as lie beneath it. A short discourse cannot admit many things on this inexhaustible subject; I will mention a few, which should engage the thoughtful and pious, while they move upon the face of the deep.

When we expose water for any time to the sun and air, we perceive that it soon loses its salutary qualities, becomes offensive, and is even pestilential. How is it that the ocean is preserved from corruption, so that it is a fit and pleasant abode for the innumerable creatures, which live and play in it; and its very vapours are not only harmless, but even salutary to men, who sail on its bosom or live on its shores? This is effected in the wise providence of God by the immense body of salt; by which the waters are impregnated, and that continual motion, in which they arc preserved by wind and tide.

With respect to living creatures, the ocean is doubtless in a great measure a world unknown to us. We are ignorant of the treasures and of the inhabitants, which lie hid in its dark and unfathomable caverns; but, judging the most reachable parts of the ocean by those, which we can penetrate and examine, or judging of the waters by the land, we may believe every part well inhabited. It is said that every portion of air, every handful of earth, and every drop of water, is animated with living creatures, chiefly too small to be discovered by the naked eye. It is generally observable also in the watry world, that in proportion to the body of waters, collected together in a pond or lake, a sea or ocean, is the size of creatures found in them. What vast and wonderful creatures, therefore, is it supposeable from analogy, must inhabit those largest oceans on the globe, which the adventurous mariner has been able but very imperfectly to explore.

Without entering the field of conjecture, enough has been discovered of the inhabitants of the deep to claim our grateful wonder and praise to their great Creator. The variety of kinds and of species is almost infinite; large and small; some to devour, and others to be their victims; some excellent for their strength, others for their beauty, and others for their usefulness and comfort to man. *There is that leviathan, whom God hath made to play therein* (Psalm civ, 26). *He maketh the deep to boil like a pot; he maketh the sea like a pot of ointment. He maketh a path to shine after him; one would think the deep to be hoary.* Thus he is described by Job (xli, 31, 32).

To pass by other surprising works of God in the deep, astonishing is that inexhaustible supply of fish, which several thousands of enterprising men are annually employed in taking on the banks of Newfoundland, without appearing in the least to diminish their quantity in the course of century. How worthy also of grateful notice is the circumstance that fish are found on the Grand Bank, not young and old, but all in full size, as if kind Providence had nurtured them in other places, perhaps inaccessible by hook and line, and had conducted them on the spot, as a convenient place of delivery to his dependent creature man. Who can fail to observe the merciful goodness of God, who has caused those fish, and those animals and birds, which are most useful to man, the fastest to multiply and the most to abound; while noxious creatures propagate slowly, and seldom appear to annoy us? *How manifold are your works, Lord God Almighty, in wisdom hast thou made them all!*

Such are some of the *works* of God, of which our seafaring brethren are spectators. In the deep also, they see many *wonders* of his providence.

We all indeed are dependant on the providence of God for our being, and for any comfort and success, which we enjoy in the world. The husbandman must look to God for his seed time and harvest, for the former and the latter rain; and for all which he gathers for man and beast. Yet the scene of providence occasionally appears more marked with affecting changes on the water, than on the land. A wind or storm, from which we take safe refuge in our houses, brings the mariner into the jeopardy of his life. He has no place of retreat; he must meet the howling tempest, and subsist as he can amid the war of elements. Hence with just concern he watches the sky, and perhaps, with the Prophet of Israel, apprehends important change from a cloud, rising out of the sea, no bigger than a man's hand. Frequently his fears are realized; and he perceives the vessel at the mercy of the winds, suffering no control from those on board, and hastening to the shore and to almost certain destruction. *Many* in this assembly have at times felt this to be their own situation; and did you not also look up with the conviction that God only could deliver you? You *cried unto the Lord in your trouble? and he brought you out of your distresses. He made the storm a calm, so that the waves thereof were still. Then were you glad, because you were quiet; so he brought you to your desired haven.* Then *praise the Lord for his goodness, and for his wonderful works to the children of men.*

It is not uncommon for us to hear the mariner talking over his dangers and hair-breadth escapes. Surely they were so many occasions of divine kindness and interposal in his behalf. At one time the wind died away, or shifted to another point, so as just to save him from a rock or shore. Will he ascribe this to chance? or to Him, *who gathereth the wind in his hand?* At another time a friendly vessel picked him up in the midst of the ocean, floating on an oar, or exposed in an open boat. Will he call this a lucky accident, and be grateful only to his human deliverer? or also to Him, whose watchful providence brought the deliverer timely to his relief? In regard to all these occasions, let him say with devout emotion, *I have seen the wonders of the Lord in the deep.*

We sometimes hear our brethren, who draw treasures out of

the water, remarking that they have been lucky and made excellent fares. Let them not forget whose *blessing* it is, *which maketh rich.* Let them not ascribe too much to their own skill or industry; though a blessing commonly attends the industrious. Let them be very cautious, lest the Prophet's description of some in his time should be applicable to them: *They take up all of them with the angle, they catch them in their net, and gather them in their drag; therefore they rejoice and are glad: therefore they sacrifice unto their net, and burn incense unto their drag; because by them their portion is fat and their meat plenteous* (Hab. i, 15, 16).

Are the *works and wonders of God in the deep* so great, so surprising and affecting? Then suffer not your minds to grow careless and unobserving of them. Things which are familiar we are apt to behold only with a glance, and to think little of them. But let not this be the case with you. When you look upon the vast ocean think how great He is, who made it; how mighty He is, who hath assigned to it a habitation, and fixed his bars, where *its proud waves are stayed* (Job xxxviii, 11). Let what you behold lead you to think also of the *wisdom* of God; it is wonderfully declared by that amazing multitude of living things, with which the waters are filled; and also by that divine art, with which God preserves the water in a salutary state, purifying it with salt, fanning it with breezes, and swelling it with tides.

Let it be a point of great interest and importance with you to realize *the providence of God;* that this great family in the deep are all fed by their Maker. Of them particularly the Psalmist speaks—*These wait all on God, that he may give them their meat in due season.* But especially bring the idea of divine providence home to yourselves; and while you lie on the bosom of the waters, waiting and seeking your subsistence, look upward with a sense of your dependance; acknowledge, gratefully acknowledge it. How strikingly is your case described in that same excellent psalm, to which I have just referred; I mean the 104th, which I recommend to your particular attention—*That thou givest them,* says David, *they gather.* How pleasingly does this text show the providence of God and human industry consistently working together! *You* pull the treasure out of the water; but, I may say, GOD brings it to your hook.

You are about to take leave of your families; then prayerfully leave them with God; and while absent, commend them every day to his mercy and care. This you can do, and this all, that you can immediately do for them. For a season your wives must lose the solace of your conversation, and your children the benefit of your counsels; but your prayers, if fervent and sincere, may avail them much. Bearing your families habitually on your hearts before God, humbly submitting them both to his care and his disposal, you will be well prepared to meet them again, whether they have been visited in your absence by the smiles or strokes of his providence. What changes may occur God only knows. The experience of some of you in the past season was truly affecting.

While diligent in your occupation, seeking treasures hid in the sea, remember there is a dearer treasure, which you ought to be ever seeking. While you perceive your dependence on the *providence* of God to secure your temporal subsistence, for this infinitely more precious treasure, this *meat, which endureth to eternal life,* feel and acknowledge your dependance on the *grace* of God. Because removed from our worshiping assemblies, and from some of the means of grace, do not for a moment think that you may be remiss in religion. Rather double your diligence to improve the means, which you still may have. You will by no means neglect to carry with you what the brave and pious Admiral NELSON calls his cabin companion, a *bible.* With this be familiar; consult it constantly as your guide, and repair to it as your solace from fatigue, and your support in danger.

Beloved, I wish above all things that you may prosper and be in health, especially that your souls may prosper: and I commend you to God, and to

the word of his grace, which is able to build you up, and to give you an inheritance among all them, which are sanctified.

A prayer to be used, when commencing a voyage.

O Lord our God, thou art very great; thou art clothed with honour and majesty; who coverest thyself with light as with a garment; who stretchest out the heavens like a curtain; who layest the beams of thy chambers in the waters; who makest the clouds thy chariot, and walkest upon the wings of the wind. Thou laidst the foundations of the earth, that it should not be removed for ever. Thou coveredst it with the deep as with a garment. O Lord, how manifold are thy works! in wisdom hast thou made them all: the earth is full of thy riches; so is this great and wide sea. While we go down to the sea in ships and do business in great waters, O teach us with grateful admiration to observe the works of the Lord and thy wonders in the deep. May we tremble before that *power,* which commandeth and raiseth the stormy wind, which lifteth up the waves thereof; and adore that *mercy,* which preserveth us from destruction, while we mount up to the heaven and go down again to the depths, and our soul is melted because of trouble. Often hast thou quieted the tempestuous waves, when we were ready to sink beneath them, and hast brought us to our desired haven. O that we might praise the Lord for his goodness and for his wonderful works to the children of men!

Most merciful Father, we implore thy blessing upon our little family in this floating dwelling. Enable us to live together, as a band of brothers; to cherish for each other the kindest affection; to bear one another's burthens, and to fulfil the law of love: ever remembering that God is love; and that they who dwell in love, dwell in God, and God in them. Let no strife for a moment enter among us, nor any profane or filthy conversation defile our lips and provoke thy displeasure. By a cheerful and modest deportment, by serious and improving discourse, by reading thine inestimable word, and by social and secret prayer, may our hearts be solaced in the absence of our domestick endearments, and our minds improved, notwithstanding many of our religious privileges are suspended.

The dear families, which we have left behind, we commend to thy gracious care. Be the light and the health of their countenance; preserve them from disease and death; from sin and spiritual ruin. Sustain our beloved partners under the cares and burthens, which are increased upon them by our absence; and grant to them wisdom from above to guide the house and to train the children in the nurture and admonition of the Lord. May the children be dutiful to them; and our sons prove as plants, grown up in their youth, and our daughters as corner-stones, polished after the similitude of a palace. And, gracious God, indulge us to return once more to the embraces of those who are most dear to us upon earth, and to join them in grateful offerings to the God of our salvation. If this be denied us in thy wise and good providence, we desire humbly to submit to thy holy will. If death and sudden death be designed for us, O deny us not thy grace to prepare for the great event; grant that it may be always our great concern, to seek first the kingdom of God and his righteousness, and so to prosecute our path through the ocean and through life, that we may finally attain the haven of everlasting rest, through Jesus Christ our great high priest and intercessor. Amen.

Rebecca Cox Jackson

"THE DREAM OF WASHING QUILTS"

*R*ebecca Cox Jackson, born in 1795, was a free black woman who made her living as a seamstress in Philadelphia. Raised in an independent black Methodist church, she experienced a personal conversion and the call to preach in her mid-thirties. After she discovered that her brother Joseph Cox, who acted as her scribe, was editing her letters, she sought the gift of literacy so that she could bear witness to her own visions. One day, as she was praying with her Bible in her lap, she discovered that she could make out the words and subsequently pledged to read no other book, as an act of devotion to God.

> Jackson reminds us that the faith that comes from perfect love casts out fear and invites us to turn our faces to the sun that always arises from behind the cloud.

In her autobiographical writings, she details her visions and her quest to discern and follow unconditionally the inner voice that she believed to be "the true Spirit of God," despite opposition from her husband and other family members. During the 1840s, in obedience to this voice, she joined the Shaker community at Watervliet, New York, and later, as an eldress, established the first black Shaker community in Philadelphia.

"The Dream of Washing Quilts" recounts a vision she received in April 1831, just a year after her conversion. It is full of mystical detail—three quilts, three cities, three pictures, and three claps of thunder; bridges and gates and streets and golden balls. But most of all, it is full of joyful confidence. In the springtime of her faith, Jackson imagines herself singing as she washes her quilts, then swinging to the top of a steeple and claiming a beautiful white cottage. Jackson reminds us that the faith that comes from perfect love casts out fear and invites us to turn our faces to the sun that always arises from behind the cloud.

"THE DREAM OF WASHING QUILTS"

A dream. I was washing. I was squatting down, washing three bed quilts and singing as I was awashing. And this same sister came to the south door and said, "What are you adoing here?" "I am awashing." "Ain't you afraid to be here?" "No." "Why, you are in great danger."

I then looked and saw I was in a place walled all around with stone. The place was four square. I was in the center of it. There was no window in it, only one door. That was in the southwest corner, opened in. The south door she stood in, which brought her behind me, rather to my left. My face was east. Under me was a pool of water. This walled place was full of water like a bowl. Nobody could get to me. There were three pieces of boards about one yard in length. They were all one size. On one of them I sat. On the one at my right side sat a tub. In it was two quilts, which I had washed in this pool, though I knowed not I was in such a dangerous place till she spoke. Yet I did not feel to move till I had done my washing. So I sat still singing until I was done.

Then I picked up my tub with my three clean quilts in, put the tub on my head, came out with great ease and went eastward, came into a street ran north and south. I then stopped, turned around to see where I had come from, found I was standing by a gate as though I had come through it, saw a bridge alongside the gate. This bridge was over a stream of water. I could not tell whether I had come through this gate or over the bridge.

While I stood here awonder, I looked up, saw the gate post on the south side had a steeple on it, and on the top of the steeple was a gold ball. As I looked from the top to where I stood, I found a little white cord hanging right by my right hand. I caught hold of it, made a squat then leaped into the air, placed my right foot on the ball, with my left foot swinging in the air. I was above all earthly things. I saw three cities, one in the east, one in the south, one in the west. These cities were clean and beautiful. Then I leaped down with as great ease as I ascended.

Then I heard this same sister speak behind me, "What are you doing here?" "Why, I have been on that pinnacle." She doubted. I caught hold of the cord and leaped upon it again. This I done three times—I had done it twice before she came. I then went through the gate and along this stream of water until I headed it. This was the same way I had come with my clean quilts in the tub upon my head, but I did not see this water nor this gate nor this bridge until I got into the street that ran north and south. This street which I came in from the washing ran east and west. Now as I returned the same way, it brought me westward, and when I headed this stream, I went south—but when I found myself at that gate, I had not tub nor quilts. So now I went south. After I got far in the south, I looked up to the heavens, saw three pictures all of one size and of one appearance, very majestic, long, and beautiful, of the male order. They were some distance apart. They faced the north. Each one was on a black cloud. And there was three heavy claps of thunder. Each clap came out of each cloud. I found I had traveled a long distance—no house nor shelter near, as far as my eyes could see, and I saw a heavy thunderstorm rising. I wondered what I should do. It was said, "Turn back." I turned, and when I turned in the same road that I came—for I never turned out of the road in all my journey—being turned on my right (that is, on my right hand side off the road, east), I saw a beautiful white cottage into which I was told to enter, which I did. And when I found myself in so beautiful a house, sheltered from the storm, I was filled with joy and rejoicing. And it was said to me, "This is yours."

Then I heard this sister holler behind the cottage, "What are you adoing here?" "Why I live here." "You live here?" "Yes, I live here." "Why, how can you live here? Nobody lives here." "Why this is my cottage, and I am as happy as a lord." "Why the sun never rises here." "The sun never rises here?" As I made this reply I advanced to the door which I came in at, which was in the south side of the cottage. (She was on the north side which made her behind the cottage—I only heard her voice.) And when I went out and looked in the west, I saw the fourth picture, like the three I saw in the south—same size, same height in the heavens—and it faced the east and was on a black cloud. And as I kept repeating, "The sun never rises here? No? Why, yonder she is arising—arising now!" "Well, she has only rose to you."

The sun, while I looked in the faces of the pictures, rose from behind the picture as though it came out of the cloud. And it rose out on the south side of this fourth picture, bearing her course toward these three pictures in the south, out of which came three claps of heavy thunder. The thunder out of the three black clouds behind the three pictures in the south, the sun out of the black cloud behind the fourth picture in the west. Then I waked.

Lisa Couturier

"THE CITY'S LAUGHTER" FROM *THE HOPES OF SNAKES AND OTHER TALES FROM THE URBAN LANDSCAPE*

Nature, as Lisa Couturier reminds us, is not reserved for rural retreats and New Hampshire farms. "New York City is Nature! Capital N!" she recalls her graduate philosophy professor exclaiming. But such exuberance is misleading. Nature is not always wild and magnificent; it may come, as it does with urban pigeons, in the form of ubiquitous outcasts or in the guise of cherished pets. Yet even the outcasts are loved. On early spring days, on park benches across the city, men and women feed the pigeons, and talk to them, and stroke their plump bodies. Or they throw seed in great handfuls, feeding both birds and rats.

These acts of devotion—perhaps especially the extravagant distribution of seed—bridge the unnatural gaps we create among ourselves. Spring brings us back on the streets, back to our windows. It invites us to wave, to say

> *Nature is not always wild and magnificent; it may come, as it does with urban pigeons, in the form of ubiquitous outcasts or in the guise of cherished pets.*

hello, to risk an awkward encounter with another human being. It promises, amidst our eccentricities and loneliness and sadness, the hope of new birth, soft feathers, and a place to know and be known.

"THE CITY'S LAUGHTER"

It's tempting to call them Pigeon Ladies, preferring, as they do, the friendship of pigeons that come to their soft, old bodies with the loyalty and discipline of homing pigeons coming home from wherever they may be in the city—on ledges, in ventilation holes, atop hard worn balconies and roofs. In warm weather, usually, pigeon ladies, and sometimes men, sit on park benches in modicums of quiet, where city sirens and horns are mere whispers through summer's leafy trees. A withered woman, her shoes hanging off her heels, taupe-colored knee-high stockings at her ankles, white legs bulging with blue veins, her drooping and torn brown coat, her shoulders teetering with pigeons, her gnarled hands stroking three cooing pigeons on her chest, while other pigeons hover around her, landing in and flying out of her ratty white hair teased into a cascading nest that drapes down her wrinkled and fair face—this vivid memory of a pigeon lady shot through me suddenly when, looking with my three cats out the window of my fifth-floor apartment, I noticed an elderly white-haired woman, with her cats, waving at me from the window of her fifth-floor apartment across the street. We met for the first time like this, with cats in sunlight, not knowing we would wave again and again for two years, not knowing we would come to look forward to the wave.

It's a habit I've had since childhood, gazing out windows. And when New Yorkers are acting like New Yorkers—which is not necessarily brash, mean, and underhanded, though there are sometimes those qualities—people-watching out your window carries with it the distinct possibility of lunchtime theater. Such was the case of the woman I came to call St. Francis, dressed in expensive black clothing, black pumps, a black leather briefcase, a black coat, and a folded black umbrella, which she carried on days it was not raining, leading me to assume she might use it for protection from the sun, which led to the further thought that she must be somehow fragile. In every way except perhaps the fragility, she was someone I would have expected to see on the Second Avenue bus heading to midtown on the way to work in the morning, when I was working, that is. But at the time I was in graduate school, and often I was home studying, which involved a certain degree of staring out the window. And so St. Francis walked down my street nearly every day over the period of six weeks or so, at lunchtime.

For some unknown reason, as my block had as many pigeons as any other block in Manhattan, this woman chose the sidewalk in front of my building as the perfect place to throw generous amounts of bird seed, for pigeons, I assumed. Although as I started to monitor Francis more vigilantly, it was not clear for whom the seed was meant. She did not stay and wait for birds to swarm her, as did other pigeon admirers readily available in the city, people I had once believed acted out of sympathy for the birds, as if in a just world even outcasts deserved something of our care. But I have watched, from old green painted park benches, pigeon people involved in more than sympathetic seed tossing. People, who, with gentle hands and warm chests, stroked their full-bodied, mild-mannered, and gentle-voiced pigeons, as though pigeon and person nourished each other, as though they understood each other's longings. Call it what you want, but consider: those believed to be sane among us show similar devotion to our dogs and cats. As domesticated pets do for domesticated people, wild pigeons do for wild pigeon people: make them happy. And peaceful, it seemed.

St. Francis, though, just threw and threw and threw, fistfuls of seed, quickly, and then, before pigeons swarmed down from their sooty, dark ledges, she left, her umbrella poking the concrete alongside her strident footsteps.

How kind, I thought, at first, when she began spreading her seed. Perhaps this was due to the fact that the seed drew to my old, black iron fire escape the pretty purplish-red-headed house finches, and, occasionally, the otherwise-located Central Park birds. But word spread among pigeons, as it will, and among rats, too. And so there were at this point kind requests from various people on the block that Francis stop what she was doing. Patient-sounding requests spoken haltingly and carefully, which is another way to describe New Yorkers, and how I most often think of them, as though we all lived, friendly and concerned, in a small village delineated by dry-cleaning establishments and Korean delis.

The requests to Francis sometimes worked, and a few days would pass without our urban saint. But she would return later in the week, the sound of her umbrella rapping the sidewalk. Until one man could no longer stand it and detailed for Francis the pigeon waste he walked through every day, not to mention the extra rats now vehemently riffling through our garbage cans. He demanded, loudly, meanly, and in her face, that she leave, find another sidewalk, maybe one in front of her building would be a good idea. This was when Francis finally spoke, in long breaths of gibberish, as she opened her black briefcase, pulled out her bag of seed and showered the man with a wild throwing.

This, anyone could see, was of course upsetting the man terribly. One might guess the man would retreat in the face of St. Francis's insanity. Instead, he became more agitated, trying to speak to a woman who could not speak to people; and all I could think of was how much Francis needed the pigeons she never waited for, the mild, soft pigeons this city offered, as refuge, as nature in its, if not wild, then outcast form.

The old woman in the fifth-floor apartment across the street has not waved in a couple of days, which is unlike her. Nearly every day for the past two years she has at some point during the day sat at the window, her five cats on or around her lap, watching me and my cats, or the street, or sky. This disconnected peering at each other has been our sole connection. Once, when she saw my calico jump up to usurp my Siamese from the coveted, southern-exposed windowsill, she opened her mouth in surprise and then pointed at her calico, as though we were living parallel lives.

It was now a week without the waving woman, and since I have not seen lights in her apartment at night, I surmise she has died, though I look for her over and over again. This is when, one afternoon, I see a pigeon thrashing against her window from inside her apartment and decide to go across the street and free the bird. It is easy, in our less-expensive buildings that have no doormen or guards, to buzz the intercom of a resident and claim you are the Chinese-food delivery person needing to be let in. This is what I do.

Her apartment door is open, swinging in a breeze originating inside. I walk in and am suddenly covered in pigeons, pigeons landing on my head, pigeons crashing into my chest and crawling up to perch on my shoulders. I hear the scuttle of their feet crossing the old wood floor and the cooing of those gathered around my legs. It is as though I'm a sculpture of some goddess they've been expecting. I shake them off. Pigeons, feathers, dust, bird excrement. Filth is everywhere, and I think, predictably, that this is what killed my old waving woman. In the living room—the room from where she sat and watched me—stained wallpaper hangs loose near the ceiling, which is cracked and which, in one corner, has opened into a hole in her roof, an entrance to the sky. On the floor underneath the ceiling sits a bucket partially filled with rainwater. In the hallway leading to her bedroom, an old gramophone and a stack of 33 rpm records cover a table. Her mattress is folded on the floor. There is no bed frame; the bedroom window is shattered. I hear baby pigeons squealing, their unmistakable cries like ungreased wheels endlessly turning, and I follow the sound to the kitchen. Above the cabinets are pigeon nests. On the windowsills are pigeon nests. Every available ledge has upon it a pigeon nest. The woman has not been gone long enough for all of this to have taken place since her departure. She has been living, who knows how long, with dozens and dozens of pigeons, monogamous mates raising their young together—the male pigeon incubating eggs by day, the female by night—here in an apartment on East Seventy-third Street. The woman has slept alongside the secret births of pigeons, secret because the sight of baby pigeons in city streets is rare. Find your way back behind the fancy brownstones, row houses, and refurbished tenement buildings of Manhattan to the sooty, forgotten, and mostly inaccessible spaces of concrete, soil, bushes, and trees, and you will find the refuge of baby pigeons. They grow there, in the shadows of buildings, backstage, until they are strong enough to conquer New York. Conquer the skies with their powerful, skillful, and beautiful flying. Have you ever noticed sunshine glowing behind the feathers of a flying pigeon's outstretched wing, as though the bird rides sunrays? Bashful does not describe city pigeons, hovering, as they do, around your cafe table during alfresco luncheons. They know—from excellent vision inside their fiery eyes—where you are. Think of them as always watching. Think of their ardent coos as songs at the windowsill.

As I stand in the sanctum of this woman, among the hundred or so pigeons she once knew, I realize she was the memory of the woman in the park, she was the one with the cascading white hair and bulging blue veins. For my waving woman, nature, quite literally, meant an exquisitely related community consisting of herself and these birds. Pigeons meant home.

I imagine that in the weeks before the woman died, she held these baby pigeons, as well as broods from the months before, and those before them, nurturing generations, as would a grandmother. That she listened to the birds and knew something of their intelligence; that she witnessed their days, their flights to and from her roof; that she knew the intoxicating colors of the birds' flashy neck feathers—tropical garden green, cabernet red, turquoise blue; that she walked to the park and above her flew her birds, her cloud lined with silver wings, until she arrived at her bench, where birds landed in her lap—how could all this not have been?

Manhattan. There are many languages spoken there. And though one of them is not "wildness" in the way it may typically be defined—as nourishing nonhuman diversity—there are, nonetheless, remnants, sparks, holdouts, representatives, entities, beings, subjects from the wild, species clinging to this landscape. The streets of

New York City are not wild with a capital *W,* though perhaps wildness is seen mostly by those who behold it regardless of its beauty; by those attempting to reconcile the great loss of diversity in one moment and, in the next, praying that further development remains within the paved boundaries we already have constructed. Maybe it helps to imagine the city as a starfish, or to appreciate, on some level, the sensuality of pigeons, the eternity of roaches, the antics of subway mice. Maybe not. "Earth laughs in flowers," said Emerson. In Manhattan, perhaps Earth laughs, a bit sarcastically, in its dark, natural, and wild outcasts.

Michael Downing

"MOON OVER MIAMI" FROM *SPRING FORWARD: THE ANNUAL MADNESS OF DAYLIGHT SAVING TIME*

*I*n the springtime, our clocks suddenly "spring ahead," and we find a new and somehow always-unexpected hour of daylight at the end of the day. On the western edge of a time zone, this might mean light in the evenings until almost 10:00. And while this seems to have many benefits—more time for recreation, for yard work after supper, for strolling along a city street—there are clearly negative effects. The farmer who had been seeing the dawn come nearer and nearer suddenly has it set back an hour. Schoolchildren are put to bed during daylight, when the birds are still singing—but they may not be going to sleep.

> *M*ay we manipulate the ways that we organize the created order?

In Spring Forward: The Annual Madness of Daylight Saving Time, *Michael Downing charts the introduction of that policy into the United States. The notion was that the extra hour would help to make America more productive, and so help the war effort during World War I. But after that motivation was gone, evidence was needed to show that the* policy did indeed save fuel, increase efficiency and productivity, or make lives better for the majority of Americans. In the years since its inception, Downing points out, no such evidence has ever been convincingly presented.

Early debates over Daylight Saving Time focused on issues of time being owned by God. Essentially, the religious question being asked was this: May we manipulate the ways that we organize the created order? It is the deep question behind a continuing debate.

"Moon Over Miami"

> As a rule, we disbelieve all facts and theories for which we have no use.
>
> —William James, 1897

The weakness of moral reasoning is that it is usually irrational. The strength of moral reasoning is that most people are irrational.

The United States adopted Daylight Saving in 1918 because it was presented as a moral necessity. The mere possibility that the war effort might be better fueled and our soldiers better supplied had persuaded even farmers, who had "endured it while the war was going on because they thought it really was a war measure," explained Representative James Strong of Kansas. "Their boys had gone to France; they were willing to do anything." When the war ended, the supporters of Daylight Saving suddenly lost this moral high ground, and they had nothing comparable to stand on during the congressional debate that ensued. They had assembled no real evidence to substantiate the economic, social, or psychological benefits they attributed to the manipulation of the country's clocks. "As a matter of fact, the law was never necessary," gloated one of Daylight's opponents in a letter to the *New York Times* after the national legislation was repealed in August 1919. "We could have beaten Germany equally well without it."

Daylight Saving had not simply fallen from grace. According to its critics, it had nearly dragged the whole world to hell with it. "We can look forward to all the European nations abolishing this wickedness and awakening as it were out of a nightmare of a species of blasphemy akin to the worship of Baal," predicted one New Jersey reader of the *Times,* distancing himself from the Daylight idolaters in New York City and Berlin. "When the Germans began the curse of daylight saving, they started on the course which ended in their great fall ... they did not care for God or man." Within weeks of the repeal, city halls across the country were besieged by requests from citizens eager to turn their clocks back to God's time before the appointed Sunday in October. "God's time is true. Man-made time is false," declared Congressman E. S. Candler of Mississippi, fueling the hellfires. "Truth is always mighty and should prevail. God alone can create daylight."

God alone knows why the overwhelmingly Christian Congress had chosen Sunday as the day to begin and end Daylight Saving each year, but this choice occasioned a lot of sermonizing against the legislation from preachers who considered the choice of Sunday further proof of the godlessness of government. For many Americans who believed that time was the provenance of the divine, Daylight Saving represented an assault on the constitutional separation of church and state. One of these latter-day Jeffersonians lived in Oxford, New York. According to a fellow parishioner who documented the episode for the *New York Times,* he had forgotten to set his clock ahead on the last Sunday of April in 1918, and "entered the church door as the pastor pronounced the [closing] benediction." As luck, or the heavens, would have it, that first day of Daylight Saving in America was Easter Sunday. "'I'll never go to church again,' he declared when the situation was explained, 'until daylight saving is abolished and we go back to God's time.'"

God is famously inscrutable, and efforts to divine the Almighty's timekeeping preferences have resulted in some impressive complications. Although Easter in 1918 fell on 31 March, Easter Sunday in 1919 was 20 April, and in 1920 it was 4 April. The arcane rules for identifying which Sunday will be Easter Sunday begin with the divination of the first Sunday after the first ecclesiastical full moon (distinct from the astronomical full moon) that occurs on or after the vernal equinox—and this calculus only applies to Catholics and Protestants. Eastern Orthodox Christians have another method entirely and, typically, designate a different Sunday as Easter. Moreover, the year 1919 was 5679 according to the Jewish calendar, and 1337 on the Islamic calendar. Given these discrepancies, how sincere was the invocation of God's time in relation to a single hour?

It was persistent. And it was not confined to pulpits or the right wing of Congress. According to the Washington Diarist for the *New Republic,* Daylight Saving Time was "distinct from natural time, which the Good Lord gave us on the first day, as is concisely reported in Genesis." This was the argument in 1919; but it was still the argument seventy years later, when the Washington Diarist published this diatribe against Daylight Saving in 1989: "What is day and what is night were clearly determined on the first day: 'And God called the light day, and darkness night,'" he continued. "Night falls, our language tells us. Let it fall when God and the sun ordain."

The God of Genesis not only sorted out night and day. He invented the week, a seven-day cycle without any astronomical significance, our only temporal unit that bears no relationship to the arrangement or operation of the sun, the earth, our moon, or any other heavenly sphere. God made it up. This innovative system of accrual relies on the ability of timekeepers to count the days, because one Sunday is otherwise indistinguishable from another Sunday or even a Friday. Sunrise effectively defines the beginning of a new day, and sunset heralds the arrival of each night. Unfortunately, God did not tell anyone exactly what time it was when darkness falls.

On 20 December 1919, with all the clocks in the country running on Standard Time, the sun set in Bangor, Maine, at 3:56 P.M. The sun would not set in New York City for another thirty-five minutes. So, at what time did night fall? What did four o'clock mean? In Miami, where clocks were synchronized with clocks in Bangor and New York—they are all in the same Eastern Standard

Time Zone—the sun did not set until 5:34 P.M. Was four o'clock ordained day or night by God?

It got worse. Looking forward to the next year's summer solstice without Daylight Saving Time, residents of cities in the north could see they were in for a rude awakening. With no adjustment of the clocks, the sun would rise over the good people of Bangor at 3:49 A.M. on 20 June. What in God's name were they supposed to do in Bangor until their factories and offices opened four or five hours later? The official start of the day in New York would occur at 4:24 A.M., leaving the dilettantes and duffers plenty of time before work to take in a play or to play a round of golf—if someone could rouse the actors and caddies. In Miami, on 20 June, the sun would not rise until 5:30 A.M. For more than an hour and a half, according to God's time, day was night in Miami. These inconsistencies not only cast a shadow on scriptural time management. They also raised a serious question about the repeal of Daylight Saving. If Florida's farmers were expected to supply neighboring stores and schools with milk and produce in 1920 operating under the 5:30 sunrise ordained by God, why had farmers in New York been unable to do the same in 1919, when Daylight Saving Time had delayed sunrise time for them until 5:24?

Annie Dillard

"UNTYING THE KNOT" AND "THE PRESENT" FROM *PILGRIM AT TINKER CREEK*

O ne night we go to bed and it is still winter; the next morning we awake and find ourselves inside spring. If we are Annie Dillard, that is enough to propel us out of bed and into the woods to stalk the new season, hoping to pinpoint the exact moment when winter ends and spring begins. But the seasons, though regular, are unpredictable, messy—they blur into one another, offering sunny skies in January and frosts in May. We cannot hold them down or contain them any more than we can contain our own awareness of this bright, burgeoning world. Too soon we snap back into self-consciousness, warily assessing what we know and how we know it.

> We cannot hold the seasons down or contain them any more than we can contain our own awareness of this bright, burgeoning world.

But spring's vitality, its headlong rush into new life, its very innocence pulls us toward moments of pure awareness, moments in which we see the glorious particulars of this world—snakeskins and puppies and adolescent *boys and sunsets and cedar trees—all illuminated by the light of eternity. Moments in which, as Dillard notes earlier in* Pilgrim at Tinker Creek, *it is "less like seeing than like being for the first time seen, knocked breathless by a powerful glance."*

In spring, the sharp edges of the world scrape against our heavy eyelids and our dulled hearts. Spring's beauty pulls us up and out of ourselves toward praise and wonder. Catch it if you can.

"UNTYING THE KNOT"

Yesterday I set out to catch the new season, and instead I found an old snakeskin. I was in the sunny February woods by the quarry; the snakeskin was lying in a heap of leaves right next to an aquarium someone had thrown away. I don't know why that some-one hauled the aquarium deep into the woods to get rid of it; it had only one broken glass side. The snake found it handy, I imagine; snakes like to rub against something rigid to help them out of their skins, and the broken aquarium looked like the nearest likely object. Together the snakeskin and the aquarium made an interesting scene on the forest floor. It looked like an exhibit at a trial—circumstantial evidence—of a wild scene, as though a snake had burst through the broken side of the aquarium, burst through his ugly old skin, and disappeared, perhaps straight up in the air, in a rush of freedom and beauty.

The snakeskin had unkeeled scales, so it belonged to a nonpoisonous snake. It was roughly five feet long by the yardstick, but I'm not sure because it was very wrinkled and dry, and every time I tried to stretch it flat it broke. I ended up with seven or eight pieces of it all over the kitchen table in a fine film of forest dust.

The point I want to make about the snakeskin is that, when I found it, it was whole and tied in a knot. Now there have been stories told, even by reputable scientists, of snakes that have deliberately tied themselves in a knot to prevent larger snakes from trying to swallow them—but I couldn't imagine any way that throwing itself into a half hitch would help a snake trying to escape its skin. Still, ever cautious, I figured that one of the neighborhood boys could possibly have tied it in a knot in the fall, for some whimsical boyish reason, and left it there, where it dried and gathered dust. So I carried the skin along thoughtlessly as I walked, snagging it sure enough on a low branch and ripping it in two for the first of many times. I saw that thick ice still lay on the quarry pond and that the skunk cabbage was already out in the clearings, and then I came home and looked at the skin and its knot.

The knot had no beginning. Idly I turned it around in my hand, searching for a place to untie; I came to with a start when I realized I must have turned the thing around fully ten times. Intently, then, I traced the knot's lump around with a finger: it was continuous. I couldn't untie it any more than I could untie a doughnut; it was a loop without beginning or end. These snakes are magic, I thought for a second, and then of course I reasoned what must have happened. The skin had been pulled inside-out like a peeled sock for several inches; then an inch or so of the inside-out part—a piece whose length was coincidentally equal to the diameter of the skin—had somehow been turned right-side out again, making a thick lump whose edges were lost in wrinkles, looking exactly like a knot.

So. I have been thinking about the change of seasons. I don't want to miss spring this year. I want to distinguish the last winter frost from the out-of-season one, the frost of spring. I want to be there on the spot the moment the grass turns green. I always miss this radical revolution; I see it the next day from a window, the yard so suddenly green and lush I could envy Nebuchadnezzar down on all fours eating grass. This year I want to stick a net into time and say "now," as men plant flags on the ice and snow and say, "here." But it occurred to me that I could no more catch spring by the tip of the tail than I could untie the apparent knot in the snakeskin; there are no edges to grasp. Both are continuous loops.

I wonder how long it would take you to notice the regular recurrence of the seasons if you were the first man on earth. What would it be like to live in open-ended time broken only by days and nights? You could say, "it's cold again; it was cold before," but you couldn't make the key connection and say, "it was cold this time last year," because the notion of "year" is precisely the one you lack. Assuming that you hadn't yet noticed any orderly progression of heavenly bodies, how long would you have to live on earth before you could feel with any assurance that any one particular long period of cold would, in fact, end? "While the earth remaineth, seedtime and harvest, and cold and heat, and summer and winter, and day and night shall not cease": God makes this guarantee very early in Genesis to a people whose fears on this point had perhaps not been completely allayed.

It must have been fantastically important, at the real beginnings of human culture, to conserve and relay this vital seasonal information, so that the people could anticipate dry or cold seasons, and not huddle on some November rock hoping pathetically that spring was just around the corner. We still very much stress the simple fact of four seasons to schoolchildren; even the most modern of modern new teachers, who don't seem to care if their charges can read or write or name two products of Peru, will still muster some seasonal chitchat and set the kids to making paper pumpkins, or tulips, for the walls. "The people," wrote Van Gogh in a letter, "are very sensitive to the changing seasons." That we are "very sensitive to the changing seasons" is, incidentally, one of the few good reasons to shun travel. If I stay at home I preserve the illusion that what is happening on Tinker Creek is the very newest thing, that I'm at the very vanguard and cutting edge of each new season. I don't want the same season twice in a row; I don't want to know I'm getting last week's weather, used weather, weather broadcast up and down the coast, old-hat weather.

But there's always unseasonable weather. What we think of the weather and behavior of life on the planet at any given season is really all a matter of statistical probabilities; at any given point, anything might happen. There is a bit of every season in each season. Green plants—deciduous green leaves—grow everywhere, all winter long, and small shoots come up pale and new in every season. Leaves die on the tree in May, turn brown, and fall into the creek. The calendar, the weather, and the behavior of wild creatures have the slimmest of connections. Everything overlaps smoothly for only a few weeks each season, and then it all tangles up again. The temperature, of course, lags far behind the calendar seasons, since the earth absorbs and releases heat slowly, like a leviathan breathing. Migrating birds head south in what appears to be dire panic, leaving mild weather and fields full of insects and seeds; they reappear as if in all eagerness in January, and poke about morosely in the snow. Several years ago our October woods would have made a dismal colored photograph for a sadist's calendar: a killing frost came before the leaves had even begun to brown; they drooped from every tree like crepe, blackened and limp. It's all a chancy, jumbled affair at best, as things seem to be below the stars.

Time is the continuous loop, the snakeskin with scales endlessly overlapping without beginning or end, or time is an ascending spiral if you will, like a child's toy Slinky. Of course we have no idea which arc on the loop is our time, let alone where the loop itself is, so to speak, or down whose lofty flight of stairs the Slinky so uncannily walks.

The power we seek, too, seems to be a continuous loop. I have always been sympathetic with the early notion of a divine power that exists in a particular place, or that travels about over the face of the earth as a man might wander—and when he is "there" he is surely not here. You can shake the hand of a man you meet in the woods; but the spirit seems to roll along like the mythical hoop snake with its tail in its mouth. There are no hands to shake or edges to untie. It rolls along the mountain ridges like a fireball, shooting off a spray of sparks at random, and will not be trapped, slowed, grasped, fetched, peeled, or aimed. "As for the wheels, it was cried unto them in my hearing, O wheel." This is the hoop of flame that shoots the rapids in the creek or spins across the dizzy meadows; this is the arsonist of the sunny woods: catch it if you can.

"THE PRESENT"

Catch it if you can.

It is early March. I am dazed from a long day of interstate driving homeward; I pull in at a gas station in Nowhere, Virginia, north of Lexington. The young boy in charge ("Chick 'at oll?") is offering a free cup of coffee with every gas purchase. We talk in the glass-walled office while my coffee cools enough to drink. He tells me, among other things, that the rival gas station down the road, whose FREE COFFEE sign is visible from the interstate, charges you fifteen cents if you want your coffee in a Styrofoam cup, as opposed, I guess, to your bare hands.

All the time we talk, the boy's new beagle puppy is skidding around the office, sniffing impartially at my shoes and at the wire rack of folded maps. The cheerful human conversation wakes me, recalls me, not to a normal consciousness, but to a kind of energetic readiness. I step outside, followed by the puppy.

I am absolutely alone. There are no other customers. The road is vacant, the interstate is out of sight and earshot. I have hazarded into a new corner of the world, an unknown spot, a Brigadoon. Before me extends a low hill trembling in yellow brome, and behind the hill, filling the sky, rises an enormous mountain ridge, forested, alive and awesome with brilliant blown lights. I have never seen anything so tremulous and live. Overhead, great strips and chunks of cloud dash to the northwest in a gold rush. At my back the sun is setting—how can I not have noticed before that the sun is setting? My mind has been a blank slab of black asphalt for hours, but that doesn't stop the sun's wild wheel. I set my coffee beside me on the curb; I smell loam on the wind; I pat the puppy; I watch the mountain.

My hand works automatically over the puppy's fur, following the line of hair under his ears, down his neck, inside his forelegs, along his hot-skinned belly.

Shadows lope along the mountain's rumpled flanks; they elongate like root tips, like lobes of spilling water, faster and faster. A warm purple pigment pools in each ruck and tuck of the rock; it deepens and spreads, boring crevasses, canyons. As the purple vaults and slides, it tricks out the unleafed forest and rumpled rock in gilt, in shape-shifting patches of glow. These gold lights veer and retract, shatter and glide in a series of dazzling splashes, shrinking, leaking, exploding. The ridge's bosses and hummocks sprout bulging from its side; the whole mountain looms miles closer; the light warms and reddens; the bare forest folds and pleats itself like living protoplasm before my eyes, like a running chart, a wildly scrawling oscillograph on the present moment. The air cools; the puppy's skin is hot. I am more alive than all the world.

This is it, I think, this is it, right now, the present, this empty gas station, here, this western wind, this tang of coffee on the tongue, and I am patting the puppy, I am watching the mountain. And the second I verbalize this awareness in my brain, I cease to see the mountain or feel the puppy. I am opaque, so much black asphalt. But at the same second, the second I know I've lost it, I also realize that the puppy is still squirming on his back under my hand. Nothing has changed for him. He draws his legs down to stretch the skin taut so he feels every fingertip's stroke along his furred and arching side, his flank, his flung-back throat.

I sip my coffee. I look at the mountain, which is still doing its tricks, as you look at a still-beautiful face belonging to a person who was once your lover in another country years ago: with fond nostalgia, and recognition, but no real feeling save a secret astonishment that you are now strangers. Thanks. For the memories. It is ironic that the one thing that all religions recognize as separating us from our creator—our very self-consciousness—is also the one thing that divides us from our fellow creatures. It was a bitter birthday present from evolution, cutting us off at both ends. I get in the car and drive home.

Catch it if you can. The present is an invisible electron; its lightning path traced faintly on a blackened screen is fleet, and fleeing, and gone.

That I ended this experience prematurely for myself—that I drew scales over my eyes between me and the mountain and gloved my hand between me and the puppy—is not the only point. After all, it would have ended anyway. I've never seen a sunset or felt a wind that didn't. The levitating saints came down at last, and their two feet bore real weight. No, the point is that not only does time fly and do we die, but that in these reckless conditions we live at all, and are vouchsafed, for the duration of certain inexplicable moments, to know it.

Stephen Graham startled me by describing this same gift in his antique and elegant book, *The Gentle Art of Tramping.* He wrote, "And as you sit on the hillside, or lie prone under the trees of the forest, or sprawl wet-legged on the shingly beach of a mountain stream, the great door, that does not look like a door, opens." That great door opens on the present, illuminates it as with a multitude of flashing torches.

I had thought, because I had seen the tree with the lights in it, that the great door, by definition, opens on eternity. Now that I have "patted the puppy"—now that I have experienced the present purely through my senses—I discover that, although the door to the tree with the lights in it was opened from eternity, as it were, and shone on that tree eternal lights, it nevertheless opened on the real and present cedar. It opened on time: Where else? That Christ's incarnation occurred improbably, ridiculously, at such-and-such a time, into such-and-such a place, is referred to—with great sincerity even among believers—as "the scandal of particularity."

Well, the "scandal of particularity" is the only world that I, in particular, know. What use has eternity for light? We're all up to our necks in this particular scandal. Why, we might as well ask, not a plane tree, instead of a bo? I never saw a tree that was no tree in particular; I never met a man, not the greatest theologian, who filled infinity, or even whose hand, say, was undifferentiated, fingerless, like a griddlecake, and not lobed and split just so with the incursions of time.

I don't want to stress this too much. Seeing the tree with the lights in it was an experience vastly different in quality as well as in import from patting the puppy. On that cedar tree shone, however briefly, the steady, inward flames of eternity; across the mountain by the gas station raced the familiar flames of the falling sun. But on both occasions I thought, with rising exultation, this is it, this is it; praise the lord; praise the land. Experiencing the present purely is being emptied and hollow; you catch grace as a man fills his cup under a waterfall.

Consciousness itself does not hinder living in the present. In fact, it is only to a heightened awareness that the great door to the present opens at all. Even a certain amount of interior verbalization is helpful to enforce the memory of whatever it is that is taking place. The gas station beagle puppy, after all, may have experienced those same moments more purely than I did, but he brought fewer instruments to bear on the same material, he had no data for comparison, and he profited only in the grossest of ways, by having an assortment of itches scratched.

Self-consciousness, however, does hinder the experience of the present. It is the one instrument that unplugs all the rest. So long as I lose myself in a tree, say, I can scent its leafy breath or estimate its board feet of lumber, I can draw its fruits or boil tea on its branches, and the tree stays tree. But the second I become aware of myself at any of these activities—looking over my own shoulder, as it were—the tree vanishes, uprooted from the spot and flung out of sight as if it had never grown. And time, which had flowed down into the tree bearing new revelations like floating leaves at every moment, ceases. It dams, stills, stagnates.

Self-consciousness is the curse of the city and all that sophistication implies. It is the glimpse of oneself in a storefront window, the unbidden awareness of reactions on the faces of other people—the novelist's world, not the poet's. I've lived there. I remember what the city has to offer: human companionship, major-league baseball, and a clatter of quickening stimulus like a rush from strong drugs that leaves you drained. I remember how you bide your time in the city, and think, if you stop to think, "next year ... I'll start living; next year ... I'll start my life." Innocence is a better world.

Innocence sees that this is it, and finds it world enough, and time. Innocence is not the prerogative of infants and puppies, and far less of mountains and fixed stars, which have no prerogatives at all. It is not lost to us; the world is a better place than that. Like any other of the spirit's good gifts, it is there if you want it, free for the asking, as has been stressed by stronger words than mine. It is possible to pursue innocence as hounds pursue hares: single-mindedly, driven by a kind of love, crashing over creeks, keening and lost in fields and forests, circling, vaulting over hedges and hills wide-eyed, giving loud tongue all unawares to the deepest, most incomprehensible longing, a root-flame in the heart, and that warbling chorus resounding back from the mountains, hurling itself from ridge to ridge over the valley, now faint, now clear, ringing the air through which the hounds tear, open-mouthed, the echoes of their own wails dimly knocking in their lungs.

What I call innocence is the spirit's unself-conscious state at any moment of pure devotion to any object. It is at once a receptiveness and total concentration. One needn't be, shouldn't be, reduced to a puppy. If you wish to tell me that the city offers galleries, I'll pour you a drink and enjoy your company while it lasts; but I'll bear with me to my grave those pure moments at the Tate (was it the Tate?) where I stood planted, open-mouthed, born, before that one particular canvas, that river, up to my neck, gasping, lost, receding into watercolor depth and depth to the vanishing point, buoyant, awed, and had to be literally hauled away. These are our few live seasons. Let us live them as purely as we can, in the present.

Robert Frost

TWO SPRING POEMS

*A*wakenings are not always pleasant—ask any mother dragging her thirteen-year-old from bed at 6:30 to meet the 7:15 school bus—and Robert Frost's southwestern wind is just such a bustling intruder. It melts the ice on the windows, rushes into the bedroom and knocks a picture askew, and sweeps paper onto the floor. But its force is tempered by grace. Southern-warmed rain returns migratory birds to New England and releases the poet from winter's grip.

As he rubs his eyes and looks around at the springtime world in the second poem, Frost echoes the sentiment of the Shaker hymn with which this section began:

> *A*wakenings are not always pleasant ... but they are tempered by grace.

"How wondrous are the ways of God! / How bountiful His hand!" And he reiterates Annie Dillard's plea that we feast on the moment. But the form of the poem—a prayer—also reminds us just how fragile such thanksgiving, such happiness, such awareness is, how often we rush by or sleepwalk through our days.

"Oh, give us pleasure in the flowers today" and wake us up, we pray.

To the Thawing Wind

Come with rain, O loud Southwester!
Bring the singer, bring the nester;
Give the buried flower a dream;
Make the settled snow-bank steam;
Find the brown beneath the white;
But whate'er you do tonight,
Bathe my window, make it flow,
Melt it as the ice will go;
Melt the glass and leave the sticks
Like a hermit's crucifix;
Burst into my narrow stall;
Swing the picture on the wall;
Run the rattling pages o'er;
Scatter poems on the floor;
Turn the poet out of door.

A Prayer in Spring

Oh, give us pleasure in the flowers to-day;
And give us not to think so far away
As the uncertain harvest; keep us here
All simply in the springing of the year.

Oh, give us pleasure in the orchard white,
Like nothing else by day, like ghosts by night;
And make us happy in the happy bees,
The swarm dilating round the perfect trees.

And make us happy in the darting bird
That suddenly above the bees is heard,
The meteor that thrusts in with needle bill,
And off a blossom in mid air stands still.

For this is love and nothing else is love,
The which it is reserved for God above
To sanctify to what far ends He will,
But which it only needs that we fulfill.

PART THREE

Growth

INTRODUCTION

"What wondrous change! what loveliness!" So begins a Shaker hymn praising spring. And, indeed, lovely change is perhaps what first comes to mind as winter releases us into the new season. "Spring is in the air," we promise one another as we anticipate the last frost, the last gray day, the last time we pull on mittens and wind scarves around our necks. We've been poring over seed catalogs since February, but now we start digging around in the garden, raking out the leaves—densely compacted into heavy, leathery sheets—that blew off the oak tree during the winter storms. We eye the green daffodil and tulip shoots and stop at garden shops on our way home from work. Although their signs sternly warn us, "Don't plant until May 15," we think maybe, just maybe, this year we can start a little earlier, and we triumphantly bear away a few pots and a flat of pansies.

Then suddenly it *is* spring and almost overnight, it seems, there are white and yellow daffodils and red-purple tulips where yesterday we saw only slender green stalks. The trees cover their brown nakedness with the leaves of golden-green that Robert Frost tells us is nature's first color. In the city we smell the difference between the cold drizzle of late winter and the light drops of spring's first shower; we look up to see the blossoms on our neighbor's cherry tree and down to spot the first weeds pushing up between the cracks in the sidewalk—and we have not the least inclination to pull them out. Life, in whatever form, seems too precious to waste.

Spring is the gardener's delight, not only because at last we can actually get our hands dirty instead of merely fantasizing over beautiful pictures, but also because something new is coming up or growing larger every day. No wonder gardeners can't resist making long lists of their favorite plants; a single word is insufficient to the season. "Daffodil" won't do for Louise Beebe Wilder; she must have *N. albicans* and Star Daffodils, *N. obvallaris* and Narcissus Golden Spur. Alice Morse Earle looks at Ladies' Delight and hears country voices chanting its names: Bird's-eye, Kitty-come, and Tickle-my-fancy. And Francis Bacon takes a deep breath and recites the blossoms of April: violets, wallflowers, gilliflowers, cowslips, fleur-de-lies, lilies, rosemary flowers, tulips, peonies, daffodils, honeysuckle, cherry and plum blossoms, whitethorns, and lilacs. Henry Howard, who taught English poets to write sonnets in the sixteenth century, transformed Petrarch's Italian verse into a catalog of his own native countryside:

The soote season, that bud and bloom forth brings,
With green hath clad the hill and eke the vale;
The nightingale with feathers new she sings;
The turtle to her mate hath told her tale....
The fishes flete with new repaired scale;
The adder all her slough away she slings,
The swift swallow pursueth the flies small
The busy bee her honey now she mings.

It is this sheer abundance, spring literally bursting at its seams, that Samuel Johnson and Dorothy Wordsworth inhale in their rambles through that same English countryside. For spring may begin in the garden, but it doesn't end there. The life that pulsates through vegetative matter pushes us out of our winter cocoons, our introspection and self-absorption, the gnarled conviction that we and we alone must carry the burdens of the world. Spring reaches the most crabbed souls—as well as those New Englanders who, as Donald Hall reminds us, are stuck in an interminable mud season. And spring pushes us toward others, for who can bear such profusion alone? We open our doors, call out greetings to neighbors who, no longer muffled from head to toe, we see clearly for the first time in months, and smile at the long-legged children, pale and lanky in their new shorts. Even the animals respond with generosity. Donald Hall describes the response of the Holstein sisterhood when a calf is born: "Not only does the mother lick the child; the whole herd tries to, and the community celebrates, enormous black and white bovines leaping as much as they are able and bellowing out of their collective triumph."

Yet spring is not simply the season of triumph, but rather of burgeoning new life. And such growth hurts. "Growing pains," we say of children who shoot up too fast, splitting their March clothes by May and showing a good two inches of ankle beneath their long trousers. But the awkwardness of knees and elbows and arms and faces grown suddenly pimply are minor inconveniences compared to the volatile tempers, sulky silences, and broken hearts that often accompany such growing pains. It is only sentimental nostalgia that paints the spring of our lives with pastels. Growth hurts and it isn't difficult to see why. Growth is life on the move, pushing through the present with barely a sideways glance, hurrying on to the next level, the next inch, the next achievement.

The blessing of spring is also its temptation, when new life becomes mere novelty and growth a headlong rush into the future. Which is why, in the flush of spring, so many wise writers recall us both to memory and to the present moment. One of the great spring rituals in the Christian tradition, Ash Wednesday, which inaugurates the season of Lent, speaks to memory and moment. In the midst of spring's busy life, we are reminded that we are but dust and ashes, that this moment is all we can surely hold, and that this moment, then, bears the weight of eternity. But Ash Wednesday also positions the moment in the past, anchors it in the life and death of Christ who gives to it and us meaning, even in the face of our own deaths. If nature's first green is a gold that we cannot hold, it is, nevertheless, one we must grasp. "Listen," says Barbara Crooker:

I want to tell you something. This morning
is bright after all the steady rain, and every iris,
peony, rose, opens its mouth, rejoicing. I want to say,
wake up, open your eyes, there's a snow-covered road
ahead, a field of blankness, a sheet of paper, an empty screen.
Even the smallest insects are singing, vibrating their entire bodies,
tiny violins of longing and desire. We were made for song.
I can't tell you what prayer is, but I can take the breath
of the meadow into my mouth, and I can release it for the leaves'
green need. I want to tell you your life is a blue coal, a slice
of orange in your mouth, cut hay in your nostrils. The cardinals'
red song dances in your blood. Look, every month the moon
blossoms into a peony, then shrinks to a sliver of garlic.
And then it blooms again.

A Shaker Hymn

"Springtime"

What wondrous change! what loveliness!
Joy o'er earth is borne;
From the sky the deep blue vaulted
Storms and clouds have gone.
When the bloom of springtime cometh
Nature pours her psalm,
Giving raptures to the echoes,
Trilling ev'ry calm.

On woodlands late so bare and cold,
Buds and blossoms rise,
Balmy breezes fan the leaflets,
Giving fresh surprise.
While the happy springtime tarries,
Fraught with ev'ry grace,
All that light and beauty cherish
Ev'rywhere we trace.

Earth's casket holds a treasure rare,
Rich with gifts to please,

And the ambient spheres concordant
With sweet harmonies.
List the merry birds that warble,
Hear the rippling stream,
Watch the genial ray of even,
These are not a dream.

Our God whose wisdom made the earth,
Guides the rolling year,
Snowflakes, roses, red leaves falling,
And arbutus dear.
But among the types of beauty
That the seasons bring,
Best of all, the heart of childhood
Loves the gladsome spring.

Francis Bacon

"Of Gardens"

*F*rancis Bacon, the seventeenth-century English essayist and statesman, was the son of Lord Keeper of the Great Seal Sir Nicholas Bacon and Anne Cooke Bacon, one of the most learned women of her day. From his father, he inherited a love of politics and from his mother, a love of fine writing and the ability to manage a great estate. Bacon's garden plan is nothing less than grand; its thirty acres are divided into a main garden bordered by trees with a tailored lawn in the front and a meadow at the rear.

Bacon's orderliness may seem a bit fussy—he specifies the height of hedges, regulates the placement of decorative glass, prefers flowers whose scent is carried on the air, and banishes ponds—but all this

> *A*ll this attention to detail has one end: to provide a place where human souls can be refreshed.

attention to detail has one end: to provide a place where human souls can be refreshed. Bacon understands the work a garden entails: tangled undergrowth must be cut away, bushes pruned, roses tended, flowers planted and watered. And he understands there is a balance between adding and taking away at the heart of all genuine growth and beauty; a fountain adds texture to a garden, but a pond may become stagnant and unhealthy; a few pieces of art enhance the pleasure of a garden, but too many statues point merely to the owner's pride. A garden not only refreshes a soul, but becomes its mirror as well.

If, as Bacon notes, it was God who first planted a garden, then we would do well to imitate his plan and to cultivate our bodies and spirits amidst its quiet greens and fresh blooms.

"OF GARDENS"

God Almighty first planted a garden. And, indeed, it is the purer of human pleasures; it is the great refreshment to the spirits of man, without which, building and palaces are but gross handiworks. And a man shall ever see that when ages grow to civility and elegancy, men come to build stately, sooner than to garden finely, as if gardening were the greater perfection.

For March, there come violets, specially the single blue, which are the earliest, the yellow daffodil, the daisy, the almond-tree in blossom, the peach-tree in blossom, the cornelian-tree in blossom, sweetbriar. In April follow the double white violet, the wallflower, the stock gilliflower, the cowslip, flower-de-luces, and lilies of all natures, rosemary flowers; the tulip, the double peony, the pale daffodil, the French honeysuckle, the cherry-tree in blossom, the damson and plum trees in blossom, the whitethorn in leaf, the lilac tree. In May and June come pinks of all sorts, specially the blush pink, roses of all kinds, except the musk, which comes later; honeysuckles, strawberries, bugloss, columbine, the French marigold, flos Africanus, cherry-tree in fruit; ribes, figs in fruit, rasps; vine flowers, lavender in flowers, the sweet satyrian, with the white flower, herba muscaria, lilium convallium, the apple-tree in blossom.

And because the breath of flowers is far sweeter in the air (where it comes and goes like the warbling of music) than in the hand, therefore nothing is more fit for that delight, than to know what be the flowers and plants that do best perfume the air. Roses, damask and red, are fast flowers of their smells, so that you may walk by a whole row of them and find nothing of their sweetness, yea, though it be in a morning's dew. Bays likewise yield no smell as they grow, rosemary little, nor sweet marjoram. That which above all others yields the sweetest smell in the air is the violet, especially the white double violet, which comes twice a year—about the middle of April, and about Bartholomew-tide. Next to that is the musk-rose, then the strawberry-leaves dying, which yield a most excellent cordial smell, then the flower of the vines, it is a little dust, like the dust of a bent, which grows upon the cluster in the first coming forth; then sweet briar, then wallflowers, which are very delightful to be set under a parlor or lower chamber window; then pinks and gilliflowers, especially the matted pink and clove gilliflower; then the flowers of the lime-tree, then the honeysuckles, so they be somewhat afar off; of bean-flowers I speak not, because they are field flowers. But those which perfume the air most delightfully, not passed by as the rest, but being trodden upon and crushed, are three, that is: burnet, wild thyme, and water mints. Therefore, you are to set whole alleys of them, to have the pleasure when you walk or tread.

For gardens (speaking of those which are indeed prince-like, as we have done of buildings), the contents ought not well to be under thirty acres of ground; and to be divided into three parts: a green in the entrance, a heath or desert in the going forth, and the main garden in the midst, besides alleys on both sides. And I like well, that four acres of ground be assigned to the green, six to the heath, four and four to either side, and twelve to the main garden. The green hath two pleasures: the one, because nothing is more pleasant to the eye than green grass kept finely shorn; the other, because it will give you a fair alley in the midst, by which you may go in front upon a stately hedge, which is to inclose the garden.

But because the alley will be long, and, in great heat of the year, or day, you ought not to buy the shade in the garden by going in the sun through the green; therefore you are of either side the green to plant a covert alley, upon carpenter's work about twelve foot in height, by which you may go in shade into the garden. As for the making of knots or figures with divers colored earths, that they may lie under the windows of the house, on that side which the garden stands, they be but toys. You may see as good sights many times in tarts.

The garden is best to be square, encompassed on all the four sides with a stately arched hedge. The arches to be upon pillars of carpenter's work, of some ten foot high, and six foot broad, and the spaces between of the same dimension with the breadth of the arch; over the arches let there be an entire hedge of some four foot high, framed also upon carpenter's work; and upon the upper hedge, over every arch, a little turret with a belly, enough to receive a cage of birds; and over every space, between the arches, some other little figure, with broad plates of round colored glass, gilt, for the sun to play upon. But this hedge I intend to be raised upon a bank, not steep, but gently sloped, of some six foot, set all with flowers. Also, I understand, that this square of the garden should not be the whole breadth of the ground, but to leave on either side ground enough for diversity of side alleys, unto which the two covert alleys of the green may deliver you. But there must be no alleys with hedges at either end of this great inclosure; not at the hither end for letting [i.e., obscuring] your prospect upon this fair hedge from the green; nor, at the further end, for letting your prospect from the hedge, through the arches upon the heath.

For the ordering of the ground within the great hedge, I leave it to variety of device; advising, nevertheless, that whatsoever form you cast it into, first it be not too busy or full of work. Wherein I, for my part, do not like images cut out in juniper or other garden stuff—they be for children. Little low hedges, round, like welts, with some pretty pyramids, I like well, and in some places, fair columns upon frames of carpenter's work.

For fountains, they are a great beauty and refreshment; but pools mar all, and make the garden unwholesome and full of flies and frogs. Fountains I intend to be of two natures—the one that sprinkleth or spouteth water, the other a fair receipt of water, of some thirty or forty foot square, but without fish, or slime, or mud. For the first, the ornaments of images gilt, or of marble, which are in use, do well: but the main matter is, so to convey the water, as it never stay, either in the bowls or in the cistern, that the water be never by rest discolored, green, or red or the like, or gather any mossiness or putrefaction. Besides that, it is to be cleansed every day by the hand. Also some steps up to it, and some fine pavement about it, doth well. As for the other kind of fountain, which we may call a bathing pool, it may admit much curiosity and beauty, wherewith we will not trouble ourselves: as that the bottom be finely paved, and with images; the sides likewise, and withal embellished with colored glass, and such things of luster, encompassed also with fine rails of low statues. But the main point is the same which we mentioned in the former kind of fountain, which is, that the water be in perpetual motion, fed by a water higher than the pool, and delivered into it by fair spouts, and then discharged away under ground by some equality of bores, that it stay little. And for fine devices, of arching water without spilling, and making it rise in several forms (of feathers, drinking glasses, canopies, and the like), they be pretty things to look on, but nothing to health and sweetness.

For the heath, which was the third part of our plot, I wish it to be framed, as much as may be, to a natural wildness. Trees I would have none in it; but some thickets, made only of sweetbriar and honeysuckle, and some wild vine amongst; and the ground set with violets, strawberries, and primroses; for these are sweet, and prosper in the shade; and these to be in the heath, here and there, not in any order. I like also little heaps, in the nature of mole-hills (such as are in wild heaths) to be set, some with wild thyme, some with pinks, some with germander that gives a good flower to the eye; some with periwinkle, some with violets, some with strawberries, some with cowslips, some with daisies, some with red roses; some with lilium convallium, some with sweetwilliams, red, some with bear's-foot, and the like low flowers, being withal sweet and sightly. Part of which heaps are to be with standards of little bushes pricked upon their top, and part without. The standards to be roses, juniper, holly, bear-berries (but here and there, because of the smell of their blossom), red currants, gooseberries, rosemary, bays, sweetbriar, and such like. But these standards to be kept with cutting, that they grow not out of course.

For the side grounds you are to fill them with variety of alleys, private, to give a full shade, some of them wheresoever the sun be. You are to frame some of them likewise for shelter, that when the wind blows sharp you may walk as in a gallery. And those alleys must be likewise hedged at both ends to keep out the wind, and these closer alleys must be ever finely gravelled, and no grass, because of going wet. In many of these alleys, likewise, you are to set fruit-trees of all sorts, as well upon the walls as in ranges. And this would be generally observed that the borders wherein you plant your fruit-trees be fair and large, and low, and not steep, and set with fine flowers, but thin and sparingly, lest they deceive the trees. At the end of both the side grounds I would have a mount of some pretty height, leaving the wall of the enclosure breast high, to look abroad into the fields.

For the main garden I do not deny but there should be some fair alleys ranged on both sides with fruit-trees; and some pretty tufts of fruit-trees, and arbors with seats set in some decent order; but these to be by no means set too thick, but to leave the main garden so as it be not close, but the air open and free. For, as for shade, I would have you rest upon the alleys of the side grounds, there to walk, if you be disposed, in the heat of the year or day, but to make account that the main garden is for the more temperate parts of the year, and in the heat of summer, for the morning and the evening, or overcast days.

For aviaries, I like them not, except they be of that largeness as they may be turfed, and have living plants and bushes set in them, that the birds may have more scope and natural nestling, and that no foulness appear in the floor of the aviary.

So I have made a platform of a princely garden, partly by precept, partly by drawing, not a model, but some general lines of it; and in this I have spared for no cost. But it is nothing for great princes that, for the most part taking advice with workmen, with no less cost set their things together, and sometimes add statues and such things for state and magnificence, but nothing to the true pleasure of a garden.

Martha Ballard

FROM *A MIDWIFE'S TALE: THE LIFE* OF *MARTHA BALLARD*

One of the tasks of spring is the tending of a garden. This may mean sprucing up a perennial bed, clearing away the signs of the decay of winter. It might mean spading up the soil to plant a vegetable garden, or setting out annuals for the summertime. In each of these cases, the work involves the meeting of human activity with the earth, and it suggests the spiritual lessons of putting in the sweat in order to reap the later harvest. Gardening—the earliest occupation assigned to humanity—is an activity based on toil and promise, which is one way of defining how one might live by faith.

Gardening—the earliest occupation assigned to humanity—is an activity based on toil and promise, which is one way of defining how one might live by faith.

In this selection from early nineteenth-century Maine, Martha Ballard closely recounts her activities during one May planting season; her work in her garden is interspersed with her vocational work, for she is a midwife throughout the Kennebec River region. By the time of this writing, Martha Ballard was seventy years old—a goodly age. Her husband is still ploughing "our fields." But when she speaks of the garden, she always speaks of it as *"My garden."* This is her space in which to do her work—not such a common thing for a woman in this period. In this space, she grows the stuff of her economy: there will be vegetables to eat this season, roots to plant in order to yield seeds for next season, seeds to sell, and herbs for her midwifery. She is asserting powerfully her own role in the renewals of spring, and her own sense of identity.

FROM *A MIDWIFE'S TALE: THE LIFE OF MARTHA BALLARD*

May 1809

1 *At John Shaws. Birth 2nd. June 16th receivd 7s and 6d of Mr Shaw.* Clear. I was Calld about midnight to John Shaws wife who is in Labour. Shee was safe delivered at 8 hour this morning of her 2nd Child and daughter. I returned home about noone. Mr Ballard went to Town meeting. Magr Samuel Howard was Chosen to represent the Town in general Coart.

9 *At home. Workt in gardin. Sophia & Dolly sleep here.* Clear part of the day. I have sett Turnips & Cabbage stumps. Daughter Ballard here. Her son Jonathan Came & informd he had shipt for Liverpoole. Setts out tomorrow. Sophia Gill & Dolly Lambard sleep here.

10 *At home. Mrs Emry here. Girls went home after breakfast. Jonathan Ballard sett out to go to sea.* Cloudy the most of the day. I have done hous work. Planted Cucumbers & three kinds squash. Removd Banking from the house &c. Knit some. Mrs Emry to see me. The girls left here this morn. Mrs Emry, two of William Stones daughters had gardin seeds of me. Mr Ballard workt at son Jonathans. Jack sett out for sea.

11 *At home. I brewed.* Cloudy. I have done houswork. Brewed. Mr Ballard workt at son Jonathans forenoon, went to sett hoops for Daughter Lambard afternoon. Informs Patty is very Lambe in her hand.

12 *At home. Bakt & planted squash & Cucumbers.* Cloudy the most of the day. I have done hous work. Bakt brown Bread. Have

not felt well. Mr Ballard mending fence round the gardin. Ephraim & William sleep here.

13 *At home. Mr Ballard to Hallowell. Had of Mr Lad 1/2 lb Tea, 2 lb Sugar, & 6 alwives. Deaths.* Cloudy the most of the day. I have fixt a bed, planted squash seeds and removd part of the Banking from East side the hous. Mr Bullin here, informed that his son Jessy buried his youngest Child yesterday. Rhoda Pollard sleeps here. Informed that Old Mr Bisbee is dead. Patty Town is very Lambe. Hannah Ballard & William sleep here.

14 *At home. Rhoda left here after dinner.* Cloudy part of the day. Raind some. Mr Ballard to meeting. Reverend Mr Stone discoarst from Romans 1st Chapter 28th vers. Hannah Ballard & Getchel Calld here. Ephraim & William sleep here.

15 *At home. Jonathan Junior returnd. Could not get a Chance to go to sea.* Clear part of the day. Showers afternoon. I have dug ground west of the hous. Planted squash, Cucumbers, musk and water mellons East side house. Began and finisht a Large wash after 3 O Clock. Feel fatagued. Son Jonathan ploughing our field. My husband workt with him.

17 *At home. Son Town left here this morning. Mr Ballard is 84 years this day. Death Mr Hains.* Clear, warm and spring like. I have workt in my gardin. Planted long squash by the hogg pen, sowd pepper grass, sett sage and other roots. Mr. Ballard mode Bush & dugg gardin. I washt his & Cyrus's old over Coats, my gound & other things. Son Jonathan had 6 Oxen taken by Execution and drove away. I do feel for but am not able to help him. Ephraim & William Sleep here.

18 *At home. Hear that Mrs Mosier is no Better.* Clear. I workt in my garden. Sett Parsley & 3 quins trees by the pigg pen. Knit some &c. Mr Ballard diging gardin & setting hop poles. Ephraim sleeps here.

19 *At home. Mr [blot]* Clear & warm. I have workt in the gardin, knit some, boiling soap. Jonathan Junior sleeps here. Mr. Wiman made us a present of 12 fish.

20 *At home. Company here. Jonathan wife gave us Butter.* Clear. I have ironed & workt in gardin. Daughter Lambard sent me 3 Lb.

pork. Mrs Farewell, Daughter Ballard & 3 Children, Patty Town took Tea here.

21 *At home. Son Ephraims wife and Patty Town here.* Clear & warm. Mr Ballard went to meeting. Walkt. Son Ephraims wife Came here before noone. Shee & Patty Town took supper with us. We are informd that Mrs. Mosier is more Comfortable. Pattys hand is better. The text from Hebrews 12, 3 vers, afternoon Psalms 62nt, 8 vs.

22 *At home. Washt & workd in gardin.* Cloudy & some rain. I have washt & workt in gardin. Sett 2 quins trees and i apple tree. Planted some of Luke's potatoes, set Leutis plants & strawberries. I have squash & Cucumbers Come up in the bed East side the hous.

23 *At home. Sowd string peas.* Cloudy morn. Sun shine the most of the day. I have done houswork and some in my gardin. Mrs Jones here forenoon. I sowed string peas N end of my gardin. Mr Ballard had ½ lbs Butter at son Jonathans. Jonathan Junior sleeps here.

24 *At home. Workt in my gardin.* Clear. I have done my hous work and dug gardin. Sowd pees &c. Mr Ballard went to son Ephraims. He sent me 7½ lb. fresh pork. Son Jonathan sent me a piece green Chees & some rice. Ephraim sleeps here.

25 *At James Catons. Birth 4th. Fell from the hors on my way home. Received 9/ at William Babcok.* Clear. I was Calld by Mr Caton at 2 hour 30 m this morning to go and see his wife. I arivd there at sun rise. Found her delivard of a son, her 11th Child, but not safe. I performd what was necessary and left her as Comfortable as Could be Expected. Arivd home before ten and sent herbs and other matters.

26 *At home. Planted Beans.* Clear, cool & windy. I have done houswork and workt in my gardin. Planted Crambury, Brown, & hundred to one beens south of the hous. Jonathan Ballard Junior sleeps here.

27 *At home. Brewd & workt in gardin.* Clear and windy. I have transplanted Cucumbers and done other work in my gardin. Mr Ballard to Hallowell. Calld at Daughter Lambards. Brot 6 lbs ¾ veal from her. Lefaett ploughd the S end of our field.

28 *At son Pollards. Birth 5th.* Clear part of the day. I was Calld by Son Pollard at 2 hour 30 m this morning to go and see his wife.

We reacht there before 5 and my Daughter was delivered at 6 of a fine Daughter, her 9nth Child, and is Comfortable. The Babe weighed 11 pounds. Sally Cleark & Preuda Snow Came at Evening, there all night.

29 *At ditoes.* Raind. My Daughter & infant Comfortable. Pruda helpt wash, Sally assisted. Shee tarried all night. All Cleverly. Son Pollard went to Watervill.

30 *At ditoes and Son Jonathan's.* Clear part of the day. I got my Daughter up, Changed her Lining &c and left her at 8. Reacht home at 11 a.m. Find my hous [without] any person in it. Daughter Pollard gave me Cake & 2¾ lb pork. I went to son Jonathan's. Carried herbs & other matters for Patty Town to Carry to Daughter Pollard. Sett squash plants East side the Gardin.

31 *At home. Works in the gardin. Mrs Mosier is no better.* Clear. I have done hous work & sett out squash plants & Cucumbers. Capt Smith & Lefaett ploughing our field. Cyrus Shearing sheep. Allin Lambard here for potatoes and Beens. Daughter Ballard sent us 13 oz Butter.

Louise Beebe Wilder

"THE COLOUR OF THE YOUNG YEAR" FROM *COLOUR IN MY GARDEN*

*L*ouise Beebe Wilder's description of her garden comes more than a century after that of Martha Ballard, but is separated by so much more than time. Ballard's garden represents her household economy, growing food for her family and herbs for her midwifery. Wilder's very formal and extensive gardens are designed for the eye. This is only possible, of course, because Wilder's resources and leisure were vast, but it also suggests an entirely different perspective. For Wilder, the garden was to be a retreat whose aesthetics spoke to the spirit. For Ballard, who is planting by the hog pens, aesthetics are irrelevant.

> *T*he garden was to be a retreat whose aesthetics spoke to the spirit.

    At the turn of the twentieth century, American landscape design was heavily influenced by gardening books from Great Britain, particularly those of Gertrude Jekyll. The designs presented in these texts were very grand and very formal, and were suited to a British climate. Louise Wilder was one of the first landscape designers to adapt the formality of the British gardens to an American landscape, and she brought to it a kind of Yankee practicality:

Every plant had to perform well, both in terms of hardiness and aesthetic contribution. The first criterion rejected the notion that an exotic plant was valuable merely because it was fragile and rare. The second criterion asserted that each individual was valuable in terms of the role it played within the whole. Thus, in her description of springtime yellow flowers, Wilder dwells on the way each plant functions as part of the whole. Beyond this, her eye is focused on what the garden might contribute to the individual soul that visits a place of beauty.

"The Colour of the Young Year"

My spring appears, Oh see what here doth grow.

—Sidney

Even a careless observer cannot but be aware that in the floral world certain colours predominate at certain seasons. In the early spring a distinct majority of the flowers are yellow and even the young leafage is instinct with yellow principle. Thoreau says that "the spring yellows are faint, cool, innocent as the saffron morning as compared with the blaze of noon," and most of these spring yellows have an ascid cast like the colour of the Winter Aconite, though there is no hint of this sharpness in the radiant, light-suggesting petals of Daffodils. These radiant and ascid yellows are in wonderful harmony with the pale young leafage, while the delicately enveloping spring light seems to draw them all into a soft illumination to honour the season of renewals and fresh hope.

As the spring advances yellow flowers become even more numerous. Tulips have sprung into being; Corydalis lutea from chinks in the wall and C. cheilanthifolia from the edge of a shady border send up spikes of yellow flowers amidst waving, fernlike foliage. Groups of tall Doronicums open their round yellow blooms among clumps of early purple Iris; yellow Alyssum edges a long border with the sky-blue Anchusa myosotidiflora and hardy white Candy-tuft.

Often the common Golden Alyssum is a bit too prominent in the spring garden. It seeds itself so generously that there is usually a good deal of it and it wears a most aggressive hue, too raw and harsh. Kept in the soothing neighbourhood of light blue or lavender flowers or freely mingled with white, it is amiable enough but it is out of harmony with the rosy blossoming boughs of its season, and here, where it wrapt the scarlet skirts of the Japanese Quince with a fiercely yellow scarf, it was like a strident voice transcending the delicate harmonies of the spring world. It is too bright and useful to be eliminated entirely, but it should be carefully placed and restricted, and more use might well be made of the pale variety called sulphureum which is of a delicate sulphur colour and quite lacks the harshness inherent in the type. This plant is in most happy accord with all its contemporaries, especially with the bright purple and lavender Phloxes and Aubrietias. Alyssum Silver Queen is said to wear the same soft colour, and seed of this kind is to be had in this country, but, while I have a sturdy colony of seedlings in the nursery, I have not yet seen it in flower.

The little Hedge Mustard or Fairy Wallflower (Erysimum rupestre, syn. pulchellum) provides us with more yellow treasure for this season. It, too, is a trifle ascid in its colour, but it is so small and pretty and has so wild and sweet a fragrance that we would not be without it, and are pleased indeed when it takes possession of a vacant cranny in the steps or walls and spreads its fine dark mat of foliage. It enjoys a stone or two to trail over but it will thrive willingly in the ordinary sunny border if the soil is not too heavy. It is a nice companion for the silvery lavender Phlox called G. F. Wilson, or if thickly set about with the bulbs of Grape Hyacinth it creates as pretty an edging as one would wish to see.

This spring there is a delightful bit of blue and gold planting in my garden—a blue and gold carpet that spreads back beneath the Lilac bushes in the angle of the high wall, woven of the Grape Hyacinth called Heavenly Blue and the little wild yellow Tulip, T. sylvestris, so full of grace and gracious sweetness. The small bulbs are closely planted, but here and there among them are set tufts of the baby Meadow Rue (Thalictrum minor) that grows only six inches tall, and spreads about its delicate greenery after the spring blossoms are past. In another angle of the garden a pretty composition in yellow and lavender bespeaks admiration. Here a well-shaped bush of old-fashioned yellow-flowering Currant stands like a great fragrant bouquet above a close ground cover of Canadian Phlox (Phlox divaricata).

But all this is but by way of preamble. The sweetest and fairest of spring's yellow blossoms has been for many weeks sending up its slender water-green spears and opening a radiant blossom here and there—"a sudden flame of gold and sweet"—until they are assembled army strong and one seems to hear the challenge:

> *King Trumpeter to Flora Queen,*
> *Hey, ho, daffodil!*
> *Blow, and the golden jousts begin!*

Begin indeed with such a burst of fluttering, soft-coloured confusion as never was and never will be until Daffodil time is again upon the land.

There they go streaming the length of one border—pale, star-like hosts with a ribbon of purple Aubrietia wound among them; there they stand, long golden trumpets, in a flutter above a cloud of silver-lilac Phlox, and again how they pick their way among the fallen Cherry blossoms.

Why plan colour harmonies for those to whom inharmony is impossible—why even choose varieties when every separate flower is a spring poem? May we not just go "dancing with the Daffodils" where ignorance is bliss? But the wise ones tell us that if we have not knowledge of how to choose our partners the dance may prove a dirge. All Daffodils do not thrive equally well in all gardens nor in all situations. The white trumpets (like N. albicans) ask for shade; the poeticus group enjoys a heavier soil and are happiest with some moisture; the dwarfs, like N. nanus and the Hoop Petticoats, should have the sharp drainage and sandy loam of the rock garden. But while these rules generally hold, it is best to experiment a little to find out which Daffodils our garden will entertain most successfully.

For naturalizing along the banks of streams none is better than the various forms of Narcissus poeticus. The old Pheasant's Eye is so inexpensive that it may be put in by the thousand and looks lovely gleaming among the young fern fronds in the short grass. The variety ornatus is also very inexpensive and blooms quite a little earlier than the Pheasant's Eye.

Daffodils belong to the radiant yellows and run the gamut from the pale, creamy N. albicans to the pure sunshine of such as Golden Spur. Their personal colour scheme is of a loveliness to be noted quite apart from their possibilities in combination with other flowers. More than any other flower they express supreme and exquisite freshness. The leaves are of that cool blue-green shade strongly suggestive of water, and the flowers themselves, radiant, crisp, vital as are no other blossoms of the year, seem their perfect accompaniment.

Daffodils are in bloom with many flowering trees and shrubs and more use should be made of these in association. Narcissus Golden Spur and N. obvallaris come early enough to bloom in the wraith shadow of the Shad Bush, or in the rosy glow of the Double-flowered Peach-trees. In my garden is a gay picture where a Peach-tree spreads its pink-clothed branches against the garden wall; beneath it are mats of silver-gray Phlox subulata G.F. Wilson and groups of yellow Daffodils.

I have found the various Star Daffodils the best for naturalizing in grass. Minnie Hume, Mrs. Langtry, Grandee, and Queen Bess are inexpensive sorts that are timed to the flowering of the orchard Cherries and with them seem to express the very fulness of the spring. I remember that the meadows about the beautiful old colonial mansion of Homewood, near Baltimore, used to be a sea of yellow Daffodils in spring—a rare treasure trove for flower-loving children. These were the fat old double sort with crumpled green-gold petals and the smell of moist earth. The poeticus varieties bloom with the Apple blossoms and may easily be naturalized in orchards where the grass need not be cut until after the Narcissus foliage has died naturally.

To-day, May 8th, a pink-flowered Japanese Cherry is in full flower, the ground beneath it carpeted with pale Star Daffodils and the edge of the bed hidden under alternate mounds of purple Aubrietia Dr. Mules and sky-blue Iris pumila caerulea. A week later Malus floribunda will shed its pink petals upon the pale gold trumpets of Narcissus beauty. Old-fashioned Bleeding Heart consorts gaily with pretty Narcissus stella superba and nodding white Checker Lilies, and to-morrow the band of purple Viola cornuta and Forget-me-not about the pool will be starred with the fragrant double blossoms of the Gardenia-flowered Narcissus.

Alice Morse Earle

"IN LILAC TIDE" FROM
OLD-TIME GARDENS, NEWLY SET FORTH

In 1901, Alice Morse Earle began her Old-Time Gardens *by evoking New England's past, writing specifically of early Plymouth, Massachusetts:*

And by every humble dwelling the homesick goodwife or dame, trying to create a semblance of her fair English home so far away, planted in her "garden plot" seeds and roots of homely English flowers and herbs, that quickly grew and blossomed and smiled on bleak New England's rocky shores as sturdily and happily as they had bloomed in the old gardens and by the ancient door sides in England. What good cheer they must have brought! how they must have been beloved!

> *The garden provides memory.*

Though this may be somewhat fanciful history, it evokes what Earle sees as a particularly potent element of gardening. For Earle, the garden does not provide medicine and food, as it does for Martha Ballard; it is not part of the household economy. Instead, it provides memory. In this selection from Old-Time Gardens—*the title itself evokes memory*—*Morse writes of the lovely emergence of perennial plants, especially that one most familiar to*

us all—lilacs, whose flowers seem to evoke springtime. Most writers of gar-
den books are pleased to dwell on the beauties of these blossoms or to recall
that they suggest rebirth or growth—all of which is quite true. But for Earle,
their re-emergence suggests something else entirely—and she withholds the
spiritual truth that she comes to until her final two paragraphs.

From "In Lilac Tide"

The universal flower in the old-time garden was the Lilac; it was the
most beloved bloom of spring, and gave a name to Spring—Lilac
tide. The Lilac does not promise "spring is coming"; it is the
emblem of the presence of spring. Dr. Holmes says, "When Lilacs
blossom, Summer cries, 'Spring is here'" in every cheerful and lavish
bloom. Lilacs shade the front yard; Lilacs grow by the kitchen
doorstep; Lilacs spring up beside the barn; Lilacs shade the well;
Lilacs hang over the spring house; Lilacs crowd by the fence side
and down the country road. In many colonial dooryards it was the
only shrub—known both to lettered and unlettered folk as Laylock,
and spelt Laylock too. Walter Savage Landor, when Laylock had
become antiquated, still clung to the word, and used it with a stub-
born persistence such as he alone could compass, and which seems
strange in the most finished classical scholar of the day.

There is no more emblematic flower to me than the Lilac; it has an
association of old homes, of home-making and home interests. On
the country farm, in the village garden, and in the city yard, the lilac
was planted wherever the home was made, and it attached itself
with deepest roots, lingering some-times most sadly but sturdily, to
show where the home once stood.

Let me tell of two Lilacs of sentiment. One [is] a glorious Lilac
tree which is one of a group of many full-flowered, pale-tinted ones
still growing and blossoming each spring on a deserted homestead
in old Narragansett. They bloom over the grave of a fine old house,

and the great chimney stands sadly in their midst as a gravestone. "Hopewell," ill-suited of name, was the home of a Narragansett Robinson famed for good cheer, for refinement and luxury, and for a lovely garden, laid out with cost and care and filled with rare shrubs and flowers. Perhaps these Lilacs were a rare variety in their day, being pale of tint; now they are as wild as their companions, the Cedar hedges.

Gathering in the front dooryard of a fallen farm-house some splendid branches of flowering Lilac, I found a few feet of cellar wall and wooden house side standing, and the sills of two windows. These window sills, exposed for years to the bleaching and fading of rain and sun and frost, still bore the circular marks of the flower pots which, filled with houseplants, had graced the kitchen windows for many a winter under the care of a flower-loving house mistress. A few days later I learned from a woman over ninety years of age—an inmate of the "Poor House"—the story of the home thus touchingly indicated by the Lilac bushes and the stains of the flower pots. Over eighty years ago she had brought the tiny Lilac-slip to her childhood's home, then standing in a clearing in the forest. She carried it carefully in her hands as she rode behind her father on a pillion after a visit to her grandmother. She and her little brothers and sisters planted the tiny thing "of two eyes only," as she said, in the shadow of the house, in the little front yard. And these children watered it and watched it, as it rooted and grew, till the house was surrounded each spring with its vivacious blooms, its sweet fragrance. The puny slip has outlived the house and all its inmates save herself, outlived the brothers and sisters, their children and grandchildren, outlived orchard and garden and field. And it will live to tell a story to every thoughtful passer-by till a second growth of forest has arisen in pasture and garden and even in the cellar-hole, when even then the cheerful Lilac will not be wholly obliterated.

A bunch of early Lilacs was ever a favorite gift to "teacher," to be placed in a broken-nosed pitcher on her desk. And Lilac petals made such lovely necklaces, thrust within each other or strung with needle and thread. And there was a love divination by Lilacs which we children solemnly observed. There will occasionally appear a tiny Lilac flower, usually a white Lilac, with five divisions of the petal instead of four—this is a Luck Lilac. This must be solemnly swallowed. If it goes down smoothly, the dabbler in magic cries out, "He loves me"; if she chokes at her floral food, she must say sadly, "He loves me not." I remember once calling out, with gratification and pride, "He loves me!"

"Who is he?" said my older companions. "Oh, I didn't know he had to be somebody," I answered in surprise, to be met by derisive laughter at my satisfaction with a lover in general and not in particular. It was a matter of Lilac-luck-etiquette that the lover's name should be pronounced mentally before the petal was swallowed.

In the West Indies the Lilac is a flower of mysterious power; its perfume keeps away evil spirits, ghosts, banshees. If it grows not in the dooryard, its protecting branches are hung over the doorway. I think of this when I see it shading the door of happy homes in New England.

I have written of the gladness of spring, but I know nothing more overwhelming than the heartache of spring, the sadness of a fresh-growing spring garden. Where is the dear one who planted it and loved it, and he who helped her in the care, and the loving child who played in it and left it in the springtime? All that is good and beautiful has come again to us with the sunlight and warmth, save those whom we still love but can see no more. By that very measure of happiness poured for us in childhood in Lilac tide, is our cup of sadness now filled.

Barbara Kingsolver with Steven Hopp

"CALLED OUT" FROM SMALL WONDER

*I*t might seem that the antithesis to Francis Bacon's orderly garden, which *began this selection of gardening essays, is the unpredictable appearance of desert wildflowers in the spring. Dependent upon winter rains and a suffi-cient seed-set, these "ephemeral annuals" may cower in the dust or burst out by the thousands into a spectacular color show, seemingly at random and at infrequent intervals. Despite their appearance of fragility, however, these desert flowers are resilient and— well, smart. As Barbara Kingsolver notes, wildflowers can alter their periods of dormancy or even their size in order to survive and they pay no attention whatsoever to human timetables.*

> *W*ildflowers pay no attention whatsoever to human timetables.

Yet, despite the differences in Bacon's garden and Kingsolver's desert, both are marvels, not only because we look at them with astonishment but also in the rich old sense of being miraculous. Both are challenged by promises broken and thrive when promises are kept, whether that promise is a steady rain or the steady hand of a master gardener. Both burst into bloom for a season and then fade away, cycling from life to death, from growth to dormancy. And both evoke from us that same sense of awe, of startled awareness that we are not in control: *"God planted them,"* we say. *And we are right.*

"CALLED OUT"

The spring of 1998 was the Halley's Comet of desert wild-flower years. While nearly everyone else on the planet was cursing the soggy consequences of El Nino's downpours, here in southern Arizona we were cheering for the show: Our desert hills and valleys were colorized in wild schemes of maroon, indigo, tangerine, and some hues that Crayola hasn't named yet. Our mountains wore mantles of yellow brittlebush on their rocky shoulders, as fully transformed as eastern forests in their colorful autumn foliage. Abandoned cotton fields—flat, salinized ground long since left for dead—rose again, wearing brocade. Even highway medians were so crowded with lupines and poppies that they looked like the seed-packet promises come true: that every one came up. For weeks, each day's walk to the mailbox became a botanical treasure hunt, as our attention caught first on new colors, then on whole new species in this terrain we thought we had already cataloged.

The first warm days of March appear to call out a kind of miracle here: the explosion of nearly half our desert's flowering species, all stirred suddenly into a brief cycle of bloom and death. Actually, though, the call begins subtly, much earlier, with winter rains and gradually climbing temperatures. The intensity of the floral outcome varies a great deal from one spring to another; that much is obvious to anyone who ventures outdoors at the right time of year and pays attention. But even couch potatoes could not have missed the fact that 1998 was special: Full-color wild-flower photos made the front page of every major newspaper in the Southwest.

Our friends from other climes couldn't quite make out what the fuss was about. Many people aren't aware that the desert blooms at all, even in a normal year, and few would guess how much effort we devote to waiting and prognosticating. "Is this something like Punxsutawney Phil on Groundhog Day?" asked a friend from the East.

"Something like that. Or the fall color in New England. All winter the experts take measurements and make forecasts. This year they predicted gold, but it's already gone platinum. In a spot where you'd expect a hundred flowers, we've got a thousand. More kinds than anybody alive has ever seen at once."

"But these are annual flowers?"

"Right."

"Well, then ... " Our nonbiologist friend struggled to frame her question: "If they weren't there *last* year, and this year they *are,* then who planted them?"

One of us blurted, "*God* planted them!"

We glanced at each other nervously: A picturesque response indeed, from scientifically trained types like ourselves. Yet it seemed more compelling than any pedestrian lecture on life cycles and latency periods. Where *had* they all come from? Had these seeds just been lying around in the dirt for decades? And how was it that, at the behest of some higher power than the calendar, all at once there came a crowd?

The answers to these questions tell a tale as complex as a Beethoven symphony. Before a concert, you could look at a lot of sheet music and try to prepare yourself mentally for the piece it inscribed, but you'd still be knocked out when you heard it performed. With wildflowers, as in a concert, the magic is in the timing, the subtle combinations—and, most important, the extent of the preparations.

For a species, the bloom is just the means to an end. The flower show is really about making seeds, and the object of the game is persistence through hell or high water, both of which are features of the Sonoran Desert. In winter, when snow is falling on much of North America, we get slow, drizzly rains that can last for days and soak the whole region to its core. The Navajo call these female rains, as opposed to the "male rains" of late summer—those rowdy thunderstorms that briefly disrupt the hot afternoons, drenching one small plot of ground while the next hill over remains parched. It's the female rains that affect spring flowering, and in some years, such as 1998, the benefaction trails steadily from winter on into spring. In others, after a lick and a promise, the weather dries up for good.

Challenging conditions for an ephemeral, these are. If a little seed begins to grow at the first promise of rain, and that promise gets broken, that right there is the end of its little life. If the same thing happened to every seed in the bank, it would mean the end of the species. But it *doesn't* happen that way. Desert wildflowers have had millennia in which to come to terms with their inconstant mother. Once the plant has rushed through growth and flowering, its seeds wait in the soil—and not just until the next time conditions permit germination, but often longer. In any given year, a subset of a species' seeds don't germinate, because they're programmed for a longer dormancy. This seed bank is the plant's protection against a beckoning rain followed by drought. If any kind of wildflower ever existed whose seeds all sprouted and died before following through to seed-set, then that species perished long ago. This is what natural selection is about. The species that have made it this far have encoded genetic smarts enough to out-wit every peril. They produce seeds with different latency periods: Some germinate quickly, and some lie in wait, not just loitering there but loading the soil with many separate futures.

Scientists at the University of Arizona have spent years examining the intricacies of seed banks. Desert ephemerals, they've learned, use a surprising variety of strategies to fine-tune their own cycles to a climate whose cycles are not predictable—or at least, not predictable given the relatively short span of human observation. Even in a year as wet as 1998, when photo-ops and seed production exploded, the natives were not just seizing the moment; they were stashing away future seasons of success by varying, among and within species, their genetic schedules for germination, flowering, and seed-set. This variation reduces the intense competition that would result if every seed germinated at once. Some species even vary seed size: Larger seeds make more resilient sprouts, and smaller ones are less costly to produce; either morph may be programmed for delayed germination, depending on the particular strategy of the species. As a consequence of these sophisticated adaptations, desert natives can often hold their own against potential invasion by annual plants introduced from greener, more predictable pastures. You have to get up awfully early in the morning to outwit a native on its home turf.

The scientific term for these remarkable plants, "ephemeral annuals," suggests something that's as fragile as a poppy petal, a captive to the calendar. That is our misapprehension, along with our notion of this floral magic show—now you see it, now you don't—as a thing we can predict and possess like a garden. In spite of our determination to contain what we see in neat, annual packages, the blazing field of blues and golds is neither a beginning nor an end. It's just a blink, or maybe a smile, in the long life of a species whose blueprint for perseverance must outdistance all our record books. The flowers will go on mystifying us, answering to a clock that ticks so slowly we won't live long enough to hear it.

Samuel Johnson

"On Spring" from *Rambler No. 5*

*S*amuel Johnson's *was one of the most capacious and rational minds in a* *century of capacious and rational minds.* His Dictionary of the English Language, *conceived and executed by himself alone, became the standard for the language.* His conversations, *recorded by his friend James Boswell, became a measure of quick wit and eloquence aimed at dispersing folly and ignorance. His is the voice of health, of reason, of moderation, of rationality, and of faith. Perhaps this accounts for his definition of spring in his* Dictionary: *"The season in which plants rise and vegetate; the vernal season."*

> *S*pring is the season in which plants rise and vegetate; the vernal season.

Nowhere does this voice shine more characteristically than in his essays—this in an age that was just inventing the essay. Many appeared in the Rambler, *a journal published twice weekly for two years, from the spring of 1750 to the spring of 1752. Johnson's "On Spring" appeared in the fifth volume, and moves out of the garden and into the English countryside. As might be the case with a springtime walk, Johnson appears to meander: From a reflection on human folly, he moves to a recollection of a man who believed that spring would always bring him relief from his trouble, to a discourse on the beauties of the season, to a sound criticism of those who are unable to be solitary, to praise for the bounties of nature. It is only in the final paragraph, where the movement of spring begins to chime with the movement of our lives, that the apparent randomness becomes direction.*

"On Spring"

Every man is sufficiently discontented with some circumstances of his present state, to suffer his imagination to range more or less in quest of future happiness, and to fix upon some point of time, in which, by the removal of the inconvenience which now perplexes him, or acquisition of the advantage which he at present wants, he shall find the condition of his life very much improved.

When this time, which is too often expected with great impatience, at last arrives, it generally comes without the blessing for which it was desired; but we solace ourselves with some new prospect, and press forward again with equal eagerness.

It is lucky for a man, in whom this temper prevails, when he turns his hopes upon things wholly out of his own power; since he forbears then to precipitate his affairs, for the sake of the great event that is to complete his felicity, and waits for the blissful hour, with less neglect of the measures necessary to be taken in the mean time.

I have long known a person of this temper, who indulged his dream of happiness with less hurt to himself than such chimerical wishes commonly produce, and adjusted his scheme with such address, that his hopes were in full bloom three parts of the year, and in the other part never wholly blasted. Many, perhaps, would be desirous of learning by what means he procured to himself such a cheap and lasting satisfaction. It was gained by a constant practice of referring the removal of all his uneasiness to the coming of the next spring; if his health was impaired, the spring would restore it; if what he wanted was at a high price, it would fall in value in the spring.

The spring, indeed, did often come without any of these effects, but he was always certain that the next would be more propitious; nor was ever convinced that the present spring would fail him before the middle of summer; for he always talked of the spring as coming till it was past, and when it was once past, every-one agreed with him that it was coming.

By long converse with this man, I am, perhaps, brought to feel immoderate pleasure in the contemplation of this delightful season: but I have the satisfaction of finding many, whom it can be no shame to resemble, infected with the same enthusiasm; for there is, I believe, scarce any poet of eminence, who has not left some testimony of his fondness for the flowers, the zephyrs, and the warblers of the spring. Nor has the most luxuriant imagination been able to describe the serenity and happiness of the golden age, otherwise than by giving a perpetual spring, as the highest reward of uncor-rupted innocence.

There is, indeed, something inexpressibly pleasing, in the annual renovation of the world, and the new display of the treasures of nature. The cold and darkness of winter, with the naked defor-mity of every object on which we turn our eyes, make us rejoice at the succeeding season, as well for what we have escaped, as for what we may enjoy; and every budding flower, which a warm situation brings early to our view, is considered by us as a messenger to notify the approach of more joyous days.

The spring affords to a mind, so free from the disturbance of cares or passions as to be vacant to calm amusements, almost every thing that our present state makes us capable of enjoying. The var-iegated verdure of the fields and woods, the succession of grateful odors, the voice of pleasure pouring out its notes on every side, with the gladness apparently conceived by every animal, from the growth of his food, and the clemency of the weather, throw over the whole earth an air of gaiety, significantly expressed by the smile of nature.

Yet there are men to whom these scenes are able to give no delight, and who hurry away from all the varieties of rural beauty, to lose their hours, and divert their thoughts by cards, or assemblies, a tavern dinner, or the prattle of the day.

It may be laid down as a position which will seldom deceive, that when a man cannot bear his own company there is something wrong. He must fly from himself, either because he feels a tediousness in life from the equipoise of an empty mind, which, having no tendency to one motion more than another but as it is impelled by some external power, must always have recourse to foreign objects: or he must be afraid of the intrusion of some unpleasing ideas, and, perhaps, is struggling to escape from the remembrance of a loss, the fear of a calamity, or some other thought of greater horror.

Those whom sorrow incapacitates to enjoy the pleasures of contemplation, may properly apply to such diversions, provided they are innocent, as lay strong hold on the attention: and those, whom fear of any future affliction chains down to misery, must endeavor to obviate the danger.

My considerations shall, on this occasion, be turned on such as arc burthensome to themselves merely because they want subjects for reflection, and to whom the volume of nature is thrown open, without affording them pleasure or instruction, because they never learned to read the characters.

A French author has advanced this seeming paradox, that *very few men know how to take a walk*; and, indeed, it is true, that few know how to take a walk with a prospect of any other pleasure, than the same company would have afforded them at home.

There are animals that borrow their color from the neighboring body, and, consequently, vary their hue as they happen to change their place. In like manner it ought to be the endeavor of every man to derive his reflections from the objects about him; for it is to no purpose that he alters his position, if his attention continues fixed to the same point. The mind should be kept open to the access of every new idea, and so far disengaged fom the predominance of particular thoughts, as easily to accommodate itself to occasional entertainment.

A man that has formed this habit of turning every new object to his entertainment, finds in the productions of nature an inexhaustible stock of materials upon which he can employ himself, without any temptations to envy or malevolence; faults, perhaps, seldom totally avoided by those, whose judgment is much exercised upon the works of art. He has always a certain prospect of discovering new reasons for adoring the sovereign author of the universe, and probable hopes of making some discovery of benefit to others, or of profit to himself. There is no doubt but many vegetables and animals have qualities that might be of great use, to the knowledge of which there is not required much force of penetration, or fatigue of study, but only frequent experiments, and close attention. What is said by the chemists of their darling mercury, is, perhaps, true of everybody through the whole creation, that if a thousand lives should be spent upon it, all its properties would not be found out.

Mankind must necessarily be diversified by various tastes, since life affords and requires such multiplicity of employments, and a nation of naturalists is neither to be hoped, or desired; but it is surely not improper to point out a fresh amusement to those who languish in health, and repine in plenty, for want of some source of diversion that may be less easily exhausted, and to inform the multitudes of both sexes, who are burthened with every new day, that there are many shows which they have not seen.

He that enlarges his curiosity after the works of nature, demonstrably multiplies the inlets to happiness; and, therefore, the younger part of my readers, to whom I dedicate this vernal speculation, must excuse me for calling upon them, to make use at once of the spring of the year, and the spring of life; to acquire, while their minds may be yet impressed with new images, a love of innocent pleasures, and an ardor for useful knowledge; and to remember, that a blighted spring makes a barren year, and that the vernal flowers, however beautiful and gay, are only intended by nature as preparatives to autumnal fruits.

Dorothy Wordsworth

FROM THE GRASMERE JOURNAL

D orothy Wordsworth was the sister of the well-known Romantic poet. She came to live with William at Grasmere Cottage when she was twenty-four years old, and from that time on she looked after him and his family—a task to which she devoted enormous energy. Even the journals that she kept somewhat sporadi- cally were meant for the pleasure of her brother. In more recent years, however, Dorothy's powers as a writer in her own right have become better known. Hers was the eye that watched for the perfect detail, the smallest stroke that showed the larger whole it signi-

*H*er journey is an inward one that suggests the wholeness of the entire human experience.

fied. It is all, Dorothy writes, "simplicity, unity, and life." Though she is reflecting upon what she sees outwardly on her springtime walks, her journey is an inward one that suggests the wholeness of the entire human experience, the writer's call to depict what we might otherwise miss, and the peculiar ability of spring to suggest the many interlacing experiences of our lives.

The following selections from the Grasmere Journal come from spring, 1802. Dorothy notes evidence of springtime in the natural world—high wind, flowers, lambs bleating, blue waters—paired with evidence of springtime in the working rural world—*smoking cottages, fisherman, farmers ploughing the fields. Readers familiar with William's "I Wandered Lonely As a Cloud" will see the same spring walk reflected here in the words of Dorothy.*

FROM THE GRASMERE JOURNAL

[*April*] *15th, Thursday* [1802]. It was a threatening, misty morning, but mild. We set off after dinner from Eusemere. Mrs. Clarkson went a short way with us, but turned back. The wind was furious, and we thought we must have returned. We first rested in the large boat-house, then under a furze bush opposite Mr. Clarkson's. Saw the plough going in the field. The wind seized our breath. The lake was rough. There was a boat by itself floating in the middle of the bay below Water Millock. We rested again in the Water Millock Lane. The hawthorns are black and green, the birches here and there greenish, but there is yet more of purple to be seen on the twigs. We got over into a field to avoid some cows—people working. A few primroses by the roadside—woodsorrel flower, the anemone, scentless violets, strawberries, and that starry, yellow flower which Mrs. C. calls pile wort. When we were in the woods beyond Gowbarrow Park we saw a few daffodils close to the water-side. We fancied that the sea had floated the seeds ashore, and that the little colony had so sprung up. But as we went along there were more and yet more; and at last, under the boughs of the trees, we saw that there was a long belt of them along the shore, about the breadth of a country turnpike road. I never saw daffodils so beautiful. They grew among the mossy stones about and about them; some rested their heads upon these stones, as on a pillow, for weariness; and the rest tossed and reeled and danced, and seemed as if they verily laughed with the wind, that blew upon them over the lake; they looked so gay, ever glancing, ever changing. This wind blew directly over the lake to them. There was here and there a little knot, and a few stragglers a few yards higher up; but they were so few as not to disturb the simplicity, unity; and life of that one busy highway. We rested again and again. The bays were stormy, and we heard the waves at different distances, and in the middle of the water, like the sea. All was cheerless and gloomy, so we faced the storm. At Dobson's, I was very kindly treated by a young woman. The landlady looked sour, but it is her way. William was sitting by a bright fire when I came downstairs. He soon made his way to the library, piled up in a corner of the window. He brought out a volume of Enfield's *Speaker,* another miscellany, and an odd volume of Congreve's plays. We had a glass of warm rum and water. We enjoyed ourselves, and wished for Mary. It rained and blew, when we went to bed.

April 16th, Friday (Good Friday). When I undrew my curtains in the morning, I was much affected by the beauty of the prospect, and the change. The sun shone, the wind had passed away, the hills looked cheerful, the river was very bright as it flowed into the lake. The church rises up behind a little knot of rocks, the steeple not so high as an ordinary three-story house. Trees in a row in the garden under the wall. The valley is at first broken by little rocky woody knolls that make retiring places, fairy valleys in the vale, the river winds along under these hills, travelling, not in a bustle but not slowly, to the lake. We saw a fisherman in the flat meadow on the other side of the water. He came towards us, and threw his line over the two-arched bridge. It is a bridge of a heavy construction, almost bending inwards in the middle, but it is grey, and there is a look of ancientry in the architecture of it that pleased me. As we go on the vale opens out more into one vale, with somewhat of a cradle bed. Cottages, with groups of trees, on the side of the hills. We passed a pair of twin children, two years old. Sate on the next bridge which we crossed—a single arch. We rested again upon the turf, and looked at the same bridge. We observed arches in the water, occasioned by the large stones sending it down in two streams. A sheep came plunging through the river, stumbled up the bank, and passed close to us. It had been frightened by an insignificant little dog on the other side.

Its fleece dropped a glittering shower under its belly. Primroses by the road-side, pile wort that shone like stars of gold in the suit, violets, strawberries, retired and half-buried among the grass. When we came to the foot of Brothers Water, I left William sitting on the bridge, and went along the path on the right side of the Lake through the wood. I was delighted with what I saw. The water under the boughs of the bare old trees, the simplicity of the mountains, and the exquisite beauty of the path. There was one grey cottage. I repeated *The Glow-worm,* as I walked along. I hung over the gate, and thought I could have stayed forever. When I returned, I found William writing a poem descriptive of the sights and sounds we saw and heard. There was the gentle flowing of the stream, the glittering, lively lake, green fields without a living creature to be seen on them, behind us, a flat pasture with forty-two cattle feeding; to our left, the road leading to the hamlet. No smoke there, the sun shone on the bare roofs. The people were at work ploughing, harrowing, and sowing; a dog barking now and then, cocks crowing, birds twittering, the snow in patches at the top of the highest hills, yellow palms, purple and green twigs on the birches, ashes with their glittering spikes quite bare. The hawthorn a bright green, with black stems under the oak. The moss of the oak glossy. We then went on, passed two sisters at work (*they first passed us*), one with two pitchforks in her hand, the other had a spade. We had some talk with them. They laughed aloud after we were gone, perhaps half in wantonness, half boldness. William finished his poem. Before we got to the foot of Kirkstone, there were hundreds of cattle in the vale. There we ate our dinner. The walk up Kirkstone was very interesting. The becks among the rocks were all alive. William showed me the little mossy streamlet which he had before loved when he saw its bright green track in the snow. The view above Ambleside very beautiful. There we sate and looked down on the green vale. We watched the crows at a little distance from us become white as silver as they flew into the sunshine, and when they went still further, they looked like shapes of water passing over the green fields. The whitening of Ambleside church is a great deduction from the

beauty of it, seen from this point. We called at the Luff's, the Bod-
dingtons there. Did not go in, and went round by the fields. I pulled
off my stockings, intending to wade the beck, but I was obliged to
put them on, and we climbed over the wall at the bridge. The post
passed us. No letters! Rydale Lake was in its own evening brightness: the Islands and Points distinct. Jane Ashburner came up to us
when we were sitting upon the wall. The garden looked pretty in
the half-moonlight, half-daylight, as we went up the vale.

Apr. 29. After I had written down the Tinker, which William finished
this morning, Luff called. He was very lame, limped into the kitchen.
He came on a little pony. We then went to John's Grove, sate a while
at first; afterwards William lay, and I lay, in the trench under the
fence—he with his eyes shut, and listening to the waterfalls and the
birds. There was no one waterfall above another—it was a sound of
waters in the air—the voice of the air. William heard me breathing
and rustling now and then, but we both lay still, and unseen by one
another. He thought that it would be sweet thus to lie in the grave, to
hear the *peaceful* sounds of the earth, and just to know that our dear
friends were near. The lake was still; there was a boat out. Silver How
reflected with delicate purple and yellowish hues as I have seen spar;
lambs on the island, and running races together by the half dozen, in
the round field near us. The copses green*ish,* hawthorn greens, cottages smoking. As I lay down on the grass, I observed the glittering
silver line on the ridge of the backs of the sheep, owing to their situation respecting the sun. Which made them look beautiful, but with
something of strangeness, like animals of another kind—as if belonging to a more splendid world. I got mullens and pansies.

May 4. Though William went to bed nervous and jaded in the
extreme, he rose refreshed. I wrote out *The Leech Gatherer* for him,
which he had begun the night before, and of which he wrote several stanzas in bed this morning. It was very hot. We rested several
times by the way—read, and repeated *The Leech Gatherer.* We saw
Coleridge on the Wytheburn side of the water; He crossed the beck

to us. Mr. Simpson was fishing there. William and I ate luncheon and then went on towards the waterfall. It was a glorious wild solitude under that lofty purple crag. It stood upright by itself; its own self and its shadow below, one mass; all else was sunshine. We went on further. A bird at the top of the crag was flying round and round and looked in thinness and transparency, shape and motion like a moth. We climbed the hill but looked in vain for a shade, except at the foot of the great waterfall. We came down and rested upon a moss-covered rock rising out of the bed of the river. There we lay, ate our dinner, and stayed there till about four o'clock or later. William and Coleridge repeated and read verses. I drank a little brandy and water, and was in heaven. The stags horn is very beautiful and fresh, springing upon the fells; mountain ashes, green. We drank tea at a farm house. We parted from Coleridge at Sara's Crag, after having looked at the Letters which C. carved in the morning. William deepened the X with C.'s penknife. We sate afterwards on the wall, seeing the sun go down and the reflections in the still water. C. looked well, and parted from us cheerfully, hopping up upon the side stones. On the Raise we met a woman with two little girls, one in her arms, the other, about four years old walking, by her side, a pretty little thing, but half starved. Young as she was, she walked carefully with them. Alas, too young for such cares and such travels. The mother, when we accosted her, told us that her husband had left her and gone off with another woman and how she *"pursued"* them. Then her fury kindled, and her eyes rolled about. She changed again to tears. She was a Cockermouth woman, thirty years of age—a child at Cockermouth when I was. I was moved, and gave her a shilling. We had the crescent moon with the "auld moon in her arms." We rested often, always upon the bridges. Reached home at about ten o'clock. We went soon to bed. I repeated verses to William while he was in bed; he was soothed and I left him. "This is the spot" over and over again.

May 6. A sweet morning. We have put the finishing stroke to our bower, and here we are sitting in the orchard. It is one o'clock. We are sitting upon a seat under the wall, which I found my Brother building up, when I came to him. He had intended that it should have been done before I came. It is a nice, cool, shady spot. The small birds are singing, lambs bleating, Cuckoos calling, the Thrush sings by fits, Thomas Ashburner's axe is going quietly (without passion) in the orchard, hens are cackling, flies humming, the women talking together at their doors, plum and pear trees are in blossom—apple trees greenish—the opposite woods green, the crows are cawing, we have heard ravens, the ash trees are in blossom, birds flying all about us, the stitchwort is coming out, there is one budding lychnis, the primroses are passing their prime, celandine, violets, and wood sorrels forever more, little geraniums and pansies on the wall. We walked in the evening to Tail End to inquire about hurdles for the orchard shed. When we came in we found a magazine and review, and a letter from Coleridge, verses to Hartley and Sara H. We read the review, etc. The moon was a perfect boat, a silver boat, when we were out in the evening. The birch tree is all over green in *small* leaf, more light and elegant than when it is full out. It bent to the breezes, as if for the love of its own delightful motions. Sloethorns and hawthorns in the hedges.

May 7. William had slept uncommonly well so, feeling himself strong, he fell to work at *The Leech Gatherer*; he wrote hard at it till dinner time, then he gave over, tired to death—he had finished the poem.

Donald Hall

"Spring" from *Seasons*
at *Eagle Pond*

*I*t *is easy to become sentimental about springtime—budding flowers and frisking lambs and cool, crisp dawns—but Donald Hall will have none of that and not just because he lives on a farm. Spring is New England's "least season," he announces, and catalogs its woes. Spring brings rain and snow and more rain and still a bit more snow. The driveway becomes impassable and mud season reigns supreme. Not to mention dozens of beavers who chew up birches and poplar trees, flooding the fields and damming up streams. The farm at Eagle Pond in the spring is nothing if not waterlogged. Furthermore, winter's accumulation of cow manure begins to thaw, the blackflies bite, and the garden pests arrive en masse: slugs, chipmunks, deer, raccoons, and—with imperturbable force—the woodchucks.*

And yet despite the mess, indeed because of it, spring also brings sweet peas from the garden and the first asparagus and generous daffodils. There are

> *I*t is the very messiness of spring, its profusion of pests and promises, that nudges us away from self-absorption.

births to celebrate: a hundred yellow chicks cheeping in their cardboard box, a Holstein calf and twin lambs, the litters of kittens. And there are memories of past springs, the hard work of farm life turning slowly into the hard work of writing. Yet it is the very messiness of spring, its profusion of pests and promises, that nudges us away from self-absorption until, like the Holsteins emerging from the barn to find themselves in a fresh, spring pasture, we too grow large with joy and turn to feed on "the green milk of Spring."

"Spring"

Spring is the least of our seasons, and it has built no constituency in New Hampshire. Our country-side attracts leaf people in Autumn who gape with good reason at the fauve hillsides; Winter's skiers who drive north from Boston, skies atop Audis, and whole families over Christmas and schoolbreaks who break rich ankles; uncountable Summer people who laze a permitted annual dally on the shore or in sailboats or simply in sun and play bridge at night by the light of state-liquor-store gin. But New Hampshire's Spring people distinguish themselves by nonexistence. In April our restaurants and motels close for the month as weary industrialists of tourism take holiday in Carolina, Georgia, or Florida. For motelers and maitred's, Spring floats a brief intermission between the anxieties of ski time, when everything glides on the temperature, and the certain labors of long Summer. Real Spring people, often identical to our own Summer people, gather at Hilton Head or sniff the sweet air of Savannah. Spring is long, tender, and luxurious in the Southeast, where the crocus shoves up its head in January and the flowering shrubs, like rhododendrons at the Masters in Augusta, waft rich odoriferous air through the warm nights.

Of the world's seasons Spring has the best press. Where are the songs of Spring? Everyplace. It is when the voice of the turtle is heard in the land. A later poet told how a young man's fancy lightly turned; another called April the cruelest month; another claimed always to mourn with ever-returning Spring; still another, resident of Italy, protested, "Oh, to be in England now that April's there."

Now I have never spent a whole Spring in Carolina or Georgia, only flown in for a brief hallucinatory visit from chill muddy April or pestiferous May to hover a moment in the saccharine air of Milledgeville, Macon, or Charlotte. But in England I have spent four Springs; I count them as a miser counts gold: two at Oxford, two in a village called Thaxted, not far from Cambridge. In England sometimes a January day can be purest Spring: warm, muddy, lazy, sunny, with crocuses starting up. Correspondingly, in weird Albion, a gale always whoops out of the northeast early in August after a warmish week, gritty wind thrashes rain through the Doctor's Garden Fete, and somebody says, "It was rather a short Summer but quite a nice one ... "

But in England April, May, and early June are lemony days of velvet-green grass in the Fellows' Garden with bowls and croquet; evenings lengthening like the promise of an afterlife; balls at the colleges that end with a group photograph in the quadrangle at six in pale dawn; ten million daffodils by the Cam at the backs of the Cambridge colleges; and at Oxford the year's climax is Eights Week, early in June. The eights are crews competing on the Isis, but never mind. Pubs stay open, girls bloom into English roses, promise gilds itself in the golden sun of arrogant youth brazen with promise, the sun never sets, the sky never clouds, strawberries and champagne endlessly arrive carried by dutiful and conservative servants who know their places. We know: The beastly Huns, not to mention the Irish and the Working Classes, will never disturb our tranquil luxury. In New Hampshire Spring begins with rain and melt. For that matter, it continues to snow, at least from time to time, late in March through April. Spring snow rattles Winter's death—or is it the triumphant final tour of Winter? Well, almost final: perhaps one more go at Hedda, for charity of course. Or Winter returns like a forty-four-year-old relief pitcher who has been practicing a knuckler in the backyard, throwing it to his mother. Now we become impatient: Let us give Winter its gold watch; let us award it an honorary Oscar or a day of its own at Cooperstown; let us push it off to a condominium in the keys of Antarctica and stop all this damned nonsense about a comeback.

Water begins it, warm rain over the wasted gray drifts of March. Long days and nights of rain wear dingy ruts in our snow-fields, or warm days of early sun release meltwater from crystals of hill and meadow, and the great crashing melt dozes creeks and streams, raising instant rivers where Summer's gulch is dry. Water is never lazy, never quiet; it talks all day and gossips all night, chatter-ing down hills through gullies to ditches at roadside. On the ponds ice rots and gray stains spread over level white. Provident ice fisher-men have removed their bobhouses by early March, but every Spring on New Hampshire's lakes some of these shacks tilt and sag and tumble through cold water to lake bottom. How many small huts, like outhouses *d'antan*, rot on pond bottoms? Ice leaves the lake one day when we do not notice; for weeks it has crept out from the shoreline, frayed from its muddy border, but when we gaze from the bridge to the pond's center, the ice looks steady and unbroken still. Then it is suddenly gone, for it sinks to the bottom while we are never looking.

Now pond and lake swell, rise, widen over meadow and bog-land, lift picnic tables from the old year's Summer and carry them a rod like pranksters, or misplace canoes, rafts, and docks improperly secured. Birch and popple that start at the water's edge now loom from water itself. Long ago our market town of Franklin routinely flooded in Spring, the Pemigewasset widening and lifting into low-set workers' housing near the mills. Now a dam constructed by Army engineers in 1940 backs the water into a valley near the town of Hill.

During wet, melt, and high water, beavers chew at anything arboreal that appears attractive. At the south end of Eagle Pond they populate a boggy place and make it boggier with dams; nearby groves prickle with cone-shaped pointy stumps. Sometimes they leave behind a tree they've chewed down if it's too big to pull, or maybe they only wanted to strip bark off. There's a worked-over beaver plantation near the house at the north end of the hayfield between Route 4 and the railroad. These must be tasty trees, popple and gray birch, because the creatures by-pass wood closer to their pond-home in order to harvest this little grove. I've counted forty-seven chewed-off stumps. The railroad trench cuts deeply below this patch, and there's a rusty B & M fence to get through when the beaver transports his timber to the pond. Near the fence a well-worn trail looks like a cowpath or a lane trodden by habitual human feet—except that this path goes under a strand of wire ten inches off the ground. Here I've found a good-sized tree caught in the fence, hanging a third of its length into the air over the track; beavers are smart but they can't solve everything. Also I've found a tree hauled a long way from its stump but caught and wedged unmovable between other stumps. When I look at the trail that the beavers wear by their haulage I'm dazzled: After they roll the treetrunk down the sandbank, they must carry it across tracks, up another bank, then down a steep slope to Eagle Pond.

We never see beaver, except a distant nose sticking up from the water, leaving a V behind it as it swims across the pond carrying a stick. When we first moved here a cousin came to the kitchen door asking permission to trap beaver on our land. I signed the paper out of family feeling and cowardice, but I felt sorry for Bucky. It took six months before rage took guilt's place: I wanted to advance my cousin capital for more traps. Beaver chewed down four birches by our swimming place and let them rot; elsewhere they flooded gardens and hayfields by building dams. The fish and game people spend half their working hours blowing up beaver dams with dynamite. Lately the price for pelts has dropped like a chewed popple and my cousin has stopped trapping and beaver multiply.

As the air warms, houseflies wake from their Winter sleep and congregate at upstairs windows. For a week of this weather houseflies are the only pest, unless the driveway is a pest, for it becomes momentarily impassable, scourge of transmissions. Mud season's yellow viscosity churns under struggling wheels without exhausting itself to a solid bottom. We stay off the dirt roads that climb Ragged and circle the pond. Bert the RD lets air out of his tires for traction but gets stuck in mud season as he never sticks in blizzards or ice storms; it is the worst driving and the worst walking of the year. Sometimes the mud freezes at night, a grid of frozen sea-ways, torture for the shocks of cars; then by noon it melts back to colloid obscenity.

Sometimes this condition lasts for weeks but usually it is quick, and when it dries the air warms and the light turns yellowish, as if the mud's churn buttered the air. For a few days we enjoy the classic look of high Spring. Crocuses stick their heads up opening fragile tentative mouths; daffodils climb beginning to unfold; the tulip rises with promise of outrage. Jane casts off Winter gloom and works at the garden in a frenzy—swooping away gray leaves matted over the borders and against the house, raking twigs broken off by ice and gravel shoved everywhere by the snowplough. Jane frees soil for the grandeur of crack and blossom, enabling flowers. She works in such a frenzy for good reason: One day when the sun passes Ragged's edge and warms the air midmorning, suddenly the black-flies are among us.

For a day or two they don't bite. Then they start biting. Our Egyptian plague, blackflies annually destroy New Hampshire's Spring. A bumper sticker turns up, NUKE THE BLACK FLIES, but drastic as the suggestion may be, it's pointless: After the last war only blackflies will prove nasty enough to survive, to evolve over a million years their own malicious culture. Oh, they bite. You hardly see them (no-see-ums is one of their names) but they have been with us forever. As Parkman describes it, in the seventeenth century—and doubtless ever since they wandered this way from the Bering Strait—Indians lived in teepees dense with smoke to discourage blackflies and mosquitoes.

In New Hampshire although the air is balmy now we wear armor outdoors: long thick socks rolled up over heavy jeans, gloves, long sleeves rolled down, and for many a beekeeper's mask and hat. Otherwise flies get in our hair and smuggle themselves into the house. We don't always feel them hit but we know afterward: Great red welts rise on our skin. My mother-in-law was once bitten between her eyes so that her two eyes shut. Dogs go raw on their bald bellies.

We dab dope on face, neck, hair, hands, wrists, and ankles; it helps, if we keep on doing it, but it does not satisfy. Blackflies buzz around us forming an angry mobile helmet; they swarm and wheel within half an inch of our faces. Sometimes in Spring I umpire softball games at the village school in Danbury, making crazy signals as my hands flip in constant involuntary motion warding blackflies. Similar wild signs emanate from pitcher, batter, and outfielders. It is spastic baseball, and if we were major leaguers we would be signaling—Take! Hit! Steal! Bunt! Run! Don't run!—on every pitch.

Mostly we stay inside. Jane makes desperate forays into her garden, transplanting this, fertilizing that, watering hastily; then she comes inside and takes a shower. Meantime tulips rise in their splendor, and daffodils that couldn't care less about blackflies dance their yellow dance on the granity hill behind the house. By the playhouse my cousin Freeman built for my grandmother Kate when she was five in 1880, with a noble slab of glacier-granite beside it, the ten thousand (really about two hundred) golden or gold and white daffodils raise bright agreeable faces. Uphill by the barn, and beside the woodshed under a sugarmaple near another boulder, and at the margin of the hayfield that runs south toward Kearsarge, Jane's daffodil armies march, onward floral soldiers. Oh, most wonderful of flowers, sun-colored welcoming the sun, vigorous handsome energetic golden trumpets of Spring heralding Summer! I stare at them dreamily all day, happy to accept their wild generosity, safe behind panes of glass.

When blackflies start to diminish mosquitoes arrive, and Spring is the least of our seasons. Here we don't suffer quite so much from mosquitoes; they are not so numerous as blackflies: As if to compensate for their numbers, of course, one mosquito can wreak havoc on a picnic or a night's sleep. But now I have gone on into Summer. Fair enough: So do the blackflies.

The first vegetable to plant is peas; we scatter the pale round seed on top of March's rags of snow. My mother remembers planting them regularly on Saint Patrick's Day, for peas like it damp and cold. When it warms in April and May the little bushes rise among black-flies, and covered with dope we pick fresh peas for the table late in June.

In the old days April and May were heavy farming times, made heavier by mud and flies. It was time to cart manure into cornfield and vegetable garden and plough it under. The big cowbarn that my great-grandfather built in 1865 still stands, south of the house a lit-tle above it. Huge blocks of granite shore its east side against Ragged's mudslide, blocks so huge you would swear cranes must have hauled them, not oxen. West the barn drops away downhill. Its main floor is the second storey, and as you look up from the house, the hill slopes enough so that there's a place to store a carriage under the grainshed that extends by the barnfloor. East of that door is the tie-up from which Holsteins strolled out to Ragged, which was their pasture, past the room for straining and cooling milk and the icehouse where we buried January's pond under sawdust for Summer. Over the cows hay lofted two storeys up.

And under the cows, west of the granite wall on bottom level, heaped the manure pile. Twice a day after milking we lifted long planks behind the cattle—rounded boards split from straight 1865 treetrunks, fastened to fixed floorboards by leather hinges made of worn-out harness—and slipped them over to open an eight-inch strip of lateral hole, the length of the tie-up. We scraped manure through this crack: Ranges of bovine excretion, down below, grew Alpine by April. For two weeks then—depending on snow, melt, and mud—my grandfather spent his days knee-deep in cowmanure. He kept a wagon for spreading it, which remained all year under the barn next to the manure pile, used every year for this one purpose only. The dump-cart remains there still, in good shape; if we wet the wheels to swell the wood tight inside iron rims, we could use it today. A small wooden seat rides on a spring next to a lever that lifted the truck bed up and slid manure off. The dump-cart under the barn flings its forearms down (arms that clutched the bony ribs of Riley and Roger, Ned's big bones, Nellie's black and Lady Ghost's pale gray) as if in despair on the humusy dirt of the floor where my grandfather let them fall in April of 1950. Beside it slope the diminishing Alps of manure from later that year, before his heart attack in November and the cows' December departure forever and ever. We use it still; it makes great topsoil.

He carted many loads to fertilize his fields. In the last decades of his life he did it alone, except for a few years when Anson came back, the hired man who had worked for them when my mother was a girl. He departed, one day in the 1920s, for twenty-five years. Anson suffered from a learning disability; in the old days we used a scientific term that we pronounced mow-ron. My grandfather wore boots and overalls, which hung on a hook under the barn, used only for this purpose, and with his shovel filled the cart and then drove it into the fields he planted with millet and fieldcorn and to the big garden plot. He spread it with the aid of gravity, and sometimes Anson, and with one shovel. When some was left over from the cropfields, he spread it on hayfields.

Mostly it was cowmanure. The horse's stall got dug out once or twice a week, horsemanure shoveled through a trap door down beside the Holsteins'. From the sheepbarn once or twice a year my grandfather extracted the rich mixture of sheepmanure and straw; my grandmother used some for her flowers. The crazy compost of the chickenhouse floor was too strong—chickenmanure, straw, and the decomposed detritus of all the garbage the hens had pecked at over the year: dry skeletal corn cobs, pale shreds of carrot tops and pea pods, even specks of old eggshells—and it would burn seed up.

There was even a little nightsoil, for my grandfather never quite accepted the indoor bathroom. In 1938 my grandparents added this innovation, struck off from the dining room: a narrow cold dingy miraculous toilet, washstand, and bathtub perpetually in trouble, water freezing in the Winter and spiders working their way up from bathtub drain all Summer. The bathroom supplemented but did not replace the outhouse. This old facility did not require a trudge through rain or snow. Although suitably far from living quarters, it situated itself under the continuous roof of the extended farmhouse. To reach it we exited the kitchen through the door to the toolshed, then through another door into the woodshed; we turned a corner at the back of the woodshed, and the outhouse door took the farthest corner. My grandfather, however, kept a roll of toilet paper near the cowmanure under the barn, and during chores if he was taken short he squatted there. I think he preferred the barn. Surely the notion of indoor defecation seemed obscene; even the outhouse was a little close to home. When he was old and sick he used the plumbing, I think with some distress.

When manure was spread on the fields, it was time to pull the plough from the long shed between chickencoop and sheep-barn where he stored plough, hayrack, mowing machine, and horsedrawn rake under cover from Winter weather. I suppose he ploughed five acres for garden, fieldcorn, and millet. I never knew my grandmother to buy a vegetable. Row after row of peas, beans in many varieties, bush beans and pole starring Kentucky Wonders, beets, tomatoes, carrots, parsnips, potatoes, and Golden Bantam corn. Millet, or sometimes Hungarian, was sweet heavy-grained grass that he scythe-mowed every afternoon in July and August for his cattle; it helped to persuade the cattle down from the hill's sweet grass for afternoon milking: Apparently millet and Hungarian were cow-delicious. (I tried them myself and they were sweet.) Field-corn, chopped up and siloed in September, provided nutriment for cattle all Winter long.

After ploughing when the time was right—usually after the last full moon around Memorial Day—it was time to plant. Soon enough it was time to weed, long hours with a hoe—my grandmother too—making sure that the vegetables started strong. No help from a Rototiller, but horse and harrow helped out between the spaced rows of corn.

Late Winter and early Spring was the time for new animals. Chicks were easiest. Before my time the hens hatched their own. At some point around the Great War the chicks began to come by parcel post, and in spring the P.O. down at Henry's store filled up with noisy rectangular boxes, cheep-cheep-cheep. Everybody kept chickens. We brought ours back to the shed and opened the boxes, each packed to sequester a hundred live chicks. Brooding factories packed the eggs before hatching, and the tiny creatures cracked through their shells on their journey here, in the baggage cars of trains or in depots and post offices. The factories packed more than a hundred to be sure they delivered a hundred. Always a few eggs arrived unhatched and dead and one or two neonates lay stiff and dry among the riotous throng that rolled and teetered and chirped infant cries. We kept them warm and noisy in the shed until the nights were warmer; then they thrived in the yard behind the henhouse, a hundred new lives pecking into ancient dirt, eating grain from V-shaped feeders, drinking water I carried from the trough at roadside.

My grandfather bred his sheep so that lambs came in May after the mothers were out to pasture and the nights warm, but sometimes a lamb was born in the barn while it was still cold, which distressed him. New births every Spring were economically essential; sheep brought money disproportionate to the time they took, and twin lambs were a cause for rejoicing.

In the Winter the quantity of milk decreased rapidly as the great Holsteins swelled up with their babies, to dry out in the weeks before birth. Earlier when each cow came into heat, my grandfather left his bull alone with the chosen member of the black and white seraglio. Cedric Blasington, the farmer just down the road, lacked a bull himself; from time to time he led a distraught cow to our barn. My grandmother took her daughters up-attic to distract them while the service was performed, but they knew something was going on; they peeked to see cows jumping about in excitement. In Spring when the cows birthed my grandfather midwifed, tying a rope around the emerging calf to pull as the bossy pushed. Sometimes he had to enter a cow as far as he could reach to assist in a breech or posterior birth. One of the great sights on a farm is the joy of the

Holstein sisterhood when a calf is born. Not only does the mother lick the child; the whole herd tries to, and the community celebrates, enormous black and white bovines leaping as much as they are able and bellowing out of their collective triumph.

When the first vegetables edge up from cracked mud and earth, the farmer's enemies assemble: weeds, drought or flood, slugs and cutworms, an entomologist's army of insects—and the imperturbable tribe of the woodchuck. Other pests include deer that browse a vegetable garden to devastation; chipmunks that eat the bulbs of flowers; bears that prefer the hives of the honeybee; foxes, weasels, fishers, and skunks that kill chickens; dogs and coyotes that kill sheep and lambs; and coons, shrewdest of vegetarian predators, that harvest our corn, taking the ripest ears on the morning before we boil water and walk into the cornpatch to pick supper.

Woodchucks are season-long, beginning in late Spring as soon as peas emerge, and do battle with the superiority of numbers, reinforcements, and stupidity. I don't suppose that my grandfather had much trouble from chucks until sometime in the 1920s when he understood that he could no longer keep a dog. A dog that runs loose eliminates the woodchuck problem; woodchucks have a dog problem. Hunter and Tripp herded sheep and helped find the cattle when they stayed up-mountain eating on late summer afternoons; they also protected vegetables and chickens from predators. But cars proliferated on Route 4 and got faster and faster until they reached speeds like 35 mph. At the north end of the farm a car approaches the house over a little ridge, unable to stop in time if the driver sees a creature in the road. The Model T killed Wesley's dogs. So my grandfather burying Tripp in his woe knew that the internal combustion engine forbade him the pleasure, companionship, and utility of dogs.

It would not have occurred to him to keep a pet inside and walk it on a leash. He loved his dogs; they earned their keep. Cats did too. The notion of a cat indoors made my grandmother wrinkle her nose—something she did frequently apropos rum, baseball on Sunday, ballroom dancing, and Frenchmen—although on rare occasions the senior barncat might be allowed entrance early in Autumn when frost chased fieldmice inside in numbers greater than traps could handle. Once the barncat ate improvident mice to its full, it was out on its ear.

The barn was dense with cats. Silage and grain encouraged rodent-presence, and without a resident cat-militia mice and rats would have eaten the grainshed hollow. My grandfather when he milked (like all farmer-grandfathers everywhere) swiveled a teat and squirted milk into the gaped jaws of kittens and cats who sat waiting for his performance, a little row of organic Staffordshire cats with pink mouths stretched wide. In the 1940s one old gray mother-tabby, shrewd about Route 4 and automobile behavior, teats hanging low from three-litter years, held perpetual sway, but her cleverness was an acquired characteristic, not transferable by Lamarckian genetics to her countless kittens. As a boy I buried one a week in the cats' graveyard between sheepbarn and vegetable garden.

Now we reverse old ways. Cats and dogs live indoors and our barns loom gray and silent without animals; I walk Gus along Route 4, on his chain; every day Jane and I drive or walk him to the triangular meadow by the pond or to a flattish stretch of New Canada Road or to cut-over acres of woodlot someplace where cars are few and Gus can run loose. Ada guards the indoor house as Mio, Catto, Bella, and Amos did before them, performing effective duty against generations of mice, moles, voles, chipmunks—and one rat.

When we moved here a dozen years ago, we planted a garden that became a Woodchuck Resources Center. As a boy I would sit for an hour at dawn and another at dusk until I got a good shot at a woodchuck. My rifle was a short-barreled handmade old octagonal Mossberg .22 carbine, built for target shooting mostly. I practiced my eye by assassinating tin cans with my father and then when I was in my teens killed many woodchucks and buried them among the roadkilled kittens. But in my fifties I lack patience to sit for an hour waiting for the fat imbecilic figure of a woodchuck to stick its head out of its hole, sniff the air, and draw fire. Without patience, without a dog, our garden disappeared down woodchuck jaws year after year—peas eaten down as they ripened, beets gnawed into the earth, Kentucky Wonders nipped in the bud. Old holes were rein-habited each year, and each year fresh sand heaped in fields near the garden reported growth in the chuck population. Suburban wood-chucks from Massachusetts built second homes in New Hampshire. Five or six times a day I wandered across Route 4 swinging my ele-gant rifle, looking for a woodchuck to shoot. Usually I saw nothing; occasionally I shot from a distance and missed; once I killed a crea-ture sunning himself behind the ruins of the sheepbarn.

Mostly they just ate us out. We tried folk remedies: dried blood, Kitty Litter, and planting marigolds. I bought one of the gas bombs Agway sells, but I wasn't sure how the subway system worked and I was wary of trying it. I raised a good fence, which helped, but I couldn't use an electric fence because of the difficulties of stringing wire across Route 4. I stayed away from leg traps. On a visit to Agway, complaining about our woodchucks, I heard a story from a clerk: A year before, somebody had dropped around for one remedy and another, continually complaining and failing, getting madder and madder. He tried gas bombs and lost some chickens; he tried a leg trap and took a neighbor's shepherd to the vet with a broken leg. One day he arrived as red as the beets he had lost and bought sticks of dynamite and caps and went home and blew up his garden and hayfield. His garden was gone, his fields looked like Saipan—but he sure got that woodchuck.

Finally I bought a Hav-a-Heart trap, which Has its Heart by capturing the animal intact when he trips a pedal going after food. I baited it with vegetables and fruit and caught two or three wood-chucks every Spring. These captures discouraged the tribe and allowed us three quarters of our garden. Of course the trap leaves the gardener with a problem: What do you do with the victim? Rumor suggests that some folks sneak live woodchucks by night into the gardens of local Democrats. I solved the problem my own way. When I caught Woody I took my Mossberg out of the closet and shot him through the head as he quavered in my Hav-a-Heart trap.

A cousin of mine used to eat one woodchuck a year. Because he lived by himself without an oven, he prevailed upon my grandmother to bake it. No one else in this house would touch the meat. Every Spring when I shot my first woodchuck in the Hav-a-Heart, I meditated eating him. I knew, after all, what filled his stomach and gave him leg muscle; I had ordered his victuals by seed from Burpee. Every Spring when the first chuck lay dead but unburied, I would look again at Irma S. Rombauer's woodchuck recipe in *Joy of Cooking*. Every year when I reread the part about wearing rubber gloves to skin the beast on account of the mites, I fetched the shovel from the toolshed and dug a hole deep enough so that dogs would not annoy the corpse.

I do not farm; less and less do I farm; physical work grows more and more alien. It isn't a general laziness; often I work a hundred-hour week. I keep a farmer's hours and a farmer's work week but avoid physical labor and raise no crops and milk no milk. I sit at my desk and put words on paper. When we first moved here to stay, I dreamed about replacing my grandparents. Mostly my dreams offered reasons and justifications: dreams for repairing trouble. My favorite was the morning when we woke (as I dreamed it) to discover that my grandfather and grandmother—very old but still living with us on the farm, still tending their hens, sheep, and cattle—were missing, nowhere to be found; what's more, the animals were gone. With the imperturbability that outfits some dreams, I decided that the old people must have dropped dead someplace while they were working; their bodies must be concealed by tall grass. We were about to give up the search and go back to our own work when we saw them coming toward us, still a couple of hundred yards away, walking up the narrow dirt road from Andover (the road was clearly dirt, road paved before I was born), waving and shouting to catch our attention: They were leading back to the barn a whole straggling line of ostriches, zebras, elephants, tigers, crocodiles. In my dream I understood that, because they were too old to continue farming, they had traded their Holsteins and merinos and

Rhode Island reds for zoo animals, for orangutans and lions, and I knew as I woke that I felt poetry to be as exotic, beautiful, scary, and useless as leopards and peacocks.

In May and June the green comes back.

Winter's white is beautiful when it begins but degenerates by March to gray snow that melts mud-brown. Spring begins as monochrome as November, but from the gray-brown, faint green arises in grass that the sun heats. Then with more sun-light green mounts, gathers, swells, and explodes, its onrushing upthrusting fibrous joy cavorting from the ground, yellow-green to butter the soul's bread with. Down from the verdant twigs of the trees, green descends toward green uprising, dog's-ear leaves first unwrapping their tender delicate early edible green, pale and lemony Spring-leaf green, later to darken or weather into the green-shutter leaves of August.

Not until Spring's end does the bounty of Summer foreshadow itself in knuckled fingers of asparagus that hoist themselves through tall grass underneath the lilac. After a rain and a hot day, asparagus leaps so rapidly that it goes by if we do not harvest it daily. Every year we miss a dozen that go to seed and grow tall as corn, wispy small trees in the breeze. The first freshness of the year's crop, they are green heaven to the mouth. And now peas bush and thicken, now rhubarb grows green elephant ears over its strange ropey red-corded stalks. Best of all, the old single roses by the driveway's bottom turn green-leafed and bud a thousand tiny green buds that will welcome Summer, just after solstice every year, with pink flowers and white. When they bloom they overpower the air with sweetness, then shatter almost immediately. My grandmother loved her old roses, and her small round gardens, marigolds under the kitchen window and poppies at the edge of the hay-field by the barn. They rise green now making ready their sweet violence.

Spring's greatest outburst happened earlier in the old days, and because it was the greatest I have saved it for last. In April between mud and blackflies, just before manuring and ploughing, my grandfather turned the cattle out to pasture. (Although it no longer happens on this farm, it never stops happening.) All Winter they stood upright in their stalls daylong, tied to wooden poles by steel chains. They lay down to sleep; they had plenty to eat; twice a day my grandfather unchained them to walk a few feet from tie-up to watering trough. They walked stiffly, down the one step and across frozen mud to the cement oblong trough to dip their pink noses into the just-unfrozen water. The surface froze every night and my grandfather lifted out big oblong pieces of ice. In January, in the shade and short daylight, Winter's icy litter left a series of trough-lids, like a sheaf of transparent pages. When the cattle drank their fill they stared around them, maybe dimly aware that they last saw this place twelve hours earlier, then each gave way to the next thirsty bossy and stiffly returned to the stalls where my grandfather left grain to encourage and reward their expeditious return.

One day in April their lives changed utterly. My grandfather kept an eye on the pasture grass, ready to spring his cattle loose. Snow and ice remained on the north side of sugar-maples and boulders, and in much of the pasture lowish sun penetrated only briefly and grass remained gray-brown, but where a clearing opened up in a high pasture, or where in lower patches new sun felt its way through a forest gap, live green grass rose edible in April. With crocuses came grass and with grass cow's paradise.

One day he untied them as if for the trough but maneuvered around them to open the pasture gate past the trough, portal to a hundred and thirty acres of Ragged Mountain: granite, hemlock, sugarbush, oak, elm, birch, and abundant grass. At first when he pushed and whooped them toward the gate they moved sluggishly. When they discovered themselves let out to pasture again, free to wander, free to eat all day long, their capacity for joy—these slow-moving mountains that usually made a name for lethargy and passivity, stoic mothers untouched and unflappable—turned huge as their bodies: They jumped, they rubbed great sides against treetrunks, they leapt, they bellowed abruptly, they bounced. For a few moments the great Holsteins were eight kittens frolicking on the stomach of mothercat Ragged Mountain, play-fighting and romping. Then they let down their great heads into the sweet tender upgrowth of new grass and fed on the green milk of Spring as we all do, even in New Hampshire where Spring is the least of our seasons.

PART FOUR

Pilgrimage

INTRODUCTION

In April, Geoffrey Chaucer tells us, "folk do long to go on pilgrimages" and spring does seem to engender the desire to pack our bags and set off on a long trip. Perhaps the urge stems simply from practical reasons: as the snow and ice disappear, it is easier to move about. No need to pack the extra blanket, candle, tin can, shovel, and bag of sand that grandma insisted would keep us safe should the car slide into the ditch during a blizzard; no worry, either, about icy roads or frozen engine blocks. And by late winter we feel a physical compulsion to get out of the house and smell the air in the next county, if not the next state or province. As spring stretches and stirs itself into wakefulness, our bodies respond. We look up and around; we get out the bikes and pull our helmets from the back of the closet where they've cradled mismatched mittens and raveling scarves for the last three months. We tug off our boots and put on our sneakers. We need to move.

If winter enshrouds the soul in a chrysalis, then spring sees its reemergence. If we've used the quiet, solitary days of winter well, we approach spring with a soul that has had its inner resources tested and strengthened. We exit the cold stillness and pick up the threads of a busy, active life with fortitude and joy. Pilgrimages help us make that transition. Chaucer's travelers might well encounter the remnants of wintry ice on their way to Canterbury, as do college students on their annual trek to the Gulf—for the notion of pilgrimage lingers in our bones even when we've suppressed its spiritual significance.

But whether the goal is Canterbury Cathedral or Fort Myers, a pilgrimage always has a goal, a destination. It is not merely a vacation, even less a springtime ramble, but a trip that is marked by definite intent. In Islam, the compulsory pilgrimage to Mecca, enjoined on every adult Muslim once in a lifetime, is called the hajj—and the very word means "to set out with a definite purpose." It is because a pilgrimage has both goal and purpose that we do well to select one whose route and destination are worth our time and effort, for the journey will shape our souls for the year to come. For David Brill, the destination is Mount Katahdin, the route the Appalachian Trail. For African American slaves, both goal and path was freedom itself—and freedom is the watchword that wings its way through their songs.

Pilgrimage, then, sets our eyes forward. During a season when we may be almost overwhelmed by the cacophony of sound and color, new life bursting out everywhere, pilgrimage lifts our sight to the horizon, to hope, and reminds us that there is more to come.

But pilgrimage also connects us to the past, for pilgrims always travel to places that are deeply rooted in tradition, in memory, in past acts that still shape our present lives. The hajj commemorates the forgiveness of Adam and Eve, the sacrifice of Ishmael by Abraham, and the obedient life of the Prophet Muhammad—all events central not just to Islamic history but also to the daily practice of observant Muslims. The Canterbury pilgrimage brought travelers back to the courage of Saint Thomas à Becket.

If spring pilgrimages set our eyes forward and press our hearts to remember, they also connect us to other people, for pilgrimages are not solitary adventures, even when they are taken alone. David Brill begins his walk along the Appalachian Trail with an acquaintance, Dan Howe, who becomes a friend. The Lady Sarashina finds that the pilgrimage into her own heart leads toward love. And the

Chinese poet Po Chü-i notes that such journeys tend to equalize society's discriminations:

> *The city walls rise up to greet*
> *Spring's luminous twilight hours;*
> *The clamour of carts goes down the street:*
> *This is the Fair of Flowers.*
> *Leisure and pleasure drift along,*
> *Beggar and marquis join the throng,*
> *And care, humility, rank, and pride*
> *In the sight of flowers are laid aside.*

At first, it might seem a paradox that pilgrimage, which sets our feet—or our hearts—in motion, is so grounded in a destination, a particular route, memory, and community. But that is only if we think of motion as directionless or circular. The movement of pilgrimage is both away from our former selves, our former positions and also, more importantly, a movement toward something better. Pilgrims divest themselves, at least for a short time, of the comforts of home, the stability of everyday circumstances, the illusion that they can dictate life on their own terms. They give themselves up to the journey, the hope, the goal of understanding their own deep commitments, so that when they return home, they may live more freely but also more confidently.

In the Christian tradition, Lent provides just such a pilgrimage, one that begins in the last days of winter, that sets our eyes toward Easter but recalls the suffering and death of Christ and our own sins that set him upon the cross. Lent takes Christian believers step by step through remembrance, confession, and repentance in order to help them live once again in the freedom of grace and forgiveness.

When an insect emerges from its chrysalis, it is called an imago—a perfect insect, fully formed, having completed all its metamorphoses. But no Muslim returns from the hajj, no Christian from a Lenten pilgrimage perfected, complete. Which is why we need the repeated pilgrimages of spring. As Lionel Basney reminds us, "We don't move toward heaven in one gigantic, decisive step after another. We move in small, repetitive, cumulative patterns—learning to make a habit of what we do well, and repenting, again and again, what we do badly."

Yet it is these small journeys that constitute the larger one on which we have all embarked. In *Pilgrim's Progress*, John Bunyan's Christian falls into the slough of Despond, wanders off into bypaths, pushes his way through Vanity Fair, resists Mr. Worldly-Wiseman, and fights the giant Apollyon, but these adventures are not ends in themselves; each one moves him along the path toward the Celestial City and prepares him to face the River of Death. And Dante the pilgrim circles through the mire of the seven deadly sins in the Inferno and trudges up Mount Purgatory in his necessary but preparatory pilgrimage toward Paradise. It is only in the last verse of the last canto that, confronted by the three eternal circles in their abyss of light, by the supernal face of God, he understands the truth of his own life, now balanced and turning "as in a wheel whose motion nothing jars / by the Love that moves the Sun and the other stars."

A Shaker Hymn

"WELCOME SPRING"

What beautiful treasures the Gospel unfolds,
As the seasons and years pass away,
In the march of progression we're moving along,
In the increasing light of our day;
And while we're inspired of its glory to sing,
Our hearts are made glad by the sweet breath of spring.

Chorus:
    Lovely spring: Beautiful spring!
    The woods with vocal welcomes ring,
    And we a grateful offering bring
    To our God who sends the spring.

We will not recline on the deeds of the past,
And think that perfection is won,
But start every day in the battle of life,
As if it had newly begun;
Each conquest some gem of the spirit will bring,
As winter is lost in the life-giving spring.

Chorus:

> *Lovely spring: Beautiful spring!*
> *The woods with vocal welcomes ring,*
> *And we a grateful offering bring*
> *To our God who sends the spring.*

Sweet emblems of innocence, growth of the year,
Oh, teach us God's laws to obey!
A morning of life when in purity spent,
Insures a bright crown for the day;
And unselfish labor its increase will bring
To our beautiful home in the eternal spring.

Chorus:

> *Lovely spring: Beautiful spring!*
> *The woods with vocal welcomes ring,*
> *And we a grateful offering bring*
> *To our God who sends the spring.*

Geoffrey Chaucer

FROM "THE GENERAL PROLOGUE" TO THE CANTERBURY TALES

*P*erhaps the most famous pilgrimage in the Western world is the fictional one undertaken by Geoffrey Chaucer's Canterbury pilgrims. In the late fourteenth century, when Chaucer wrote his masterpiece, it was not uncommon for men and women, and even children, to pack their bags in the spring and journey through the English countryside on their way to the cathedral in Canterbury. The shrine they would visit was that of Saint Thomas à Becket, a worldly-wise courtier turned archbishop who was not afraid to tell his king to repent. Henry II, enraged, ordered his murder, and the archbishop was killed in 1170 within the sanctuary of the cathedral itself.

*S*tories can penetrate to the heart of who we are and who we want to be.

By the fourteenth century, the pilgrimages to Canterbury had taken on a festive, but somewhat routine, air. Chaucer transforms this rather common springtime rite into an extraordinary picture—and critique—of late medieval life. In the General Prologue, as he introduces us to the Canterbury pilgrims, he also gently uncovers their foolish vices and self-deceptions. The tales and interactions that follow tell us more about the pilgrims and particularly about the way in which stories can penetrate to the heart of who we are and who we want to be.

Although Chaucer's pilgrims do not reach Canterbury, we might imagine them entering the great cathedral, joining the line as it winds up the long aisle, and ascending the steps to the casket. And we might imagine a moment of self-awareness—and a moment of grace—that blesses the end of this pilgrimage.

From "The General Prologue"

When that April with his sweet showers
The drought of March hath pierced to the root,
And bathed every plant in such liquor
From which power, engendered is the flower;
When Zephirus too with his sweet breath
Inspired hath in every holt and heath
The tender crops, and the young sun
Hath in the Ram his half-course run,
And small birds make melody,
That sleep all night with open eye
(So does Nature spur them in their hearts),
Then folk do long to go on pilgrimages,
And travelers look to seek foreign shores,
And distant shrines, famous in other lands;
And especially from every shire's end
In England, to Canterbury they go,
The holy, blissful martyr for to seek,
That hath helped them when they were sick.

Lady Sarashina

FROM THE DIARY OF LADY SARASHINA

*T*he Lady Sarashina, one of a group of Japanese women writers from
the tenth and eleventh centuries, was born in 1008 during the Heian
period. Her father was a provincial assistant governor, her mother belonged to
an aristocratic family, and Sarashina herself spent some time at court. Her
diary, marked by an intense awareness of her surroundings and her emotions,
captures the complex interplay between a conventional outer life and deep
inner longings. It is also something
of a travelogue, recording her pilgrimages to Buddhist holy sites,
many of which she undertook in
response to her dreams.

> *T*heir quiet intimacy,
> their journey together
> into a tranquil spring
> night seems almost
> too fragile to record on
> paper.

In this selection, however, the
pilgrimage Sarashina embarks
upon is not to a distant monastery
or temple but into the labyrinths of
her own heart. Unhappy at court,
depressed by the artificiality that
surrounds her, fortified only by the
tales she loves to read, she meets a man with whom she begins a delicate
exchange of poems, in the traditional thirty-one-syllable uta form. Their
quiet intimacy, their journey together into a tranquil spring night seems

almost too fragile to record on paper. But it is, in fact, her writing that sears the memory of that brief, shared pilgrimage into her heart—and ours.

FROM *THE DIARY OF LADY SARASHINA*

One very bright night, after the full moon, I attended the Princess to the Imperial Palace. I remembered that the Heaven Illuminating Goddess was enthroned within, and wanted to take an opportunity to kneel before the altar. One moon-bright night I went in privately, for I know Lady Hakasé who was taking care of this shrine. The perpetual lights before the altar burned dimly. She grew wondrously old and holy; she seems not like a mortal, but like a divine incarnation, yet she spoke very gracefully.

The moon was very bright on the following night and the Princess's ladies passed the time in talking and moon-gazing, opening the doors of the Fujitsubo. The footsteps of the Royal consort of Umetsubo going up to the King's apartment were so exquisitely graceful as to excite envy. "Had the late Queen been living, she could not walk so grandly," some one said. I composed a poem:

> She is like the Moon, who, opening the gate of Heaven,
>> goes up over the clouds.
> We, being in the same heavenly Palace, pass the night
>> in remembering the footfalls of the past.

The ladies who are charged with the duty of introducing the court nobles seem to have been fixed upon, and nobody notices whether simple-hearted countrywomen like me exist or not. On a very dark night in the beginning of the Gods-absent month, when sweet-voiced reciters were to read sutras throughout the night, another lady and I went out towards the entrance door of the Audience Room to listen to it, and after talking fell asleep, listening, leaning, when I noticed a gentleman had come to be received in audience by the Princess.

"It is awkward to run away to our apartment. We will remain here. Let it be as it will." So said my companion and I sat beside her listening.

He spoke gently and quietly. There was nothing about him to be regretted. "Who is the other lady?" he asked of my friend. He said nothing rude or amorous like other men, but talked delicately of the sad, sweet things of the world, and many a phrase of his with a strange power enticed me into conversation. He wondered that there should have been in the Court one who was a stranger to him, and did not seem inclined to go away soon.

There was no starlight, and a gentle shower fell in the darkness; how lovely was its sound on the leaves! "The more deeply beautiful is the night," he said; "the full moonlight would be too dazzling." Discoursing about the beauties of Spring and Autumn he continued: "Although every hour has its charm, pretty is the spring haze; then the sky being tranquil and overcast, the face of the moon is not too bright; it seems to be floating on a distant river. At such a time the calm spring melody of the lute is exquisite.

"In Autumn, on the other hand, the moon is very bright; though there are mists trailing over the horizon we can see things as clearly as if they were at hand. The sound of wind, the voices of insects, all sweet things seem to melt together. When at such a time we listen to the autumnal music of the koto we forget the Spring— we think that is best—

"But the winter sky frozen all over magnificently cold! The snow covering the earth and its light mingling with the moonshine! Then the notes of the hitchiriki vibrate on the air and we forget Spring and Autumn." And he asked us, "Which captivates your fancy? On which stays your mind?"

My companion answered in favor of Autumn and I, not being willing to imitate her, said:

> *Pale green night and flowers all melting into one*
> *in the soft haze—*
> *Everywhere the moon, glimmering in the Spring night.*

So I replied. And he, after repeating my poem to himself over and over, said: "Then you give up Autumn? After this, as long as I live, such a spring night shall be for me a memento of your personality." The person who favored Autumn said, "Others seem to give their hearts to Spring, and I shall be alone gazing at the autumn moon."

He was deeply interested, and being uncertain in thought said: "Even the poets of the Tang Empire could not decide which to praise most, Spring or Autumn. Your decisions make me think that there must be some personal reasons when our inclination is touched or charmed. Our souls are imbued with the colors of the sky, moon, or flowers of that moment. I desire much to know how you came to know the charms of Spring and Autumn. The moon of a winter night is given as an instance of dreariness, and as it is very cold I had never seen it intentionally. When I went down to Isé to be present as the messenger of the King at the ceremony of installing the virgin in charge of the shrine, I wanted to come back in the early dawn, so went to take leave of the Princess in a moon-bright night after many days' snow, half shrinking to think of my journey.

"Her residence was an other-worldly place awful even to the imagination, but she called me into an adequate apartment. There were persons who had come down in the reign of the Emperor Enyu. Their aspect was very holy, ancient, and mystical. They told of the things of long ago with tears. They brought out a well-tuned four-stringed lute. The music did not seem to be anything happening in this world; I regretted that day should even dawn, and was touched so deeply that I had almost forgotten about returning to the Capital. Ever since then the snowy nights of winter recall that scene, and I without fail gaze at the moon even though hugging the fire. You will surely understand me, and hereafter every dark night with gentle rain will touch my heart; I feel this has not been inferior to the snowy night at the palace of the Isé virgin."

With these words he departed and I thought he could not have known who I was.

In the Eighth month of the next year we went again to the Imperial Palace, and there was in the Court an entertainment throughout the night. I did not know that he was present at it, and I passed that night in my own room. When I looked out opening the sliding doors on the corridor I saw the morning moon very faint and beautiful. I heard footsteps and people approached—some reciting sutras. One of them came to the entrance, and addressed me. I replied, and he, suddenly remembering, exclaimed, "That night of softly falling rain I do not forget, even for a moment! I yearn for it." As chance did not permit me many words I said:

> *What intensity of memory clings to your heart?*
> *That gentle shower fell on the leaves—*
> *Only for a moment our hearts touched.*

I had scarcely said so when people came up and I stole back without his answer.

That evening, after I had gone to my room, my companion came in to tell me that he had replied to my poem: "If there be such a tranquil night as that of the rain, I should like in some way to make you listen to my lute, playing all the songs I can remember."

I wanted to hear it, and waited for the fit occasion, but there was none, ever.

In the next year one tranquil evening I heard that he had come into the Princess's Palace, so I crept out of my chamber with my companion, but there were many people waiting within and without the Palace, and I turned back. He must have been of the same mind with me. He had come because it was so still a night, and he returned because it was noisy.

> *I yearn for a tranquil moment*
> *To be out upon the sea of harmony,*
> *In that enchanted boat.*
> *Oh, boatman, do you know my heart?*

So I composed that poem—and there is nothing more to tell. His personality was very excellent and he was not an ordinary man, but time passed, and neither called to the other.

David Brill

"FEAR" FROM *AS FAR AS THE EYE CAN SEE: REFLECTIONS OF AN APPALACHIAN TRAIL HIKER*

O ne of the great pilgrimages available to hikers in North America is the Appalachian Trail. Most "thru-hikers" begin the 2,100 mile trek at Springer Mountain in Georgia, and hike for at least five laborious months toward Maine, ending on the summit of Mount Katahdin. Along the way, they climb over a hundred peaks; walk more than five million steps; and cross bridges, interstates, ponds, and swamps with chest-high water. They begin in spring and end in near winter, and so pursue, allegorically, the shape of their own lives.

> *A* pilgrimage means change, and change means vulnerability, and vulnerability may bring with it fear.

David Brill waited for ten years before he wrote about his own five-month trek in 1979. He wanted not only to write about the hike itself, but to write about the ways that the hike had changed him—and to do that, he needed both time and perspective. In the following selection, the opening chapter of the book, Brill reflects on the preparations for the trip north. Certainly this involves a *great deal of physical preparation, as well as accumulating the essentials that he will carry. But in addition, Brill finds that a pilgrimage—any pilgrimage—involves an emotional and spiritual preparation, for a pilgrimage means change, and change means vulnerability, and vulnerability may bring with it fear. "I was afraid of the vast mystery of nature," Brill writes.*

But it is spring, and if he does not find the sweet breaths of Chaucer's zephyrs, he finds that he too is emerging and growing, as he changes from "visitor to resident of the wilderness."

"FEAR"

> *I'm lying under a wind-and-rain-buffeted tarp in a mountain gap in Georgia. I can hear wind gusts begin miles away, then gather intensity and plow through the gap, and with each gust the tarp sounds as if it's about to rip from its tethers. The trees creak, and I can hear limbs crack. I am terrified and awed by the power and violence of nature, and I realize that there's nowhere I can go to escape it. I never appreciated how vulnerable I'd feel away from the shelter of a roof and four sound walls.*
> —April 24, 1979, Tesnatee Gap, Georgia

A month earlier I had resigned my job as manager of a Washington, D.C., tennis shop and had committed myself and my meager $1,500 in savings to completing the trail. I wanted to become one of several hundred "thru-hikers" who had navigated the route from end to end in one summer, but other reasons, too, had drawn me toward the trail. Among them was the desire to confront and overcome my fears, but in the wake of the storm, I realized that I had only begun to identify them. Moreover, I acknowledged that I couldn't hope to banish my fears until I had pushed deeper into the eastern wilderness and probed much further into myself.

Though fear is a solitary condition, at least I had not had to endure the storm alone. I had shared my camp with Dan Howe, a twenty-three-year-old former architectural planner for a large oil corporation who had swapped his business suit and fast-track career for a pair of lug-soled boots, a backpack, and 2,100 miles of adventure. When we had set out on the trail, we had known each other just over a month and had met face to face only a half-dozen times.

Dan and I had first met during a program on the Appalachian Trail at a Washington-area backpacking shop. The program featured Ed Garvey, a well-known thru-hiker and author who had hiked the trail in the early 1970s. I had arrived for Garvey's talk fully reconciled to the notion that I would begin and finish the trail by myself, despite the fact that my previous backpacking experience had been limited to four or five overnighters; the longest duration had been three days. Over the previous months, I had telephoned every friend I had, and even a few casual acquaintances, in hopes of cajoling one or more of them into taking up the trail with me.

Most of them, like me, were in their first year out of college but, unlike me, had devoted their energies to charting career paths rather than ambling along wilderness trails. While they regarded the Appalachian Trail as a romantic pursuit, they also recognized its potential for stalling a career climb, and one by one they declined my invitation. So I had attended Garvey's presentation with the dim hope of finding a partner there.

As Garvey concluded his presentation, he asked if anyone among the thirty people in the audience intended to attempt the trail that summer. Tentatively, I raised my hand and then quickly scanned the room. One other hand waved in the air, and it belonged to a sandy-haired, bearded man who appeared to be about my age. After the meeting disbanded, I approached him and introduced myself, trying not to seem too eager or needy and realizing that to ask him abruptly if he would commit to spending the next five months with me was tantamount to proposing marriage on a first date.

Within a half-hour, Dan and I sat at a nearby tavern drinking beer and discussing our hopes, dreams, and expectations for our months on the trail. As we talked, I discovered that we had planned to begin the trail at about the same time—late April—and that we shared many common attitudes. Both of us had lived through the turbulent years of the late 1960s and early 1970s, and we both had emerged with a sense that if society failed to provide the peace and stability we sought, we might find it in nature.

While I had begun the trail seeking nature's healing powers, over the first four days I had found only disappointment, discovering that nature was capable of more violence than I had ever experienced in civilization. I found disappointment, too, in discovering the fear that dwelt within me.

In the throes of the storm, I had lain awake, my heart thumping like that of a snared rabbit, while Dan slumbered peacefully beside me. Through the long night, my head churned a maelstrom of doubt and anxiety, and I began to suspect that I possessed neither the courage nor the stamina to reach Mount Katahdin more than two thousand miles to the north. I also suspected that I had invested my hopes in a folly that would break me the way the wind had cracked away the branches of the surrounding trees and that I would limp back home wounded by failure. Those feelings may have been amplified by the storm, but they had just as surely accompanied my first tentative steps on the trail four days earlier.

Early on the morning of April 21, my parents had driven Dan and me up a ten-mile stretch of gravel road to Nimblewill Gap, which reaches within three miles of Springer Mountain and represents the nearest road access to the southern terminus of the Appalachian Trail.

An alternate route to the top follows an approach trail, which begins at Amicacola Falls State Park and ascends nine miles to Springer. We had heard stories about the stiff vertical ascent from the park to the trailhead, reputed to be among the trail's most difficult sections. This was especially the case for neophyte hikers who lacked the fitness and stamina that hundreds of miles on the trail would later provide. Among the dozens of hopeful thru-hikers who abandon the trail each year, in fact, many stumble back down the mountain—defeated—before ever reaching the summit of Springer. We didn't want to be among them, and by starting our hike at Nimblewill, we reasoned, we would at least make it as far as the official starting point.

We arrived at the gap in my parents' new sedan, and Dan and I climbed from the car smelling of soap and shampoo, fresh from our last hot shower for many days. Once out of the car, Dan, a seasoned woodsman who had logged countless miles on backcountry trails, hefted his pack from the trunk and slid effortlessly into its straps. The process wasn't quite as easy for me.

First, there was the actual heft of my pack. I realize now that there is no more reliable method for gauging a hiker's confidence than studying the contents of his pack. The least experienced hikers labor under a yoke of fear and worry, cluttering their packs with devices they hope will duplicate the security of more familiar environments. Veteran hikers, whose packs are characteristically Spartan, have discovered that a well chosen poem or quotation, which weighs nothing once committed to memory, can provide more solace in the face of fear than a welter of gadgets and trinkets.

Since I was a novice, my backpack burgeoned with expendable items that catered either to my fears or to my vanity but which served no purpose other than to occupy space with their bulk and stress my knees with their weight. While Dan's pack weighed a respectable thirty-five to forty pounds, mine surpassed fifty-five. I had read and reread backpacking how-to books, which sang the praises of light-weight packs bearing only the essentials. In the months before the outset of my hike, I had loaded the pack dozens of times, and each time I tried to assess honestly the merit of each item I slipped into the pockets. Gradually, I had pared the pack down to forty pounds. As the day of departure approached, however, my doubts and fears reversed the trend, and I found myself sneaking small items back into the pack until the scales again topped fifty-five.

On the eve of the hike, I had down-loaded the pack one last time, and I resolved to leave it just as it was. To assuage my fears, though, I had stashed the discarded items in the trunk of the car. As I wrestled the pack onto the ground in Nimblewill Gap and glimpsed them for the last time, each suddenly seemed essential, and I realized that once the trunk was closed, I would be forced to live without them.

Wouldn't the two-pound pair of binoculars in their leather case bring me closer to wildlife and help me identify the denizens of my new environment? Wouldn't the plastic egg-carrier and fifty feet of braided marine rope prove indispensable? What about the extra cook pot, aluminum plate, and oven mitt? Would one pair of long trousers be enough, and did I need a third pair of wool socks? Would the sheath knife, with its six-inch blade, protect me from wild beasts, or would my Swiss Army knife be sufficient? Would the package of firecrackers and can of dog repellent chase marauding bears from our camps? Would the metal pocket mirror, which doubled as a signal mirror, become an invaluable grooming aid or even save my life if I became lost? Wouldn't the one-pound hammock help make my leisure hours more comfortable? Would my health fail without the three-month supply of vitamins and the bulky first-aid manual?

As I deliberated, Dan shifted impatiently, and I resolved finally that the egg-carrier, binoculars, oven mitt, sheath knife, and marine rope would stay behind. The mirror, the first-aid guide, the fire-crackers, the hammock, the extra pair of socks and trousers, the supplemental pot and plate, the vitamins, and dog repellent, I reasoned, would justify their weight.

At the time, my pack, as heavy as it was, seemed far less burdensome than the emotional and physical challenge that awaited me, and as I glimpsed the trailhead, I first registered the full impact of what I was about to do. I had been raised by conservative and protective parents, who tended not to venture far from the cloister of their snug middle-class environment. From the time I was young, my life had been predicated on safe decisions. Now I was about to embark on a five-month journey through the unknown where I would face risks more real than any I had known before.

Fueling my fears was the knowledge that once I entered the backcountry I would leave behind the familiar trappings of the civilized world—electric lights to chase away the darkness, television sets and radios to help fill the idle hours, modern appliances to ease the chores of daily life—and the comfort they provided. I had fully enjoyed the morning's hot shower and the meal at the hotel restaurant. I felt no shame in ascending into the mountains inside the climate-controlled environment of the car, and I wasn't at all sure I could endure life without those and other amenities.

In some ways, the act of climbing from the car was tantamount to exiting the womb: I faced a strange and forbidding new world. At least in the first instance I had been blessed with conscientious parents who shepherded me clear of major pitfalls. Once I entered the woods, I knew that there would be nothing to shield me from hardship and danger except my own resources, which I had never really tested.

When the time to leave came, I embraced my parents and hoped they would offer some advice or guidance, yet I realized that I was about to enter a realm they knew little about.

"Be careful," said my mother, with tears welling in her eyes.

"Yes, and have fun," Dad advised, as I took the first of the five million steps that would lead me to Mount Katahdin. After a few hundred feet, I turned one last time to see the white sedan disappear in a cloud of dust as it descended the gravel road. For the first time in my life, I was truly on my own.

Within an hour and a half, we reached Springer, a rounded mountain cloaked in hardwood trees, their branches tipped with opening buds, and we discovered a sign-in book wedged into a mailbox planted on the summit. We took the register to a grassy clearing and basked for a few minutes in the eighty-two-degree sunshine as we read the entries logged by other hikers who had begun the hike in previous days and weeks. Dan and I noted that eight hikers, all bound for Maine, had signed in over the weekend, and we were two of the nearly five hundred who would set out on the northward pilgrimage that summer. At that point, none of us knew who would be among the one hundred or so who would reach our goal.

I penned a brief message about my dream of reaching Katahdin and then signed my name. Under it I drafted the thru-hiker symbol: a capital T nestled under and joined with the crossbar of a capital A. Beside it I printed the letters GA, the designation for Georgia, with an arrow pointing to the letters ME, the abbreviation for Maine, and added the year: 1979. In so doing I became an official Appalachian Trail thru-hiker.

Before continuing north, Dan and I posed for pictures beside a forest service sign. It listed Springer Mountain and its elevation of 3,782 feet along with the distance to a few major mileposts ahead. The last entry was Mount Katahdin, mileage two thousand miles (since the sign had been erected, trail relocations had added about one hundred miles). From the perspective of the wooded hills of Georgia at the base of the Appalachian spine, the northern terminus wouldn't have seemed more remote if it had been located on the surface of the moon.

For the next several days we traversed the three-thousand-foot peaks of the Chattahoochee National Forest. I count those days among the most difficult I have endured. I spent most of them absorbed in the rigors of survival in an environment that seemed foreign and hostile. In short, I was consumed by apprehension and fear.

I was afraid of my own ineptitude. I fumbled with my new stove, lost track of items stored in my pack, and listened at night as mice gnawed through my foodbag before I learned to hang it out of their reach. I had no idea how to bushwhack down a mountainside to locate a water source, what to do to protect myself on an exposed ridge in a thunderstorm, how to patch myself back together after I had sliced myself with my pocketknife, how long to boil lentils and rice, how much stove fuel to carry for the days and nights between supply stops, and how much and what type of food I would need to keep from starving.

I was afraid of my own weakness. My lungs burned, my thighs

were seared, and my feet throbbed as my boots rubbed my tender heels to blisters on the first few steep ascents, and I wondered if I had the fortitude to keep pushing on through the pain. When late April storms drenched the woods, I dreaded leaving the dry warmth of my shelter to set out for fifteen miles through the downpour. I was afraid, too, of facing my friends back home if I failed to meet those challenges and had to pack it in.

I was afraid of being alone. Dan's woods-sense far exceeded my own, and I stuck by him like moss on a log, worried that if I let him out of my sight, I would never catch up to him and would be left to earn my proficiency through hardship and failure. As it turned out, Dan taught me much, and we remained a team to the very pinnacle of Mount Katahdin. During our five months on the trail, we propped each other up when our spirits flagged, fought like badgers when our egos pulled in different directions, and shared our food, our shelter, and our thoughts. When the trip ended, we had spent more than 150 days and nights together and had forged a friendship that will endure no matter how much time and distance separate us.

I was afraid of the vast mystery of nature. The chilling echo of hoot owls, the distant drumming of male ruffed grouse beating the air with their wings, the constant rustling in the brush around our camps after we'd extinguished our evening campfires were all unfamiliar sounds that fueled my fear.

And I was afraid when, under a tarp in Tesnatee Gap, I first experienced the raw power of nature.

The fear inspired by that first spring storm—and all the fears that accompanied me along my first miles on the trail—soon fused into a pervading sense of dread. As I watched Dan confront the trail's challenges with courage and confidence, I began to resign myself to the belief that I wasn't quite suited for an extended stay in the woods. One evening, while I sat on a log downcast and preparing to tell him that I had decided to leave the trail, a toy collie strayed into camp. Though I didn't realize it at the time, I was about to learn the first, and perhaps the most enduring, lesson about life on the trail. Put simply, if one is receptive and open to change, the trail—and in a larger sense, nature itself—seems always to answer one's questions and meet one's needs. It sounds mystical, and I wouldn't believe it if I hadn't experienced it so many times along my journey.

Just behind the dog, a woman in her late fifties labored up the trail, the huge pack she carried dwarfing her slight frame. Her legs appeared much too frail to support her own weight, much less the weight of the pack, and her face, framed by silver shoulder-length hair, registered the pain of every step.

She paused for a few minutes, leaning on her walking stick, and told us that her name was Elizabeth and that she was hiking alone. Her destination, like ours, was Mount Katahdin. She told us that her husband had died the previous year and that she had taken up the trail to ease her grief and to chart a new direction for her life. She said she covered twelve to fifteen miles per day, beginning at dawn and continuing until dark.

She declined our invitation to join us in our camp, saying that she hoped to cover a few more miles before it became too dark to navigate the boulder-strewn trail. Soon she called to her dog and resumed her slow, deliberate pace.

Later, as Dan and I sat beside the fire plotting our mileage for the next several days and as I struggled with the decision to continue on or abandon the trail, I couldn't shake the memory of Elizabeth. It had taken me five hours to cover the twelve miles to camp that day; she had been plodding along for nearly twice that long. At the end of each day, my twenty-three-year-old thighs and feet ached. How, then, must hers have felt? I had shuddered as the storm blew through our camp, and I had flinched in the darkness when the trees creaked and wild animals crept unseen through underbrush. Yet I had the comfort of a companion. How did she contend with such fears during her solitary days and nights on the trail? How had she become so brave?

Frankly, in spite of her apparent courage, I had dismissed Elizabeth's goal of completing the trail as foolhardy. Yet one evening some five months later, while Dan and I camped in the woods of central Maine, a toy collie entered camp. As soon as we saw it, we looked at one another and smiled. Then we turned and looked up the trail. A slender figure soon emerged from the trees. It was Elizabeth.

Although the previous five months had wrought physical changes in all of us, the rigors of trail life had completely transformed Elizabeth. Her face was wan and haggard, and dark circles had formed under her eyes. Her legs seemed to have lost what little muscle tone they had had, and her silver hair had billowed into a tangled mass. Her gait seemed even more painful and unsteady than when I had first seen her.

Once she joined us in camp, she explained that she had made it as far as New England before realizing that at her pace, she could not hope to reach Katahdin before the end of October, when Baxter State Park officials bar access to the mountain because of unpredictable weather. She had decided to "flop," as do many of the slower-moving hikers, and travel to Katahdin, then hike south to where she had left off. I later learned that she reached her goal.

When I refer back to my journal entry on the night we first met Elizabeth in Georgia, I find a message of hope. There I termed her "Our Lady of the Trail" and wrote that "she seems weak and distant and unaware of the difficulty of the task that awaits her. We have heard about other hikers who have already gotten discouraged and gone home. But after these few days, she is still here, still moving north. How, I don't know. She will always be an inspiration to me."

Thereafter, Elizabeth became my guiding spirit, like a figurehead on an old wooden ship leading frightened sailors through uncharted seas. When my confidence began to fail, I would think of her and her frail body, facing the wilderness alone with no one to ease her fears or share her discoveries. From then on I resolved that although I could not conquer my fears outright, I could at least confront them squarely. As I did, they seemed to lose their power over me.

As the weeks passed, my blisters began to heal, and my thighs grew hard and strong. My camp routine became well enough ingrained that I could fetch water, fire the stove, cook and eat dinner, and hang my food without a wasted motion. My pack and its contents became more familiar to me than my dresser drawers at home, and I eventually discarded the spare socks, extra cook pot and plate, vitamins, firecrackers, dog repellent, and several other pounds of extraneous gear. I gave the extra trousers to a fellow hiker who had ripped the seat out of his own, and soon my pack dipped to a manageable thirty-five pounds.

From then on I carried only the essentials. As the load in my pack decreased, my initial fear of the wilderness mellowed, and I began walking my fifteen to twenty miles each day alone, fascinated with the process of spring awakening around me. I even began to regard thunderstorms, which weeks earlier had pitched me into panic, as among nature's most formidable and entertaining displays, more potent and grand than anything I had witnessed in civilization. Many evenings, as storms approached, I scrambled to an open perch on a ridge-line from which to watch them, as their charcoal-gray sentries floated across dusky skies stretching to the horizon. I sat captivated as their silver talons raked nearby mountain peaks and their thunder shook the earth. As I watched, I began to realize that my transformation from visitor to resident of the wilderness had begun and that there was much yet to learn about my new home.

Anonymous

A GATHERING OF AFRICAN
AMERICAN SPIRITUALS

*T*he spirituals and songs that came out of slavery times expressed, at their core, the human desire to be free. Recently it has been argued that many of these songs, in fact, played a vital role in the winning of freedom. "Go Down, Moses" was used by Harriet Tubman to announce an impending escape, and "Swing Low, Sweet Chariot" was similarly employed by other conductors on the Underground Railroad. "Follow the Drinking Gourd," with its reference to the North Star and the Big Dipper, worked as a musical set of directions to help the escaped slaves head north.

> *F*reedom, in the spirituals and songs, is often connected to springtime.

Freedom, in the spirituals and songs, is often connected to springtime. Both "Go Down, Moses" and "Oh Mary, Don't You Weep" evoke the time of the Passover and the escape from Egypt, when Pharaoh's soldiers in pursuit of the escaped Hebrews are destroyed in the Red Sea. "Follow the Drinking Gourd" is, in fact, set in springtime, "When the sun come back, / When the firs' quail call." Another familiar spiritual, "Were You There When They Crucified My Lord?" sets its events during Holy Friday, ending with the melancholy of death, with no mention of an Easter resurrection.

Sadness and joy, despair and hope, bondage and freedom—these are the poles between which the harmonies of the African American spirituals vibrate. That they are so frequently connected to spring inclines the ear and the heart to joy, hope, and freedom.

"Go Down, Moses"

When Israel was in Egypt's land,
    Let my people go;
Oppress'd so hard they could not stand,
    Let my people go.

(Chorus)
    Go down, Moses, Way down in Egypt land,
    Tell ole Pharaoh, Let my people go.

Thus saith the Lord, bold Moses said,
    Let my people go;
If not I'll smite your first born dead,
    Let my people go.

No more shall they in bondage toil,
    Let my people go;
Let them come out with Egypt's spoil,
    Let my people go.

When Israel out of Egypt came,
    Let my people go;
And left the proud oppressive land,
    Let my people go.

O, 'twas a dark and dismal night,
*   Let my people go;*
When Moses led the Israelites,
*   Let my people go.*

'Twas good old Moses and Aaron, too,
*   Let my people go;*
'Twas they that led the armies through,
*   Let my people go.*

The Lord told Moses what to do,
*   Let my people go;*
To lead the children of Israel through,
*   Let my people go.*

O come along, Moses, you'll not get lost,
*   Let my people go;*
Stretch out your rod and come across,
*   Let my people go.*

As Israel stood by the water side,
*   Let my people go;*
At the command of God it did divide,
*   Let my people go.*

When they had reached the other shore,
*   Let my people go;*
They sang a song of triumph o'er,
*   Let my people go.*

Pharaoh said he would go across,
  Let my people go;
But Pharaoh and his host were lost,
  Let my people go.

O, Moses, the cloud shall cleave the way,
  Let my people go;
A fire by night, a shade by day,
  Let my people go.

You'll not get lost in the wilderness,
  Let my people go;
With a lighted candle in your breast,
  Let my people go.

Jordan shall stand up like a wall,
  Let my people go;
And the walls of Jericho shall fall,
  Let my people go.

Your foes shall not before you stand,
  Let my people go;
And you'll possess fair Canaan's land,
  Let my people go.

'Twas just about in harvest time,
  Let my people go;
When Joshua led his host divine,
  Let my people go.

O let us all from bondage flee,
 Let my people go;
And let us all in Christ be free,
 Let my people go.

We need not always weep and moan,
 Let my people go;
And wear these slavery chains forlorn,
 Let my people go.

This world's a wilderness of woe,
 Let my people go;
O, let us on to Canaan go,
 Let my people go.

What a beautiful morning that will be,
 Let my people go;
When time breaks up in eternity,
 Let my people go.

O bretheren, bretheren, you'd better be engaged,
 Let my people go;
For the devil he's out on a big rampage,
 Let my people go.

The Devil he thought he had me fast,
 Let my people go;
But I thought I'd break his chains at last,
 Let my people go.

O take yer shoes from off yer feet,
    Let my people go;
And walk into the golden street,
    Let my people go.

I'll tell you what I likes de best,
    Let my people go;
It is the shouting Methodist,
    Let my people go.

I do believe without a doubt,
    Let my people go;
That a Christian has the right to shout,
    Let my people go.

"Oh Mary, Don't You Weep"

Oh Mary, don't you weep, don't you moan,
Oh Mary, don't you weep, don't you moan.
Pharaoh's army got drownded,
Oh Mary, don't you weep.

One of dese mornings, bright and fair,
Take my wings and cleave de air,
Pharaoh's army got drownded,
Oh Mary, don't you weep.

One of dese mornings, five o'clock,
Dis ole world gonna reel and rock,
Pharaoh's army got drownded,
Oh Mary, don't you weep.

Oh Mary, don't you weep, don't you moan,
Oh Mary, don't you weep, don't you moan,
Pharaoh's army got drownded,
Oh Mary, don't you weep.

"Follow the Drinking Gou'd"

(Chorus)
Foller the drinkin' gou'd
Foller the drinkin' gou'd
For the ole man say,
"Foller the drinkin' gou'd."

When the sun come back,
When the firs' quail call,
Then the time is come
Foller the drinkin' gou'd.

The riva's bank am a very good road,
The dead trees show the way,
Lef' foot, peg foot goin' on,
Foller the drinkin' gou'd.

The riva ends a-tween two hills,
Foller the drinkin' gou'd;
'Nuther riva on the other side
Follers the drinkin' gou'd.

Wha the little riva
Meet the grea' big un,
The ole man waits—
Foller the drinkin' gou'd.

Lionel Basney

"MEDITATIONS FOR LENT"

*A*s *Lionel Basney writes, the season of Lent is a time for repentance, a time for assessing, and then turning in right directions. One of the central images he uses in these Meditations is that of a young C. S. Lewis, who, upon first arriving at Oxford, leaves the train station in the wrong direction.* Only when he senses that he has gone wrong does he turn around and then see the beautiful spires of the city. In Basney's hands, this becomes an emblem of what Lent calls us to.

> *T*he season of Lent is a time for repentance, a time for assessing, and then turning in right directions.

Basney's longest prose work was An Earth-Careful Way of Life *(1994), a book which calls powerfully for environmental stewardship. In it he argues that it will not do to make small adjustments, to hope for help from new technologies, or to eternally search out new sources of fossil fuels. We, as a society, must turn around completely; we must radically alter the way we use the resources of the planet we have been given. That prophetic call emerges from Basney's Lenten awareness.*

Spring is a time of growth, of new life, of green things, of joy. Basney acknowledges all of this and, in fact, closes with another image that goes beyond the annual joys of spring to suggest an eternal, unchanging joy. "Lent is the time when we renew our hope of glory," he writes. But to renew that hope, he argues, we do not merely trump up our emotions. We repent. We repent sincerely. That is what makes the springtime hope of glory possible.

"MEDITATIONS FOR LENT"

The Season: First Sunday in Lent

As I walked through the wilderness of this world, I lighted on a certain place ...
—*The Pilgrim's Progress*

Every Jan. 1 we hang a large calendar on the kitchen wall and begin to write reminders in the daily squares—birthdays, vacations, committee meetings, coffee duty. Slowly—actually, not all *that* slowly—the squares fill with a thicket of notes. Appointments come and go; the year turns. Then it is Dec. 31. We take the calendar down, heavy with memories, and lay it aside until tax time.

The new calendar comes with some appointments preprinted—the Fourth of July, Thanksgiving, Yom Kippur. Easter is there, in the spring, which means that Lent comes now, in late winter. And when you look out the window, there is Lent's image, its feel: you see the unbroken gray sky, the trees, still gaunt, and you feel your need of Easter.

Of course, for our sisters and brothers in Santiago and Johannesburg, Lent comes in late summer and Easter on the porch of fall. But the seasons' turn is important however it comes, for it reminds us that our lives proceed in circles. Lunch won't last you long; you'll be hungry again (thank goodness) in a few hours. The encouragement you give a friend today will need to be renewed tomorrow.

The same holds true for our spiritual lives. We don't move toward heaven in one gigantic, decisive step after another. We move in small, repetitive, cumulative patterns—learning to make a habit of what we do well, and repenting, again and again, what we do badly.

Lent is for repentance. Repentance is a hard idea and a hard job. Yet the calendars of our lives fill with the gray scribbling of our mistakes and bad habits. We have been selfish when we should have been generous, impatient when we should have been patient, cold when we should have been warm.

Of course a believer's life has many moments of repentance. We may say a general confession on Sunday, and this is important. But our sins get so mixed up with the dailiness of our lives that they disappear from view. It is good, healthy, to have a time when our job is to bring them to mind.

I have been a gardener all my adult life, in a small way (seasons again). I spade, plant, mulch, weed, pick, peel, slice, and can the results—and then I get tired of the whole business. I go out some-time in October, pull up the gray, dilapidated plants, the ones with no life left in them, and stand for a moment in the garden's empti-ness and quiet.

Lent is the time to clean the garden—to pull up the old habits, the ones with no life in them. We look forward to Easter, to new seed, the fresh flower. But first, the cleaning up.

The Burden: Second Sunday in Lent

Behold I saw a man clothed with rags ... a book in his hand, and a great burden upon his back.

Lent is the time for repentance.

It's a hard idea and not a popular one. A theologian tells me repentance is not a popular topic even among theologians. Perhaps that is why we sometimes hear preaching meant to make us feel sorry not for our sins but for ourselves.

We live in a therapeutic culture. Among us sin is something to be cured, like a headache. The goal is not to draw closer to God but to feel free to enjoy ourselves. We may even see repentance as mor-bid, as pointlessly depressing.

But to believe that everything wrong with us can be fixed with an aspirin is to think too little of ourselves. For it would mean we had no really good possibilities in us to begin with—that the most anyone could expect of us was to do a little business, have a little fun.

But love has always thought better of us than this. Our parents dreamed we would become exemplary people, brave, distinguished. And God expects even more—that we will become his friends, charged with the energy and freedom of his love. Lent is the time when we renew our hope of glory.

When we do, however, we see, too, that we aren't what God hoped we would become. Something is in the way; something is deeply, not superficially, wrong.

John Bunyan opens *The Pilgrim's Progress* with a picture of it: Christian stands at the start of his journey "with a great burden upon his back." In Barry Moser's wonderful recent watercolor, the burden is bigger than Christian, a heap of bags and bundles. It bends Christian in half.

Christian cannot wish it away or shrug it off. It falls off when he stands at the cross, the sign that only Christ's dying and rising make repentance work at all.

Yet we need another picture, not for the fact of sin but for all the daily examples of it and how we cope with them. Maybe that picture is the canvas bag I carry my books and papers in. Shapeless, endlessly stretchable, it is always in my hand, heavier as the week goes on.

Eventually I sit down and unpack it. There is the letter I didn't answer, the favor I didn't do, the injustice I didn't repair. There are the opportunities for charity I put off.

Sometimes I find I have done well: there is a note of thanks from a student. But I had to pull out all the trash to find it.

The Turn: Third Sunday in Lent

For it is an hard matter to go down into the Valley of Humiliation.

The Bible speaks of repentance often. The two common biblical words for it, one Hebrew, one Greek, have similar meanings. Both mean turning—turning around, turning away from our sins and back to God. It's a decisive image: you change direction; you face the other way.

What do we repent of? In the Bible it is often idolatry—putting the wrong thing at the center of our lives. Or it is an outright wrong, done on impulse or by design. It is the favorite anger, the nurtured grudge, the stab of envy, the pet dream of greed or lust or power. It is our preoccupation with ourselves.

We recut the world as we want it to be. And because we are only small parts of the world, the recutting is always a lessening. We make other people less, in our minds, so that we can dream of using them; we make the world less, in our minds, so that we can waste it freely. If we could, we would junk the world and start over.

This is why repentance can be hard: it hurts to let go of the dream of having the world all our way. Jesus is (as always) honest about the cost: it can feel, he said, like cutting off your hand.

Yet there is a danger here: seeing how serious *repentance* is, we may overdramatize *repent-ing* and discourage ourselves before we start.

No doubt some of us—the ones who run concentration camps or who gut pension funds and ruin whole communities—do need to make public, dramatic repentances. For many of our faults, though, turning around can begin with a small step. It may be like acknowledging the wrong we have done a friend: it's hard to do, but we have the friendship to rely on. It is the friendship God has shown us that encourages us to try.

Repenting is like turning around. C. S. Lewis once recalled his first arrival, as a student, at the Oxford train station. He set off for town, unfortunately in the wrong direction. It was not until minutes later, when he stopped and turned around, that he saw "far away, never more beautiful since ... the fabled cluster of spires and towers."

There it is—the world as God meant it to be. The sight, all by itself, will change something in us. But we will still need to walk back to the crossroads and set off in the right direction.

The Task: Fourth Sunday in Lent

*This Vanity Fair is no new erected business, but a thing of
ancient standing.*

It's an odd thing, but in our feel-good society we're having a feel-bad moment.

You catch it on the talk shows. "Feel any remorse over that?" Geraldo asks, after his guest has described some bizarre bit of behavior. Talk shows have a gloss of moral earnestness. Of course, the guests are being paid to confess. And they often come from an economic class that makes it easy for Geraldo to condescend to them without offending his viewers.

There are more serious examples. What should we do about grave historical wrongs? Jewish groups have been demanding for decades that the Vatican apologize for its conduct during the Holocaust. African Americans are asking the United States government to apologize for slavery.

These wrongs cannot be doubted: the Holocaust and slavery were Vanity Fair at its most lethal. Yet we may wonder if an apology is the right response. Governments, after all, are more temporary than nations. If the U.S. Congress apologizes, does that mean that the United States has apologized? And what will this mean the next time you meet someone of another skin tone in the grocery store or are asked to make right an injustice at work?

We are caught up, all of us, in sins larger than ourselves. And we often wonder whether we are responsible and how we should respond.

For example, like it or not we are all involved in the excesses and dangers that we call the environmental crisis. For the most part, the scientific community agrees, now, that the global economy is overstressing the creation. We are using more and wasting more than the earth can afford.

Here is a large, systemic wrong we must face. I often talk with people about it, and they always ask, "What can any of us do?" It's a natural, sensible Lenten question, and it has a direct answer: Do the

nearest good thing you can. Put yourself to the nuisance of recycling; turn your thermostat down; shorten your shower. Sell your
fourth car and then your third and drive your children to their
appointments yourself. Or let them drive you.

This is the work we call restitution—making right what we
have done wrong. Small, specific, practical turnings.

No matter how large the wrong, there is comfort in a small turning. Fairly soon, in a day, in a week, you see that something is better.

The Freedom: Fifth Sunday in Lent

*These Mountains are Immanuel's Land, and they are
within sight of the City.*

So we set about repentance, restitution: we make time, name our
faults, turn to God in faith and expectation. What then?

The answer, I think, is that we feel at home again. Perhaps it is
like waking up. We get back the world we know and naturally love,
but freed now from the cramp and fog of our preoccupation with
ourselves. And we feel again that we have a true, absorbing place in
God's world as well as work to do.

Maybe that doesn't seem enough: "I repent, and then I get a
work assignment?" Sometimes we do feel other things—the warmth,
the exhilaration, of God's love. Sometimes we feel like Ebenezer
Scrooge on the Christmas morning of his redemption—"light as a
feather, happy as an angel."

But Scrooge took his rediscovered joy straight to his counting-
house and raised his clerk's salary. If we don't put our joy to work, if
we don't reinsert it into our daily responsibilities, we can make it
into an idol. We can make it into a yardstick. We come to think that
if we aren't feeling exhilarated, then there is something wrong with
our faith or our repentance.

This is like thinking that if we aren't feeling crazy in love, there
is something wrong with our marriages. But that excitement is a
sometimes thing. It isn't the heart of the matter: the marriage is, that
patient melding of lives and selves. That is where we are at home.

That is where we have work to do, the best kind of work—work that frees us, that lets us forget ourselves.

Let me give you a picture. Many years ago I watched a child take a stack of scrap paper and a pencil and begin to tell a story. It started with a little girl, but in a minute it reached toward talking trees and airplanes, battles and magic lakes. All the time the child was speaking the story, her hand floated across the paper, drawing picture after picture. The sheets spread at her feet like a river delta.

She drew in the perfect freedom of the story. It was as if the drawing flowed out of her imagination, down her arm, through the pencil, out onto the paper.

When the story ended, she dropped the pencil and left. There would be more stories when she wanted them. They were where she was at home, where she did her work, the kind God did when the world was made.

The Promise: Sixth Sunday in Lent

And the trumpets sounded for him on the other side.

All the time, while waiting, praying through Lent, we are expecting Easter.

Standing in the empty garden, we wait for the first green shoots. Unpacking the bag, we imagine a time when there will be nothing in it but good things. Plodding down the road, we look for the city's spires.

For 30 years, give or take a month, I lived in a small, rural town. It stands scattered in a river valley and up the valley's steep west wall, which is itself part of the mountains behind it.

In my boyhood, in the early 1950s, trains still ran on the straight track in the flat of the valley. I grew up within hearing of the train whistle, that powerful wail of longing and comfort.

I live even more deeply in the country now, and one of my pleasures is to waken in the morning, before light, hearing the deep throb of the locomotive not many hundreds of yards away and its air horn trumpeting.

The whistle blows because the tracks cross a main road, the one that reaches from town out to the Interstate highway. A century ago, the crossing was its own little town. The town has vanished now, though the foursquare, substantial brick house where the stationmaster lived still stands.

When I hear the morning train I imagine that it is calling for the town that used to be there. So we live as believers, thinking of the place we started from, Eden, the home we can't get back to.

I also imagine the little crossing town restored—a family living again in the stationmaster's house, the master coming out with his pocket watch to meet the evening train. So we dream of the place we are traveling toward, Bunyan's Celestial City, the new Jerusalem.

Lent is the time when we renew our hope of glory. The hard job of repenting prepares us. There will be a day when the train will call, and it will be answered with a shout of welcome from the community of God's love, whole again, restored.

Scott Cairns

TWO POEMS OF TURNING
AND DELIGHT

*C*haucer concludes his Canterbury Tales *with a retraction. It is a state-ment of his own faith, his desire that his vocation as a writer be found pleasing to God, and a wish that if his readers find "anything in it that pleases them, that thereof they thank our Lord Jesus Christ, from whom proceedeth all wit and all goodness." Chaucer's portraits and stories throughout the* Tales *reveal moral faults primarily as foolish failings—although he is not blind to the havoc wickedness can work in the world. Similarly, Scott Cairns, in the first of these two poems, recognizes the silliness of sin and, in his gentle dismissal, makes us more aware and more ashamed of how often we indulge it. But repentance, as the second poem makes clear, can turn us in a new direction, send us out into the fields, and set us on a pilgrimage of delight.*

> *R*epentance can turn us in a new direction, send us out into the fields, and set us on a pilgrimage of delight.

Adventures in New Testament Greek: Metanoia

Repentance, *to be sure,*
but of a species far
less likely to oblige
sheepish repetition.

Repentance, *you'll observe,*
glibly bears the bent
of thought revisited,
and mind's familiar stamp

—a quaint, half-hearted
doubleness that couples
all compunction with a pledge
of recurrent screw-up.

The heart's metanoia,
on the other hand, turns
without regret, turns not
so much away, *as* toward;

as if the slow pilgrim
has been surprised to find
that sin is not so bad
as it is a waste of time.

The Theology of Delight

Imagine a world, this ridiculous,
tentative bud blooming
in your hand. There in your hand, a world
opening up, stretching, after the image of
your hand. Imagine
a field of sheep grazing, or a single
sheep grazing and wandering in the
delight of grass, of wildflowers
lifting themselves, after their fashion,
to be flowers. Or a woman, lifting her hand
to touch her brow, and the intricacy of the
motion that frees her
to set the flat part of her hand carelessly
to her brow. Once, while walking, I happened
across a woman whose walking had brought her
to a shaded spot near a field. Enjoying
that cool place together, we sat watching sheep
and the wind moving the wildflowers in the field.
As we rose to set out again, our movement
startled the flock into running; they ran
only a little way before settling again
to their blank consideration of the grass.
But one of them continued, its prancing
taking it far into the field where,
free of the others, it leapt for no clear reason,
and set out walking through a gathering
of flowers, parting that grip of flowers with its face.

PART FIVE

Dance

INTRODUCTION

If you had been a traveler in the English countryside many years ago, you might, as William Wordsworth did one morning, have heard "blithe notes of music, suddenly let loose / On the thrilled ear" and, looking down upon a village green seen the Maypole shining "Like a mast / Of gold ... as if the rays / Of morning, aided by exhaling dew, / With gladsome influence could re-animate / The faded garlands dangling from its sides." For if spring begins to stir quietly, imperceptibly, beneath the mud in March, it bursts into song and dance as it pelts through May toward the summer sun.

In the sonnet that frames the concerto "Spring" from *The Four Seasons,* Antonio Vivaldi, too, begins with song and ends with dance:

> *Springtime is upon us.*
> *The birds celebrate her return with festive song,*
> *and murmuring streams are softly caressed by the*
> *   breezes.*
> *Thunderstorms, those heralds of Spring, roar,*
> *casting their dark mantle over heaven,*
> *Then they die away to silence,*

> *and the birds take up their charming songs once*
> *more....*
> *Led by the festive sound of rustic bagpipes,*
> *nymphs and shepherds lightly dance beneath the bril-*
> *liant canopy of spring.*

And James Thomson, an eighteenth-century English poet, summons up the Edenic spring, sending Adam and Eve out to work in the garden, full of merriment and great content:

> *Mean time the song went round; and dance and*
> *sport,*
> *Wisdom and friendly talk, successive, stole*
> *Their hours away: while in the rosy vale*
> *Love breath'd his infant sighs, from anguish free,*
> *And full replete with bliss.*

Dance is a particularly apt metaphor for our spiritual lives, because it evokes one of the most elusive but sought-after virtues: balance. As we dash between work and home, scrambling for some "leisure" time while we meet the demands of spouses, children, an exercise regimen, and household chores, we often mutter, "I just need to find some balance here." But when we seek that balance by parceling out our energies—a bit here, a bit there—as if life could be measured on a scale or rotated as easily as the tires on our car, we miss the unexpected lurches and breathtaking turns that make it all worthwhile.

The balance we need is better imaged by the dance—two bodies in motion, toe to toe, leaning into one another, giving and taking, always slightly askew as they whirl about the floor. It is this rhythmic, patterned, yet surprising dance of life that leads us into "the charming agonies of love." It may be unrequited love as Spenser's Thomalin, limping along with Cupid's arrow in his heel, discovers. Or it may be the deep, quiet love that finds its whole world in the sight of a beloved woman kneading dough at the kitchen counter.

But the dance might also take us into parenthood, through the shock of infertility and the delicate equilibrium of an open adoption, or into the slow uncoiling of old age, or to that most melancholy of duets—divorce. Through each movement we follow old patterns and improvise new steps, we stumble, we regain our poise, we are caught up in the music and the motion—so much so that we are able to dance even in times of trouble.

In the fourteenth century, the recurring plague epidemics decimated England and the Continent; nearly a quarter of the population died. From such devastation rose the Dance of Death, played out in dramas and later memorialized by Hans Holbein in a set of famous woodcuts. As Death danced his way across the stage, accompanied by fiddlers and other folk musicians, he beckoned to reluctant partners—kings, queens, farmers, tradespeople, even children—each of whom eventually took his hand. And yet they danced not toward death but with Death and toward God. For Death was but a messenger, a partner, dancing the soul to the world beyond.

And, indeed, all the dances of life—and of death itself—are but rehearsals for the Great Dance. In *Perelandra,* C. S. Lewis's retelling of the first three chapters of Genesis, Tor the king and Tinidril the queen, unlike Adam and Eve, refuse to succumb to the temptations laid out before them. In particular, they resist the lure to control their own destinies, to live on the "Fixed Land." As Tinidril says, "Why should I desire the Fixed except to make sure—to be able on one day to command where I should be the next and what should happen to me? It was to reject the wave—to draw my hands out of Maleldil's, to say to Him, 'Not thus, but thus'—to put in our own power what times should roll toward us ... as if you gathered fruits together to-day for to-morrow's eating instead of taking what came. That would have been cold love and feeble trust. And out of it how could we ever have climbed back into love and trust again?" And Tor echoes, "No fixed land. Always one must throw oneself into the wave."

Because Tinidril and Tor throw themselves into the wave, because they trust themselves to the hand and plan of their loving God, they experience the joy that shimmers through the air, "as if there were dancing in Deep Heaven."

And, indeed, there is dancing in Deep Heaven, a Great Dance that began before time and will continue forever, a Dance in which "plans without number interlock, and each movement becomes in its season the breaking into flower of the whole design to which all else had been directed. Thus each is equally at the centre and none are there by being equals, but some by giving place and some by receiving it, the small things by their smallness and the great by their greatness, and all the patterns linked and looped together by the unions of a kneeling with a sceptred love."

It is the fittingness of the Great Dance—small things valued for their smallness, great things valued for their greatness, all things looped together in love—that draws our hearts through all the perplexities of our daily dances. Though we stumble and step on our partner's toes and crash into the furniture, the music urges our feet back into the rhythm, back into the dance. The ancient Hebrew prophet Jeremiah made this promise:

> The Lord hath redeemed Jacob ... therefore they shall come and rejoice in the light of Zion, and shall run to the bountifulness of the LORD, even for the wheat, and for the wine, and for the oil, and for the increase of sheep, and bullocks: and their soul shall be as a watered garden, and they shall have no more sorrow. Then shall the virgin rejoice in the dance, and the young men, and the old men together: for I will turn their mourning into joy, and will comfort them, and give them joy for their sorrows.

A Shaker Hymn

"VERNAL SEASON"

Springtime glories round us teeming,
Fill our hearts with joyous cheer,
Sunshine brightly o'er us beaming,
Makes all nature glad appear;
Lovely season bright and vernal,
Ever welcome to our clime,
Emblem of a growth eternal,
And of destinies sublime.

Every blossom blade and leaflet
Springing from the verdant sod,
Blends with song of bird and streamlet,
Voicing praise to nature's God.
From this wondrous world of beauty
Lessons new our souls can draw,
'Till our daily life and duty
Shall be ruled by perfect law.

What a prospect lies before us
On the hillside, in the vale,
Heavenly blessing resting o'er us,
Tells that promise cannot fail.
Hands that toil in consecration
Shall with precious fruit be blest,
Hearts that dwell in pure relation
Find a home of peace and rest.

Isak Dinesen

"Some African Birds" and "I Will Not Let Thee Go Except Thou Bless Me" from *Out of Africa*

In 1914, twenty-nine-year-old Karen Blixen arrived in East Africa from Denmark to establish a pioneer coffee plantation near Nairobi, Kenya. For most of the next fifteen years she worked on her farm, absorbing the dramatic landscape and making friends with both Africans and colonials. Her memoir, Out of Africa, *was published under the pseudonym Isak Dinesen in 1938.*

In the selections that follow, Dinesen celebrates the beginning of the rainy season as the vast grass plains turn freshly green, the birds dance on sky and land, and the farmers hold up their faces for great gulps of life-giving rain. This is the season in which stars are unwelcome, for they herald a dry spell that may foreshadow a crippling drought. Spring rain in Africa is not a romantic luxury but an economic necessity.

Although Dinesen's eye looks outward across Ngong farm, her ear is tuned to more subtle inward spiritual resonances: the cranes dance a sacred ballet, connecting heaven and earth "like the winged angels walking up and

> Spring rain in Africa is not a romantic luxury but an economic necessity.

down Jacob's Ladder," and the fragile community, bound together by the memory of drought, cries out with Jacob to the piercing rainfall—and to life itself—"I will not let thee go except thou bless me."

"SOME AFRICAN BIRDS"

Just at the beginning of the long rains, in the last week of March, or the first week of April, I have heard the nightingale in the woods of Africa. Not the full song: a few notes only,—the opening bars of the concerto, a rehearsal, suddenly stopped and again begun. It was as if, in the solitude of the dripping woods, some one was, in a tree, tuning a small cello. It was, however, the same melody, and the same abundance and sweetness, as were soon to fill the forests of Europe, from Sicily to Elsinore.

We had the black and white storks in Africa, the birds that build their nests upon the thatched village roofs of Northern Europe. They look less imposing in Africa than they do there, for here they had such tall and ponderous birds as the Marabout and the Secretary Bird to be compared to. The storks have got other habits in Africa than in Europe, where they live as in married couples and are symbols of domestic happiness. Here they are seen together in big flights, as in clubs. They are called locust-birds in Africa, and follow along when the locusts come upon the land, living high on them. They fly over the plains, too, where there is a grass-fire on, circling just in front of the advancing line of small leaping flames, high up in the scintillating rainbow-coloured air, and the grey smoke, on watch for the mice and snakes that run from the fire. The storks have a gay time in Africa. But their real life is not here, and when the winds of spring bring back thoughts of mating and nesting, their hearts are turned towards the North, they remember old times and places and fly off, two and two, and are shortly after wading in the cold bogs of their birth-places.

Out on the plains, in the beginning of the rains, where the vast stretches of burnt grass begin to show fresh green sprouting, there are many hundred plovers. The plains always have a maritime air, the open horizon recalls the Sea and the long Sea-sands, the wandering wind is the same, the charred grass has a saline smell, and when the grass is long it runs in waves all over the land. When the white carnation flowers on the plains you remember the chopping white-specked waves all round you as you are tacking up the Sund. Out on the plains the plovers likewise take on the appearance of Sea-birds, and behave like Sea-birds on a beach, legging it, on the closing grass, as fast as they can for a short time, and then rising before your horse with high shrill shrieks, so that the light sky is all alive with wings and birds' voices.

The Crested Cranes, which come on to the newly rolled and planted maize-land, to steal the maize out of the ground, make up for the robbery by being birds of good omen, announcing the rain; and also by dancing to us. When the tall birds are together in large numbers, it is a fine sight to see them spread their wings and dance. There is much style in the dance, and a little affectation, for why, when they can fly, do they jump up and down as if they were held on to the earth by magnetism? The whole ballet has a sacred look, like some ritual dance; perhaps the cranes are making an attempt to join Heaven and earth like the winged angels walking up and down Jacob's Ladder. With their delicate pale grey colouring, the little black velvet skull-cap and the fan-shaped crown, the cranes have all the air of light, spirited frescoes. When, after the dance, they lift and go away, to keep up the sacred tone of the show they give out, by the wings or the voice, a clear ringing note, as if a group of church bells had taken to the wing and were sailing off. You can hear them a long way away, even after the birds themselves have become invisible in the sky: a chime from the clouds.

"I WILL NOT LET THEE GO EXCEPT THOU BLESS ME"

When in Africa in March the long rains begin after four months of hot, dry weather, the richness of growth and the freshness and fragrance everywhere are overwhelming.

But the farmer holds back his heart and dares not trust to the generosity of nature, he listens, dreading to hear a decrease in the roar of the falling rain. The water that the earth is not drinking in must bring the farm, with all the vegetable, animal and human life on it, through for rainless months to come.

It is a lovely sight when the roads of the farm have all been turned into streams of running water, and the farmer wades through the mud with a singing heart, out to the flowering and dripping coffee-fields. But it happens in the middle of the rainy season that in the evening the stars show themselves through the thinning clouds; then he stands outside his house and stares up, as if hanging himself on the sky to milk down more rain. He cries to the sky: "Give me enough and more than enough. My heart is bared to thee now, and I will not let thee go except thou bless me. Drown me if you like, but kill me not with caprices. No *coitus interruptus,* heaven, heaven!"

Sometimes a cool, colourless day in the months after the rainy season calls back the time of the marka mbaya, the bad year, the time of the drought. In those days the Kikuyu used to graze their cows round my house, and a boy amongst them who had a flute, from time to time played a short tune on it. When I have heard this tune again, it has recalled in one single moment all our anguish and despair of the past. It has got the salt taste of tears in it. But at the same time I found in the tune, unexpectedly surprisingly, a vigour, a curious sweetness, a song. Had those hard times really had all these in them? There was youth in us then, a wild hope. It was during those long days that we were all of us merged into a unity, so that on another planet we shall recognize one another, and the things cry to each other, the cuckoo clock and my books to the lean-fleshed cows on the lawn and the sorrowful old Kikuyus: "You also were there. You also were part of the Ngong farm." That bad time blessed us and went away.

The friends of the farm came to the house, and went away again. They were not the kind of people who stay for a long time in the same place. They were not the kind of people either who grow old, they died and never came back. But they had sat contented by the fire, and when the house, closing round them, said: "I will not let you go except you bless me," they laughed and blessed it, and it let them go.

An old lady sat in a party and talked of her life. She declared that she would like to live it all over again, and held this fact to prove that she had lived wisely. I thought: Yes her life has been the sort of life that should really be taken twice before you can say that you have had it. An arietta you can take *da capo,* but not a whole piece of music,—not a symphony and not a five-act tragedy either. If it is taken over again it is because it had not gone as it ought to have gone.

My life, I will not let you go except you bless me, but then I will let you go.

Edmund Spenser

"MARCH" FROM *THE SHEPHERD'S CALENDAR*

*E*dmund *Spenser's* Shepherd's Calendar *(1579), dedicated to Spenser's fellow poet and patron, Sir Philip Sidney, is a delightful set of meditations initiated by the advent of each successive month. The meditations are meant to show some comedy—in this selection, for example, Thomalin rails against the perils of love because Cupid has wounded him—but they are also meant to suggest some serious thoughts about love, age, fortune, the nature of poetry, the health of the church, and even Queen Elizabeth herself.*

Beneath their railing, one senses that it would only take a small shift in circumstances to lead them on a very different line— because it is, after all, springtime.

Since spring is beginning, the thoughts of Willie and Thomalin turn to love, and it seems that each has been unhappy. Thomalin's experience has left him with a festering sore in his heel, suggesting that his suit has been spurned. Willie too seems wary, eager to learn the signs of Cupid's presence so that he may avoid his arrows. And yet, though both fear and hope to avoid Cupid, their conversation seems inevitably drawn to the questions of love, and beneath their railing, one senses that it would only take a small shift in circumstances to lead them on a very different line—because it is, after all, springtime.

March

Argument:

In this Ecologue, two shepherd boys, taking occasion of the season, begin to discourse of love and other pleasure, which to springtime is most agreeable. The special meaning hereof is, to give certain marks and tokens so as to recognize Cupid, the Poets' God of Love. But more particularly, I think, in the person of Thomalin is meant some secret friend, who scorned Love and his knights long, till at length he himself was entangled, and unaware, was wounded with the dark of some beautiful regard, which is Cupid's arrow.

Willie:
Thomalin, why sit we so,
As if overcome with woe
  Upon so fair a morrow?
The joyous time now cometh fast,
That shall allay this bitter blast,
And slake the winter's sorrow.

Thomalin:
Truly, Willie, thou warnest well:
For winter's wrath begins to quell,
  And pleasant spring appeareth.
The grass begins to be refreshed,
The swallow peeps out of her nest,
  And the cloudy skies do cleareth.

Willie:

See you not the hawthorn shrub,
How, bragging, it begins to bud,
        And put out his tender head?
Flora now calls forth each flower,
And bids make ready Maia's bower,
        Who now is uprisen from her bed.
There shall we sport in delight,
And learn with Lottie to wax light,
        Who scornfully looks at us askance.
There we will bold Cupid awake,
That now sleeps low in Lethe's lake,
        And pray him to lead our dance.

Thomalin:

Willie, I expect you are besot:
For lusty Cupid sleepeth not,
        But is abroad at his game.

Willie:

How knowest thou that he is awake?
Did you yourself his slumber break?
        Or go secretly to the same?

Thomalin:

No, but it happened that I him spied
Within a bush, where he did hide,
        With wings of purple and blue.
And were it not that my sheep would stray,
His secret marks I'd to you say,
        Wherein by chance I him knew.

Willie:

Thomalin, have no care for your sheep,
Myself a double eye will keep,
    Alike to my flock and to thine.
For I too at home have a sire,
A stepdame too as hot as fire,
    Who duly each day will count mine.

Thomalin:

Nay, but your watching will not serve,
My sheep, even so, may chance to swerve,
    And fall into some mischief.
For indeed, it is but the third morrow,
Since I fell asleep with sorrow,
    And waked again with grief:
While I slept, an unhappy ewe,
Whose clouted leg her hurt did show,
    Fell headlong into a dell.
There, unjointed, she set her din
Though if her neck had unjointed been,
    She would have no more to tell.
The ewe was so wanton and so mad,
(And by my sleep, less good than bad),
    She wants no longer to graze on green.

Willie:

Let be, as may be, what is past:
What is to come, let that be forecast.
    Now, tell me what thou hast seen.

Thomalin:
It was upon a holiday,
When shepherds' grooms have leave to play,
  I cast to go a-hunting.
Long wandering up and down the land,
With bow and arrows in either hand,
    For birds in bushes' hunting.
At length within an ivied bush
(Where Cupid was in hiding, hushed)
  I heard a busy bustling.
I bent my bolt against the bush,
Listening if anything did rush,
    But then heard no more rustling.
Then peeping close into the thick,
I saw the moving of something quick,
    Whose shape appeared not.
But whether it was faerie, fiend, or snake,
I called my courage to awake,
    And manfully thereat shot.
With that sprang forth a naked swain,
With spotted wings like peacock's train,
    And laughing leapt up a tree.
His gilded quiver upon his back,
And silver bow, which was but slack,
    Which lightly he bent at me.
That seeing, I levelled again,
And shot at him with might and main,
    Arrows thickly, as though it hailed.
So long I shot that my store was spent
So to stones around me I hasty, bent,
    And threw—but naught availed.

He was so nimble, and so bright,
From bough to bough he leapéd light,
    And often the stones he caught.
Therewith, afraid, I ran away.
But he, that seemed before only to play,
    A shaft in earnest sought.
He hit me, running, in the heel,
Though then I little hurt did feel—
    But soon it sore increased.
And now it rankles more and more,
And inwardly it festers sore,
    Nor know I how to cease it.

Willie:
Thomalin, I pity thy plight.
Indeed, with Cupid thou didst fight;
    I know him by that token.
For once I heard my father say
How he him caught upon a day
    Whereof his will was broken.
Entangled in a fowling net,
Which he for carrion crows had set,
    That had our pear tree haunted.
He said, He was a winged lad,
But bow and shafts he did not have
    To hold him that day, daunted.
But see, the sky thickens apace,
And stooping Phoebus lowers his face:
    It's time to haste us homeward.

Willie's moral:

> *To be wise and also to love,*
> *Is granted only to God above.*

Thomalin's moral:

> *On honey and of gall, in love, there is store;*
> *The honey is much, but the gall is more.*

Paul Laurence Dunbar

A Gathering of Poems

In these three springtime poems, Paul Laurence Dunbar traces the dance of love from the warm intimacy of daily life through a walk in the meadow to the sweet, sad memory that a May breeze invokes. Love is all of these—and more—he suggests. It arises as inevitably as spring itself: "For life is life and love is love, / 'Twixt maid and man or dove and dove."

Yet the ubiquity of love does not coarsen or cheapen it. The most ordinary sight—Dinah kneading bread—is enough to capture his heart. And the loss of love is enough to turn the sweetness of May into fatal perfume.

> The most ordinary sight—Dinah kneading bread—is enough to capture his heart.

Dinah Kneading Dough

I have seen full many a sight
Born of day or drawn by night:
Sunlight on a silver stream,
Golden lilies all a-dream,
Lofty mountains, bold and proud,
Veiled beneath the lacelike cloud;
But no lovely sight I know
Equals Dinah kneading dough.

Brown arms buried elbow deep
Their domestic rhythm keep,
As with steady sweep they go
Through the gently yielding dough.
Maids may vaunt their finer charms—
Naught to me like Dinah's arms;
Girls may draw, or paint, or sew—
I love Dinah kneading dough.

Eyes of jet and teeth of pearl,
Hair, some say, too tight a-curl;
But the dainty maid I deem
Very near perfection's dream.
Swift she works, and only flings
Me a glance—the least of things.
And I wonder, does she know
That my heart is in the dough?

Spring Song

A blue-bell springs upon the ledge,
A lark sits singing in the hedge;
Sweet perfumes scent the balmy air,
And life is brimming everywhere.
What lark and breeze and bluebird sing,
　　　Is Spring, Spring, Spring!

No more the air is sharp and cold;
The planter wends across the wold,
And, glad, beneath the shining sky
We wander forth, my love and I.
And ever in our hearts doth ring
　　　This song of Spring, Spring!

For life is life and love is love,
'Twixt maid and man or dove and dove.
Life may be short, life may be long,
But love will come, and to its song
Shall this refrain for ever cling
　　　Of Spring, Spring, Spring!

In May

Oh to have you in May,
  To talk with you under the trees,
Dreaming throughout the day,
  Drinking the wine-like breeze,

Oh it were sweet to think
  That May should be ours again,
Hoping it not, I shrink,
  Out of the sight of men.

May brings the flowers to bloom,
  It brings the green leaves to the tree,
And fatally sweet perfume,
  Of what you once were to me.

Ts'en-Ts'an, Ssü-K'ung T'u, and Wang Ch'ang-Ling

A GATHERING OF CHINESE LOVE POEMS

*T*hese love poems breathe out longing, desire, and loss.

Ts'en-Ts'an, an eighth-century poet who was also a provincial governor, speaks for all parted lovers: if only a spring breeze might touch both faces, spanning the miles and bringing their souls together. For Ssü-K'ung T'u, writing a century later, spring itself is a siren, singing a story of beauty and love that is old and yet new and summoning the poet into her embrace. Wang Ch'ang-Ling, a contemporary of Ts'en-Ts'an's, invokes in just a few lines a desperate trinity: spring, war, and love.

> *I*n spring we can dare to hope again, and in spring we see clearly all we have to lose.

Taken together, these poems refuse to sentimentalize spring but they recognize its potent hold on our imagination. In spring we can dare to hope again, and in spring we see clearly all we have to lose.

A Dream of Spring

Ts'en-Ts'an

Last night within my chamber's gloom some
    vague light breath of Spring
Came wandering and whispering, and bade my
    soul take wing.

A hundred moonlit miles away the Chiang crept
    to sea;
O keeper of my heart, I came by Chiang's ford
    to thee.

It lingered but a moment's space, that dream of
    Spring, and died;
Yet as my head the pillows pressed, my soul had
    found thy side.

Oh! Chiang Nan's a hundred miles, yet in a
    moment's space.
I've flown away to Chiang Nan and touched a
    dreaming face.

Return of Spring

SSÜ-K'UNG T'U

A lovely maiden, roaming
  The wild dark valley through,
Culls from the shining waters
  Lilies and lotus blue.
With leaves the peach-trees are laden,
  The wind sighs through the haze,
And the willows wave their shadows
  Down the oriole-haunted ways.
As passion-tranced, I follow,
  I hear the old refrain
Of Spring's eternal story,
  That was old and is young again.

Tears in the Spring

WANG CH'ANG-LING

On whom as yet Sorrow has laid no scar,
Climbs the Kingfisher's Tower. Suddenly
She sees the bloom of willows far and wide,
And grieves for him she lent to fame and war.

Elizabeth Vander Lei

"PICTURE POSTCARDS"

*I*n the Edenic curse, the joys of childbirth are forever linked with pain—even in springtime. "In sorrow thou shalt bring forth children," God tells Eve (Genesis 4.16). Reading the curse, we tend to identify that sorrow with physical distress. But as Elizabeth Vander Lei shows, the birth of a new family can be emotionally painful, a mix of joy and sadness, endings and beginnings. Though Jesus himself later affirmed that the sorrows of childbirth are followed by the joys of the child—"A woman when she is in travail hath sorrow, because her hour is come: but as soon as she is delivered of the child, she remembereth no more the anguish, for joy ... " (John 16.21)—he never negates the pain that precedes the joy.

> *There* is grace and joy and laughter, but also sorrow and pain and weeping.

It is this balance—or perhaps unity—that Vander Lei explores in her story of "open adoption." There is certainly joy here, but also recognition that one family is being formed, at least in part, because another has been broken. There is grace and joy and laughter, but also sorrow and pain and weeping. Like Robert Burns and William Blake, Vander Lei shows that the springtimes of our experience are not all robins and violets; they are grace couched in need and pain.

"Picture Postcards"

Perusing our photo albums, you might think that in our life before kids Paul and I did nothing but travel and that we spent most of our time taking pictures. Albums of our European train tour include not only the obligatory images—Big Ben, the Eiffel Tower, the Rhine—but also photos that attest to our seriousness as photographers: the single perfect rose, hay bales casting shadows on an alpine meadow, bikes lining a narrow Dutch street. The Southeast Asia trip: wild orchids, rice paddies, water buffalo. But no picture records the brown, oily liquid that streamed from the plane's fuselage on our descent to Bali. Who takes photos of such things? For what purpose—to show our mothers? "See, we very nearly died. But didn't." The South American trip: Galapagos iguanas and blue-footed boobies, schools of darting fish—mere flashes of color. We surreptitiously snapped photos of the armed guards who shadowed our tour group in Peru, protecting us from guerilla fighters. But what of the quality of light on Machu Picchu at dusk—golden, diffuse, ancient? None of our photos comes close.

The trip to South America proved to be our last vacation for a while. Returning home, we had to face facts: what started on the Southeast Asia trip as a nonchalant willingness to become parents had hardened into careful documentation of reproductive cycles and, finally, cold certainty that something was wrong. Together and alone we visited doctors' offices; we told absolutely no one about our gathering despair. After a few months of visits to the lavish offices of a doctor who claimed distinction as one of the top five reproduction specialists in the nation, we quit. Procedures and pills that merely encouraged nature had quickly given way to cutting-edge technologies, and we lost our will to explore the boundaries of reproductive medicine. We went home and sobbed out the news to our parents, leaving them to leak it to the rest of the family.

A few weeks later, an envelope bearing my mother's distinctive handwriting arrived in the mailbox. Ripping it open, I already suspected its contents: my mother is a clipper—newspaper articles, recipes from magazines, instructions for appliances—she cuts out anything that needs saving, sending, or attempting. Sure enough: "Thought this might encourage you" angled across the first of two full newspaper pages containing an article about a couple who had adopted a baby and befriended the baby's birthmother, too. The adoptive parents, the birthmother, the social worker—all spoke glowingly, almost reverently, about this "open adoption." The color photos that accompanied the article showed them—all of them— gathered around the family table, calmly eating breakfast. Queasy, disoriented, I forced myself to read the article all the way through before I tossed it in the trash. "What did you think?" my mother asked a few days later. I didn't say. I didn't say that it seemed like some kind of a modern-day sideshow—a topic for women's maga- zines and raucous talk-shows rather than a lifestyle I might find appealing.

Over the next months, Paul and I waded through our emo- tions and options. For reasons rooted in an admix of desperation, altruism, and theology, we chose adoption. Meetings and home vis- its, self-evaluations and reference letters, personality tests and finger- prints, we completed them all and become state-certified adoptive parents. All we needed was a baby. The path to a baby, to parent- hood, to pediatrician appointments, birthday parties and Little League games led straight to a pregnant girl, a prospective birth- mother. She would choose the family for her unborn child from "the matchbook"—a collection of photos and letters from prospec- tive adoptive parents. She would interview the couple and decide if they were right—but for whom? The baby? Her? Her family? What would she be looking for? For our photo we hunted out a local park and posed with sand toys. In the letter we described our house and listed our pets.

The first week of February, our social worker calls, "A birth- mom has picked you. Can you meet her on Thursday?" Of course. I hang up and wonder what prospective parents wear to such a meeting. Something formal-but-not-dressy, reassuringly-parental- but-not-frumpy. In such clothes we sit, expectantly, on the couch in the adoption agency's small conference room. A knock on the door. We stand up to greet first our social worker, then Nenetta's social worker, and finally, Nenetta. My thoughts whirl and clash: She's pretty—the baby will be, too. My dress is wrong; she'll think we're boring and old. Boring and old: does that make us perfect or terrible? She carries a half-finished Diet Pepsi. Should she be drinking Diet Pepsi in her condition? Do I have a right to say anything about that? Wait—she *is* pregnant, right? When I had imagined Nenetta I had focused on an enormous, magnificently pregnant belly—the whole reason for our meeting. But Nenetta carries herself easily, naturally.

We all sit. The two social workers consult their notes to guide the conversation: "So, Elizabeth, you come from a large family. How did you enjoy that growing up?" "Nenetta's sister is a nursing student; Nenetta plans to go to college in the fall. What will be your major, Nenetta?" And so it goes, questions and answers, big smiles, bobbing nods of understanding. That is, until Nenetta's social worker prompts, "Nenetta, do you have that picture of Chad? They might like to see what the baby's birthfather looks like." Nenetta's shoulders slump and she blushes; the rest of us stiffen. Nenetta sighs, "Okay, it's a little embarrassing. I forgot that they would want to see his picture." She opens her purse slowly, removes an envelope, and slides out a photo: it's a wallet-sized head shot, once ripped into quarters, now carefully taped back together.

As I remember it, I laugh first and hardest, remembering the bitter-sweet satisfaction of disposing of ex-boyfriends. Paul quips a line from Monty Python. Nenetta grins in recognition: "Oh, my dad loves all those old British comedy shows." Maybe this will be okay. We agree to meet again, without the social workers. At California Pizza Kitchen we discuss baby names. Nenetta's already picked a name: Tyler Nolan. Paul and I list our favorites: Thomas, William, Andrew, Anthony. Nenetta likes Andrew; together we settle on Andrew Tyler as a name we can all live with. We invite Nenetta over for dinner. She likes the food and the Winnie-the-Pooh themed nursery. Yes, maybe this will be all right.

The call comes early on March 9: "Nenetta's in labor. I'll call again when I know more."

Paul and I lie in bed, staring at the ceiling: On this day we might become parents. Or Nenetta could change her mind; many birthmothers do. Do we go to work? If we stay home, what do we call it? A sick day? A vacation day? We go to work. We return to a message from our social worker: "Nenetta wonders if you would like to visit her at the hospital tonight." We eat out, more to steel our courage than to stave our hunger, and arrive, camera in hand, at the maternity ward. Nenetta, baby in arms, greets us from her hospital bed and introduces us to her parents and sister. We all smile and turn our attention to the baby. I notice immediately the name on his hospital band—Tyler Nolan and wonder what has happened to Andrew Tyler. Nenetta lays him on the bed to change his diaper. Her mother hovers, offering advice. We all admire the shape of his head; we laugh with joy as he yawns and stretches. Paul snaps a couple of photos.

A nurse ushers out everyone but the patient and her mother. The rest of us wait in the hall, desperate for conversation, avoiding each other's eyes. When we enter again, the baby is in his bassinette. Nenetta turns to me and quietly asks, "Would you like to hold him?" Yes. I pick up the baby and try to cuddle him maternally-but-not-possessively as the air in the room thickens, threatening to gag us all. After what I hope is a suitable amount of time, I return the baby to his bed. The air thins a bit, and Paul and I soon leave for home.

Three days later, Nenetta relinquishes her parental rights to Tyler Nolan, and we become the parents of Andrew Tyler. As we sign documents at the agency, our social worker suggests, "Sometimes we have a little ceremony when you receive the baby. Nenetta wonders if we could hold it at your house on Saturday." Okay. Nenetta's family parks on the street, and I watch from the kitchen window as they walk up our drive, Nenetta's father carrying Andrew's car seat and a bulging diaper bag, Nenetta cradling Andrew with both arms. I avert the rising panic by reminding myself that this is a done deal. He's ours. We arrange ourselves for pictures: Nenetta, her family, and Andrew; Paul and me with Nenetta holding Andrew. And, finally, all of us together. Smiling. I offer lemonade and cookies.

"Well, it's about time," Nenetta's social worker says as she rises. "Shall we join hands?" She says a few words, reads some scripture, and we pray. Nenetta looks at Andrew for a long time, kisses him on the forehead, and hands him to me. Tearful and smiling we hug, the baby between us. Picking up purses and cameras, Nenetta and her family say quick goodbyes. From the kitchen window I watch as they walk back to their car. At the end of the driveway, Nenetta's mother stops, her head drops, and her shoulders shake with sobs I cannot hear. The social worker comforts her, first patting her back and then embracing her, as the grief intensifies. Nenetta's father puts his arm around her and leads her to the car. I look down at Andrew and turn away.

A week later, I show off Andrew at work and drop off my letter of resignation. Work now seems a troublesome intrusion on my time with Andy. Nenetta calls regularly, and I dutifully report on Andy's development. On Good Friday, the mailbox holds an envelope addressed in Nenetta's handwriting to Andrew Tyler Vander Lei. Inside, a card: "Easter Greetings to My Son." My Son? I toss the card on the table and storm out to the backyard, slamming the door as I go. How long is this going to go on? He's our son, not hers. He's my Andy.

Nenetta continued to call throughout that spring, to stop by for short visits. In May, we took her out for dinner to celebrate her birthday and her high school graduation, leaving Andy with a babysitter for the first time. Our conversation began with the usual Andy updates, but over dinner talk turns to other things: funny stories from her childhood, the college courses she would take in the fall, her new romantic relationship. After that dinner, Nenetta stopped by the house more often, always calling first and never staying long. She brought over her new boyfriend and later, shyly, asked what we thought of him. We discovered Nenetta's favorite foods and served them. Nenetta began to hang around—clearing the table after dinner, playing with Andrew, and lingering over an espresso after Andrew was tucked in bed.

Our home video from that spring and summer is agonizing to watch: long stretches of Andrew, lying on the floor, sucking his fist and cooing, kicking his legs, reaching for a toy, struggling to roll from back to belly. Sometimes the video captures something else, too: sometimes Nenetta's toes appear in the frame—she's there, watching as intently as we are. The audio captures Nenetta's voice blended with ours as we exuberantly celebrate each accomplishment—like those mustered by first-time parents everywhere.

All that was long ago. Andrew is twelve now, staring down puberty with a mix of anticipation and fear. And Nenetta and Paul and I are still watching with the same intensity as that first spring. In face Andrew resembles his birthfather; his temperament, his build, his brown eyes are Nenetta's. Recently he spoke before a group of prospective social workers to provide a child's perspective on the open adoption experience. "So how do you feel when you see your birthmother?" one asked. Hands thrust deep in his pockets, Andrew shrugged, "I don't know. It's just normal. I mean, it's Nenetta."

Abram Van Engen

"The Portico"

A bram Van Engen's poignant narrative of loss and recovery emerges out of *the darker underside of spring—the knowledge that the return of warm weather, the recovery of longer days, the rebirth of the perennials, in fact, all of the re's that mark the season, point not only to beginnings, but to future endings. Though spring suggests joy in the recovery, nothing in the season suggests permanence. And so Van Engen will complicate Alice Morse Earle's confident assertions about springtime lilacs and their yearly renewals. For this writer, the lilacs are scarred, and withered some, and neglected. Thus the miracle of the annual renewal is all the greater, particularly because it is so very unexpected.*

> *T*hough spring suggests joy in the recovery, nothing in the season suggests permanence.

Van Engen will take on Samuel Johnson as well, powerfully challenging Johnson's own very eighteenth-century optimism about the world. Of course, Van Engen affirms, there is an annual renovation of the world. This we can observe. But how does it happen? Johnson seems pleased to simply observe that it does happen. But how? Van Engen insists. Does it just happen? Does it arise out of goodness and grace? Or—a more difficult question—does renovation have more gnarled and battered roots?

"THE PORTICO"

When I was sixteen, the fort I had so often played in as a child came down. It had to. Not only was it old and unused, it stood in the way of further development—grand plans for a fully landscaped backyard. My father and I tore it down and swept the ruins away. As soon as the spot was clear, crews came and dug and built and planted, and by the end, a beautiful garden skirted the edge of a sturdy wooden fence, sweeping toward the yard's middle where a Sunburst Locust blazed against the Indiana sky. Where the fort had once crouched beside the garage in a patch of lilac trees, we wheeled a set of garbage cans.

Taking out the trash, we passed on stepping stones through Dropwort rich with feathery pink, over a yard of green grass, and finally back through a trellis in the fence to an area hidden from view. If you stood in our kitchen and looked out the window on a fine spring day, you would see only a backyard brimming over with glorious garden—Jacob's Ladder and Jupiter's Beard, Stella Dora and Moonbeam Coreopsis, all the blossoms bulging forth along the pattern of their planting. The trellis would look like a strange and inexplicable gap, a portico to a fallen fort, an unfortunate dark hole. Beyond it, the lilacs withered and shrank from view. I figured they had died.

I often marvel at the image of spring that seems implanted in me—a vision from the kitchen window of a garden filled with hope, a renewal sweeping away all that has come before. Samuel Johnson tells us of a man who each year referred "the removal of all his uneasiness to the coming of the next spring." And Johnson himself seems no less enthusiastic. Spring "throw[s] over the whole earth an air of gaiety," offering "amusement," "entertainment," and "diversion"—a season of relief from all our woes. And that seems to be how it goes, the expectant hope if not the grand fulfillment. Spring, I always believed, was a great escape, a second chance, a breath of new air in dry and rattled bones.

It's the rattling I forgot.

In the spring of my twentieth year, my torn and tired father stepped into his car and rattled off down our gravel driveway—a separation that would become divorce. For four previous years, in the twilight of a fading marriage, he worked side-by-side with my mother, day after spring day in the fenced-in garden yard, pruning, tucking, weeding, and wheeling out the barrelfuls of dead and dying branches—out through the fence's trellis to the garbage cans that waited with their dark, gaping jaws. Many days, I drove up our driveway after school and found a garden looking easily pristine, my parents relaxing on the patio with a glass of lemonade, gazing out across the blooms that they had tended. Now, only now, I wonder what they saw as they sat in their cheap, plastic chairs. Did they see the garden blossoming forth with new and abundant life, a glorious robe of colors covering the barren, wintered earth? Did they glory in the small blossoms of the crocuses or the little blooms of Snow on the Mountain as they sprouted up from an April ground barely warm? Or did they see it always going wrong, always on the edge of failure? Did they finish for the day, pour a glass of lemonade, lean back and watch the weeds return, the branches bramble, the living begin to die and the dying fall dead in heaps that would have to be cut away, heaved into the barrel and lugged behind the fence?

In his dictionary, Johnson defines spring only as "the season in which plants spring and vegetate," the verb meaning "to arise out of the ground and grow by vegetative power." Well and good. But what tends that vegetative power? What work harnesses it into beauty and order? For Johnson, the "annual renovation of the world" seems to arise always of its own accord—no struggle, no strife, no death.

"Cursed is the ground because of you," God told Adam, and each year the sweat thickened as thorns and thistles encroached upon our garden. I left for college, and the backyard became for me a series of snapshots taken on visits home, a time-lapse video that tended toward ruin. Each trip, I'd step out of my car and gaze across its roof at a garden that had lost its glory.

When my parents separated, my mother cried after every day of work. She no longer sat on the patio. She no longer watched the garden fail. Instead, she'd slip off her gloves and throw them on the wooden bench by the back door, her face flushed, her tears brimming. She'd fling the door wide and try to hold back from crying—hold back so that her last son, home from college for three days, would not scare and take flight. But still her eyes would burst. And I would tell her to sit, to eat, to tackle the rest of the garden another day. Let it be for now. There will always be more death to strip away. Let it run its course for now. Tomorrow we will work the garden together. Tomorrow we'll work side-by-side.

But I lied. I could not take another's place, and I did not want to. I left for college, and I did not return. I did not want to don the good cheer of spring when all it seemed to bring were dark memories, weeds, and heaps of death to clear away. I stayed away.

But while I was gone things began to change—changed without my knowing it, changed in me and at home. One day, I returned—reluctantly—called home for some special reason I now forget. I drove up the gravel driveway and parked beneath our unused basketball hoop. I stepped out. I turned. I looked over my car's beige roof. And I stopped. The Chinese Dwarf Lilacs that lined the sidewalk dropped dark purple blossoms on the pavement. Pink peonies next to the house looked as large as melons and about to burst. I left my luggage in the car. I stepped into the garden. It looked marvelous. Not perfect; it would never look perfect. But its fullness bulged against the fence, leaning into the trellis that doubled as a portico. I walked through. On the other side, trash cans still marked the gravesite of my childhood fort. Next to them, the withered lilacs tangled down. But not dead. They were not dead. Off one branch hung a string of blossoms, blue and pink and full of smell, low enough to touch. I reached my hand to the petals and held them in my palm. I plucked a blossom from the branch.

When I came back through the portico, I saw my mother in the kitchen window. She had heard me rattle up. She had followed me with her gaze. She stood behind the glass, and I could see that she was smiling. A full smile. I lifted the blossom in my hand. She nodded.

"It is not good that man should be alone." Tonight, my mother would not be alone, as on other nights when she gathered with her friends, with neighbors, with a community that wandered by and sat together in our aging plastic chairs, tipping back lemonade and gazing out across a garden full of both the living and the dead. Keeping company. Bearing up.

Each spring now I see a garden full of life, and it reminds me also of death. Blooms bathed in sweat burst and fall and must be swept through the trellis in the fence, the portico of a fallen fort. Life passes to death and death comes to life, and every year I ask again, which of these two will triumph, which will prevail in the end?

I went inside. Instantly, I was covered by the smell of portabella mushrooms simmering in a pool of onions and butter for the meal my mother knew I loved. I hugged her. There were tears in her eyes, but she was not afraid that they would drive me away. I would not drive away. Tonight, we would eat together. Tomorrow, we would work side-by-side.

We put the lilac blossom in water and set the table.

Nancy String fellow

"SOCIAL SECURITY" FROM REPORT FROM GRIMES CREEK AFTER A HARD WINTER

*I*t is easy enough to think of flowers, birds, frisking lambs or even of Ash Wednesday, Lent, and Easter during the spring. But we hardly think of April 15—Tax Day—as a rite of spring. But, of course, it is.

For Nancy Stringfellow, however, the advent of the federal government is not a bumbling intrusion into her spring. Rather, it is a cause for celebration, for this April marks the receipt of her first social security check. And with that check comes the freedom to live in her cabin on Grimes Creek, the freedom to remain independent. As she evokes the world of elderly women before the dawn of pensions—a world confined by poverty and good intentions—we are caught in the undertow of desperation. Yet this spring at Grimes Creek, the flood waters will recede, the star flowers will erupt, and one retired widow will dance on its banks.

> *We* hardly think of April 15—Tax Day—as a rite of spring. But, of course, it is.

"SOCIAL SECURITY"

April, laughing her girlish laughter, is upon me. The water is completely gone from the basement. Old Grimes is still threatening the lane, and I park my car outside the gate, lest I get trapped by a sudden surge of water. Everything is coming up with a whoop and a holler. The earth shimmers with movement. Mysterious jewelled bugs venture forth. Ants stream over the ground in columns. Spiders pop in and out of holes, sidle along twigs, cast lines into the wind and swing out like the Flying Wallendas.

Lichen doily the rocks, and in every crevice green fingers of moss are reaching toward the sun. So beautiful and strange. Some are thick green velvet pincushions, some mounds of green stars. Scallops of soft green hair betray the Nereids peeking from their granite catacombs. Sit down and look at a patch of moss, and suddenly you are in Tolkien land, wandering in a green forest, strange branches waving above you, soft carpets beneath your feet. Sometimes a star flower erupts in the midst, terrifyingly tall, blindingly white. And tiny insects are wending their way through the trees to their Promised Land, following their own special star.

The birds are coming on strong now, the whole place has been divided up among them like a checkerboard, and every bird is in its own private square, hollering Mine! Mine!

April is also the month my Social Security payments begin. Such a lovely little brown paper envelope, meaning, indeed, security. I remember other days. In the raw new land of South Idaho it was shove and scrape, and if you had bad luck or lost your strength you were done for. I was raised in mortal fear of disability or of some natural disaster. We walked a thin tightrope with no net. Two years of crop failures could wipe out the savings of ten years. That of course was part of the reason for large families. More hands to work the land. Someone to help you when your strength was going. Children were sometimes your only security against dying in a ditch. There was no cushion.

I remember the bewildered old ladies, widows who had lost their husbands, and whose small hoard of savings had been swept away by illness and death. Sometimes they had no one left to turn to, and then it was the County Poor Farm, with bare endless corridors and echoing board floors. Cheerless Charity. Sometimes they had children or relatives who took them in and sheltered them, but the extra mouth was a burden, and they knew it. Old ladies sitting in the far corner of the room when company came, thinning hair dragged back into a tight bun, knobby hands folded in aproned laps. Soft list slippers slit to ease the painful bunions. Apologetic, silent, arthritically awkward. Or drudging from one task to another, pathetically anxious to please a harried daughter-in-law. Relicts, they called them. Flotsam from an earlier culture, bleached, dry, juiceless, and helpless. Women who had once been strong and beautiful, and suffered from that memory.

And there were the ones who still had a measure of strength, but were trapped in that dreadful bind that women were trapped in so little time ago. Not enough education to teach, too old to be a clerk or a waitress. There was little other opportunity. Poverty was a sandpit, and they could not scale the walls. They fought, sometimes gallantly, sometimes bitterly, but mostly they lost. Their lives subsided into an empty endless waiting. Even when their families cared for them and kept them safe they still lacked their independence. For as much as your people care for you, and you for them, absolute financial dependence is a terrible, a crippling, thing. Social security helped change that. It gave the elderly a measure of dignity. Not to have to ask for little things, silly little things that made you remember you were still a woman. To be able to buy a lipstick, to ease your drying skin with a pot of cream. And a small but solid contribution to the monthly bills. Enough so that you could have a room of your own. With luck, a place of your own.

Here in my mountains I am remarkably fortunate. Living is cheap. I have seven acres of room. Room for dignity and freedom, privacy to cry when I am sad and dance when I am gay. It all comes in that little brown paper wrapper, and it lets me spit in anybody's eye.

William Blake and Robert Burns, with Gerard Manley Hopkins

A GATHERING OF POETRY

*I*t may seem odd to bring together William Blake and Robert Burns. Blake is the mystical visionary poet, writing of heaven and hell. Burns is the poet of the Scottish highlands, writing in dialect of the countryside, of the River Devon, of love beside quiet woods. Though they lived at almost the same time—Burns was only two years younger than Blake—the differences in their poetry are vast.

And yet there is at least this one connection: In their handling of the season of spring, they are both utterly subversive. Each acknowledges the symbols and sentiments that are so often attached to the season. But each then turns those on their heads to suggest

> *Though spring points to the dance of juice and joy, it does not therefore deny grit and pain.*

spiritual meanings quite different from what one might expect in an era of poetry devoted to the wonders of the natural world. For Blake, spring suggests a crisis between that which is idealized and that which is real and observed. For Burns, spring almost mockingly suggests the enormity not of abundance but of loss.

Both Blake and Burns want to point out that springtime images can also teach us through contemplating their obverse. It is not only in winter that a life can be barren. It is not only in autumn that we can experience

and sense loss. Though spring points to the dance of juice and joy, it does not
therefore deny grit and pain.

To Spring

from *Poetical Sketches*

WILLIAM BLAKE

O thou, with dewy locks, who lookest down
Thro' the clear windows of the morning, turn
Thine angel eyes upon our western isle,
Which in full choir hails thy approach, O Spring!

The hills tell each other, and the list'ning
Vallies hear; all our longing eyes are turned
Up to thy bright pavilions: issue forth,
And let thy holy feet visit our clime.

Come o'er the eastern hills, and let our winds
Kiss thy perfumed garments; let us taste
Thy morn and evening breath; scatter thy pearls
Upon our love-sick land that mourns for thee.

O deck her forth with thy fair fingers; pour
Thy soft kisses on her bosom; and put
Thy golden crown upon her languish'd head,
Whose modest tresses were bound up for thee.

The Ecchoing Green

from *Songs of Innocence*

WILLIAM BLAKE

The Sun does arise,
And make happy the skies;
The merry bells ring
To welcome the Spring;
The skylark and thrush,
The birds of the bush,
Sing louder around
To the bells' cheerful sound,
While our sports shall be seen
On the Ecchoing Green.

Old John, with white hair,
Does laugh away care,
Sitting under the oak,
Among the old folk.
They laugh at our play,
And soon they all say:
"Such, such were the joys
When we all, girls & boys,
In our youth time were seen
On the Ecchoing Green.

Till the little ones, weary,
No more can be merry;
The sun does descend,
And our sports have an end.

Round the laps of their mothers
Many sisters and brothers,
Like birds in their nest,
Are ready for rest
And sport no more seen
On the darkening Green.

Holy Thursday

from *Songs of Innocence*

WILLIAM BLAKE

'Twas on a Holy Thursday, their innocent faces clean,
The children walking two & two, in red & blue &
green,
Grey-headed beadles walk'd before, with wands as
white as snow,
Till into the high dome of Paul's they like Thames'
waters flow.

O what a multitude they seem'd, these flowers of
London town!
Seated in companies they sit with radiance all their own.
The hum of multitudes was there, but multitudes of
lambs,
Thousands of little boys & girls raising their innocent
hands.

Now like a mighty wind they raise to heaven the
voice of song,
Or like harmonious thunderings the seats of Heaven
among.

Beneath them sit the aged men, wise guardians of the
    poor;
Then cherish pity, lest you drive an angel from your
    door.

Nurse's Song

from *Songs of Innocence*

WILLIAM BLAKE

When the voices of children are heard on the green,
And laughter is heard on the hill,
My heart is at rest within my breast,
And everything else is still.

"Then come home, my children, the sun is gone down,
And the dews of night arise;
Come, come, leave off play, and let us away
Till the morning appears in the skies."

"No, no, let us play, for it is yet day,
And we cannot go to sleep;
Besides, in the sky the little birds fly
And the hills are all cover'd with sheep."

"Well, well, go & play till the light fades away
And then go home to bed."
The little ones leaped & shouted & laugh'd
And all the hills echoed.

Holy Thursday

from *Songs of Experience*

WILLIAM BLAKE

Is this a holy thing to see,
In a rich and fruitful land,
Babes reduced to misery,
Fed with cold and usurous hand?

Is that trembling cry a song?
Can it be a song of joy?
And so many children poor?
It is a land of poverty!

And their sun does never shine,
And their fields are bleak & bare,
And their ways are fill'd with thorns;
It is eternal winter there.

For where-e'er the sun does shine,
And where-e'er the rain does fall,
Babe can never hunger there,
Nor poverty the mind appall.

Nurse's Song

from *Songs of Experience*

WILLIAM BLAKE

When the voices of children are heard on the green,
And whisp'rings are in the dale,
The days of my youth rise fresh in my mind,
My face turns green and pale.

Then come home, my children, the sun is gone down,
And the dews of night arise;
Your spring & your day are wasted in play,
And your winter and night in disguise.

Now Spring Has Clad

[Inscribed to Allan Cunningham, and dated Aug. 3, 1795]

ROBERT BURNS

I.

Now spring has clad the grove in green,
        And strew'd the lea wi' flowers;
The furrow'd, waving corn is seen
        Rejoice in fostering showers;
While ilka thing in nature join
        Their sorrows to forego,
O, why thus all alone are mine
        The weary steps o' woe!

II.

The trout within yon wimpling burn
        Glides swift, a silver dart,

And, safe beneath the shady thorn,
Defies the angler's art:
My life was ance that careless stream,
That wanton trout was I,
But Love wi' unrelenting beam
Has scorch'd my fountains dry.

III.

The little floweret's peaceful lot,
In yonder cliff that grows,
Which, save the linnet's flight, I wot,
Nae ruder visit knows,
Was mine, till Love has o'er me past,
And blighted a' my bloom;
And now beneath the withering blast
My youth and joy consume.

IV.

The waken'd lav'rock warbling springs,
And climbs the early sky,
Winnowing blithe his dewy wings
In Morning's rosy eye:
As little reck't I Sorrow's power,
Until the flowery snare
O' witching Love in luckless hour
Made me the thrall o' care!

V.

O, had my fate been Greenland snows
Or Afric's burning zone,
Wi' Man and Nature leagu'd my foes

So Peggy ne'er I'd known!
The wretch, whose doom is "hope nae mair,"
What tongue his woes can tell,
Within whose bosom, save Despair,
Nae kinder spirits dwell!

Lament of Mary Queen Scots: On the Approach of Spring

ROBERT BURNS

I.

Now Nature hangs her mantle green,
On every blooming tree,
And spreads her sheets o' daisies white
Out o'er the grassy lea;
Now Phoebus cheers the crystal streams,
And glads the azure skies:
But nought can glad the weary wight
That fast in durance lies.

II.

Now laverocks wake the merry morn,
Aloft on dewy wing;
The merle, in his noontide bow'r,
Makes woodland echoes ring;
The mavis wild wi' monie a note
Sings drowsy day to rest:
In love and freedom they rejoice,
Wi' care nor thrall opprest.

III.

Now blooms the lily by the bank,
The primrose down the brae;

The hawthorn's budding in the glen,
 And milk-white is the slae:
The meanest hind in fair Scotland
 May rove their sweets amang;
But I, the Queen of a' Scotland
 Maun lie in prison strang.

IV.

I was the Queen o' bonie France,
 Where happy I hae been;
Fu' lightly rase I in the morn,
 As blithe lay down at e'en:
And I'm the sov'reign of Scotland,
 And monie a traitor there;
Yet here I lie in foreign bands
 And never-ending care.

V.

But as for thee, thou false woman,
 My sister and my fae,
Grim vengeance yet shall whet a sword
 That thro' thy soul shall gae!
The weeping blood in woman's breast
 Was never known to thee;
Nor th' balm that draps on wounds of woe
 Frae woman's pitying e'e.

VI.

My son! my son! may kinder stars
 Upon thy fortune shine;
And may those pleasures gild thy reign,

That ne'er wad blink on mine!
God keep thee frae thy mother's faes,
　　Or turn their hearts to thee;
And where thou meet'st thy mother's friend,
　　Remember him for me!

VII.
O! soon, to me, may summer suns
　　Nae mair light up the morn!
Nae mair to me the autumn winds
　　Wave o'er the yellow corn!
And in the narrow house of death,
　　Let winter round me rave;
And the next flow'rs that deck the spring
　　Bloom on my peaceful grave.

Composed in Spring

ROBERT BURNS

I.
Again rejoicing Nature sees
　　Her robe assume its vernal hues:
Her leafy locks wave in the breeze,
　　All freshly steep'd in morning dews.

Chorus
And maun I still on Menie doat
　　And bear the scorn that's in her e'e?
For it's jet, jet-black, an' it's like a hawk,
　　An' it winna let a body be.

II.

In vain to me the cowslips blaw,
    In vain to me the vi'lets spring;
In vain to me in glen or shaw,
    The mavis and the lintwhite sing.

III.

The merry ploughboy cheers his team,
    Wi' joy the tentie seedsman stalks;
But life to me's a weary dream,
    A dream of ane that never wauks.

IV.

The wanton coot the water skims,
    Amang the reeds the ducklings cry,
The stately swan majestic swims,
    And ev'ry thing is blest but I.

V.

The sheep-herd steeks his faulding slap,
    And o'er the moorlands whistles shill;
Wi' wild, unequal, wand'ring step,
    I meet him on the dewy hill.

VI.

And when the lark, 'tween light and dark,
    Blythe waukens by the daisy's side,
And mounts and sings on flittering wings,
    A woe-worn ghaist I hameward glide.

VII.

Come winter, with thine angry howl,
*   And raging, bend the naked tree;*
Thy gloom will soothe my cheerless soul,
*   When nature all is sad like me!*

Chorus
And maun I still on Menie doat,
*   And bear the scorn that's in her e'e?*
For it's jet, jet-black, an' it's like a hawk,
*   An' it winna let a body be.*

The Primrose

ROBERT BURNS

I.

Dost ask me, why I send thee here
The firstling of the infant year:
This lovely native of the vale,
That hangs so pensive and so pale?

II.

Look on its bending stalk, so weak,
That, each way yielding, doth not break,
And see how aptly it reveals
The doubts and fears a lover feels.

III.

Look on its leaves of yellow hue
Bepearl'd thus with morning dew,

And these will whisper in thine ears:—
"The sweets of loves are wash'd with tears."

Spring

GERARD MANLEY HOPKINS

Nothing is so beautiful as spring—
    When weeds, in wheels, shoot long and lovely and
        lush;
    Thrush's eggs look little low heavens, and thrush
Through the echoing timber does so rinse and wring
The ear, it strikes like lightnings to hear him sing;
    The glassy peartree leaves and blooms, they brush
    The descending blue; that blue is all in a rush
With richness; the racing lambs too have fair their
        fling.

What is all this juice and all this joy?
    A strain of the earth's sweet being in the beginning
In Eden garden.—Have, get, before it cloy,

Before it cloud, Christ, lord, and sour with sinning,
    Innocent mind and Mayday in girl and boy,
Most, O maid's child, thy choice and worthy the
        winning.

ACKNOWLEDGMENTS

We began this series of seasonal spiritual biographies with *Winter*, and come now to its conclusion with *Spring*—which seems to us just right. During this journey we have looked for ways in which each season speaks to us in terms of its rhythms, and so we conclude with a season whose rhythm is marked by a movement to warmth and light and growth and rebirth. This work is finished, we sense, and now we go out into new work—all right and appropriate.

With *Spring,* as with the other books in the series, we found a host of those willing to help, and we thank them for their generous hearts. Melissa Van Til and Stephanie Biesheuvel were responsible for much of the sometimes tedious work of scanning and typing and manipulating into computer files all the texts we found. Kathy Struck has, as always, our thanks for her work in the Calvin College Library, where she tracked down anything we asked with efficiency and grace. Our colleague Donald R. Hettinga introduced us to the work of Nancy Stringfellow via Rosalie Sorrels's CD performance. And James Vanden Bosch, our colleague and chair of our English Department, was generous as always in his willingness to run interference for us. The woodcuts of Mary Azarian again provide just the right visual balance to all the words, words, words that we love.

We are especially grateful to Irving Yucheng Lo, Professor Emeritus of East Asian Languages and Cultures and Comparative Literature at Indiana University, who generously allowed us to use his translations of Chinese poetry in both the *Winter* and *Summer* volumes. Although we never met Professor Lo in person, he was a model of kindness and grace, and we lament his passing on 5 July 2005. The poems in this volume are reprinted by permission of his widow, Lena D. Lo.

In all four books, our colleagues and former students have been liberal in their willingness to contribute to the work by offering short stories, poetry, prayers, and essays. For this volume, we wish to acknowledge three in particular. We thank Elizabeth Vander Lei, of the Calvin College English Department, for sharing the story of her first son, and Abram Van Engen, now a graduate student at Northwestern University, for his poignant essay on loss and renewal. And we thank and remember Lionel Basney, our colleague in the English Department, lost to us all too soon, but now caught up in the rebirths of that eternal spring. His devotions are reprinted by permission of his widow, Ruth Basney.

To our spouses, our loving spouses, Doug Felch and Anne Schmidt, we thank you for the ways in which you make spring— with its warmth and love and joy and celebration—perpetual.

Woodcuts by Mary Azarian, Copyright © 2005 by Mary Azarian. Reprinted by permission of the artist.

Original woodcuts may be viewed online and purchased at www.maryazarian.com or ordered from

Mary Azarian
Farmhouse Press
258 Gray Road
Plainfield, VT 05667.

PERMISSIONS

Abiel Abbot: *Sermons to Mariners.* Copyright © 1812. Public Domain.

Charles C. Abbott: "A Cheerful Fog" from *In Nature's Realm* by Charles C. Abbott. Copyright © 1900. Public Domain.

Francis Bacon: "Of Gardens" from *The Essays or, Counsels, Civil and Moral of Francis Bacon,* edited by Henry Morley. Copyright © 1883. Public Domain.

Martha Ballard: *A Midwife's Tale: The Life of Martha Ballard, Based on Her Diary, 1785-1812* edited by Laurel Thatcher Ulrich. Copyright © 1990 by Laurel Thatcher Ulrich. Used by permission of Alfred A. Knopf, a division of Random House, Inc.

Lionel Basney: *Meditations for Lent.* Copyright © 1999 by Lionel Basney. Reprinted by permission of Ruth Basney.

David Brill: "Fear" from *As Far as the Eye Can See: Reflections of an Appalachian Trail Hiker* by David Brill. Copyright © 1990 by David Brill. Reprinted by permission of the Appalachian Trail Conservancy and the author.

Scott Cairns: "Adventures in New Testament Greek: *Metanoia*" and "The Theology of Delight" from *Philokalia: New and Selected Poems* by Scott Cairns. Copyright © 2002. Reprinted by permission of the author.

Lisa Couturier: "The City's Laughter" from *The Hopes of Snakes and Other Tales from the Urban Landscape*. Copyright © 2005 by Lisa Couturier. Reprinted by permission of Beacon Press.

Barbara Crooker: "Listen" from *Literature and Belief*. Copyright © 2004 by Barbara Crooker. Reprinted by permission of the author and *Literature and Belief*.

Annie Dillard: "Untying the Knot" and selections from "The Present" from *Pilgrim at Tinker Creek*. Copyright © 1974 by Annie Dillard. Reprinted by permission of the author.

Isak Dinesen: "Some African Birds" and "I Will Not Let Thee Go Except Thou Bless Me" from *Out of Africa*. Copyright © 1937 by Random House, Inc. and renewed 1965 by Rungstedlundfonden. Used by permission of Random House, Inc.

Michael Downing: "Moon Over Miami" from *Spring Forward: The Annual Madness of Daylight Saving Time* by Michael Downing. Copyright © 2005 by Michael Downing. Reprinted by permission of Shoemaker & Hoard.

Paul Laurence Dunbar: "Dinah Kneading Dough," "Spring Song," and "In May" from *The Complete Poems of Paul Laurence Dunbar*. Copyright © 1913 by Dodd, Mead and Company. Public Domain.

Alice Morse Earle: "In Lilac Tide" from *Old-Time Gardens, Newly Set Forth* by Alice Morse Earle. Copyright © 1901. Public Domain.

Robert Finch: "Shadow on the Pond" and "Long Nook" from *Death of a Hornet and Other Cape Cod Essays* by Robert Finch. Copyright © 2000 by Robert Finch. Reprinted by permission of PublicAffairs, a member of Perseus Books, L.L.C.

Robert Frost: "To the Thawing Wind" and "A Prayer in Spring" from *A Boy's Will* by Robert Frost. Copyright © 1913 by Robert Frost. Public Domain.

Donald Hall: "Spring" from *Seasons at Eagle Pond* by Donald Hall. Copyright © 1987 by Donald Hall. Reprinted by permission of Houghton Mifflin Company. All rights reserved.

Nathaniel Hawthorne: "Buds and Bird-Voices" from *The*

Oxford Book of American Essays, edited by Brander Matthews. Copyright © 1900. Public Domain.

Thomas Wentworth Higginson: "April Days" from *Outdoor Studies [and] Poems* by Thomas Wentworth Higginson. Copyright © 1900. Public Domain.

Gerard Manley Hopkins: "Spring" from *Poems of Gerard Manley Hopkins* edited by Robert Bridges. Copyright © 1918. Public Domain.

Barbara Hurd: "Marginalia" from *Stirring the Mud: On Swamps, Bogs, and Human Imagination* by Barbara Hurd. Copyright © 2001 by Barbara Hurd. Reprinted by permission of Beacon Press, Boston.

Rebecca Cox Jackson: "The Dream of Washing Quilts" from *Gifts of Power: the Writings of Rebecca Jackson, Black Visionary, Shaker Eldress,* edited by Jean McMahon Humez. Copyright © 1981 by University of Massachusetts Press. Reprinted by permission of the University of Massachusetts Press.

Samuel Johnson: "On Spring" from *Rambler No. 5.* Copyright © 1750. Public Domain.

Jane Kenyon: "Mud Season" from *Otherwise: New & Selected Poems* by Jane Kenyon. Copyright © 2005 by the Estate of Jane Kenyon. Reprinted from *Collected Poems* with the permission of Graywolf Press, Saint Paul, Minnesota.

Barbara Kingsolver: "Called Out" from *Small Wonder* by Barbara Kingsolver. Copyright © 2002 by Barbara Kingsolver. Reprinted by permission of HarperCollins Publishers Inc.

Lucy Larcom: "Between Winter and Spring," "Apple Blossoms" and "Would You" from *The Poetical Works of Lucy Larcom.* Copyright © 1884. Public Domain.

Daniel Offord: "Returning Spring," "Welcome Spring," and "Vernal Season" from *Shaker Music, Original Inspirational Hymns and Songs Illustrative of the Resurrection Life and Testimony of the Shakers.* Copyright © 1884. Public Domain.

Noel Perrin: "Flow Gently, Sweet Maple" from *First Person Rural* by Noel Perrin. Copyright © 1978 by Noel Perrin. Reprinted by permission of David R. Godine, Publisher, Inc.

Lady Sarashina: *The Sarashina Diary* in *Diaries of Court Ladies of Old Japan,* translated by Annie Shepley Omori and Kochi Doi. Copyright © 1920 by Houghton Mifflin Company. Public Domain.

Shaker Hymns: "Spring Is Coming" and "Springtime" from *Original Shaker Music Published by the North Family of Mt. Lebanon, Col. Co., N.Y.* Copyright © 1893. Public Domain.

Ssü-K'ung T'u: "Return of Spring" from *A Lute of Jade: Being Selections from the Classical Poets of China,* translated by L. Cranmer-Byng. Copyright © 1918. Public Domain.

Nancy Stringfellow: "Report from Grimes Creek" and "Social Security" from *Report from Grimes Creek After a Hard Winter.* Copyright © 1990 by Nancy Stringfellow. Reprinted by permission of Rosalie Sorrels and Limberlost Press.

Harry Thurston: Excerpts from "March: The Day the Ice Goes Out" from *A Place between the Tides.* Copyright © 2004 by Harry Thurston. Published in Canada by Greystone Books, a division of Douglas & McIntyre Ltd. Reprinted by permission of the publisher.

Ts'en-Ts'an: "A Dream of Spring" from *A Lute of Jade: Being Selections from the Classical Poets of China,* translated by L. Cranmer-Byng. Copyright © 1918. Public Domain.

Tu Fu: "Random Pleasures: Nine Quatrains," from *Sunflower Splendor: Three Thousand Years of Chinese Poetry,* translated by Irving Yucheng Lo, edited by Wu-chi Liu and Irving Yucheng Lo. Copyright © 1975 by Wu-chi Liu and Irving Lo. Reprinted by permission of Lena D. Lo.

Elizabeth Vander Lei: "Picture Postcards." Copyright © 2005. Reprinted by permission of the author.

Abram Van Engen: "The Portico." Copyright © 2005. Reprinted by permission of the author.

Antonio Vivaldi: Translation of "Spring" by Michael Meacock. Copyright © 2005 by Michael Meacock. Reprinted by permission of the translator.

Wang Ch'ang-Ling: "Tears in the Spring" from *A Lute of Jade: Being Selections from the Classical Poets of China,* translated by L. Cranmer-Byng. Copyright © 1918. Public Domain.

Louise Beebe Wilder: "The Colour of the Young Year" from *Colour in My Garden* by Louise Beebe Wilder. Copyright © 1918. Public Domain.

Molly Wolf: Excerpt from "Two Pieces in Mud Season" from *White China: Finding the Divine in the Everyday* by Molly Wolf. Copyright © 2005 by Molly Wolf. Reprinted with permission of John Wiley & Sons, Inc.

Dorothy Wordsworth: Entries from the Grasmere Journals from *The Journals of Dorothy Wordsworth,* transcribed by William Knight. Copyright © 1897. Public Domain.

Allen M. Young: "Spring Peepers" from *Small Creatures and Ordinary Places* by Allen M. Young. Copyright © 2000 by Allen M. Young. Reprinted by permission of the University of Wisconsin Press.

NOTES

Preface

Louisa May Alcott's juvenile poem, "To the First Robin," was published in J. S. P. Alcott, *The Story of the Alcotts* (Boston: Little, Brown, 1889), 4. The lines from the Song of Solomon 2:10–13 are from the King James Version of the Scriptures. Henry Timrod's "Spring's Lessons" was first published in *The Carolinian,* and is here reprinted from Paul H. Hayne, ed., *The Poems of Henry Timrod* (New York: E. J. Hale and Son, 1873), 49–50. The definitions of "spring" are drawn from Samuel Johnson, *A Dictionary of the English Language,* 11th ed., revised and corrected (London: J. Johnson, 1799). The Alexander Pope quotation is from "An Essay on Man," Epistle 1: line 95. Gerard Manley Hopkins's "Spring" was penned in 1877; Robert Bridges, Hopkins's literary executor, printed it in *Poems of Gerard Manley Hopkins* (London: H. Milford, 1918). Christina Rossetti's "Spring" was published in her *Poems by Christina Rossetti* (Boston: Little, Brown, 1899), 34–35. Selections from the prayers from the *Vedas* and from the poet Surdas may both be found in George Appleton, ed., *The Oxford Book of Prayer* (London: Oxford University Press, 1985): #865 (285) and #873 (288). References to the

Shaker hymns are drawn from Daniel Offord, *Shaker Music, Original Inspirational Hymns and Songs* (New York: William A. Pond, 1884), 13, 28, 102–103, 151, 243–244; and *Original Shaker Music Published by the North Family of Mt. Lebanon, Col. Co., N.Y.* (New York: William A. Pond, 1893), 102, 172, 173.

Part One: Stirrings

Introduction: The stirrings of spring in Narnia are described by C. S. Lewis in *The Lion, the Witch and the Wardrobe* (New York: Macmillan, 1950), 100. Gertrude Jekyll's description of her garden is found in *Wood and Garden* (London: Longmans, Green, 1899), 44. The picture of the Michigan farm boy is from Jim Heynen's "Spring," in *The One-Room Schoolhouse: Stories about the Boys* (New York: Random House, 1993), 55. The two passages from the Psalmist are taken from the King James Version: Psalm 30:5 and 126:5.

The Shaker hymn "Spring Is Coming" is taken from *Original Shaker Music Published by the North Family of Mt. Lebanon, Col. Co., N.Y.* (New York: William A. Pond, 1893), 172.

Jane Kenyon's poem "Mud Season" was first published in *The Boat of Quiet Hours* (1986) and is taken here from *Otherwise: New & Selected Poems* (St. Paul, MN: Graywolf Press, 1996), 87.

Molly Wolf's selection is from *White China: Finding the Divine in the Everyday* (San Francisco: Jossey-Bass, 2005), 92–95.

Barbara Hurd's "Marginalia" is chapter 1 of *Stirring the Mud: On Swamps, Bogs, and Human Imagination* (Boston and New York: Houghton Mifflin, 2003), 1–9, 13–14.

Lucy Larcom's poems were collected in *The Poetical Works of Lucy Larcom* (Boston: Houghton Mifflin, 1884). These poems are taken from the *Household* edition, pages 238, 37–38, 42–43, and 46–47.

Harry Thurston's "March: The Day the Ice Goes Out" is taken from *A Place between the Tides* (Vancouver: Greystone Books, 2004), 47–67.

"Spring Peepers" is from Allen M. Young's *Small Creatures and*

Ordinary Places (Madison: University of Wisconsin Press, 2000), 31–38.

Nathaniel Hawthorne's "Buds and Bird-Voices" was first published in 1846 and is taken here from *Mosses from an Old Manse,* vol. 1 (Boston and New York: Houghton, Mifflin and Company, 1900), 205–219.

Thomas Wentworth Higginson's "April Days" is taken from *Outdoor Studies [and] Poems* (New York: Houghton, Mifflin and Co., 1900), 55–83.

"Report from Grimes Creek After a Hard Winter" is taken from Nancy Stringfellow's *Report from Grimes Greek After a Hard Winter* (Boise, ID: Limberlost Press, 1990), 1–2. The comment from Rosalie Sorrels is on page 5.

Part Two: Awakenings

Introduction: Robert Murphy, *The Peregrine Falcon* (Boston: Houghton Mifflin, 1963), 3–4. The passage from Henry David Thoreau's *Walden* is taken from the very conclusion of the text. Thomas Carew's "The Spring" has been published in R. Dunlap, ed., *The Poems of Thomas Carew* (Oxford: Clarendon Press, 1949). The lines cited here are 5–8, 11–12, 22–24. Thoreau's letter is cited from a British retrospective of his life that appeared in *The Eclectic Magazine of Foreign Literature, Science, and Art,* new series 4 (August 1866), 180–195.

The Shaker hymn "Returning Spring" is taken from Daniel Offord, *Shaker Music, Original Inspirational Hymns and Songs Illustrative of the Resurrection Life and Testimony of the Shakers* (New York: William A. Pond, 1884), 13.

"A Cheerful Fog" is taken from Charles C. Abbott's *In Nature's Realm* (Trenton, NJ: Albert Brandt, 1900), 95–108.

Noel Perrin's "Flow Gently, Sweet Maple" is from *First Person Rural* (Boston: Godine, 1978), 81–85.

"Shadow on the Pond" and "Long Nook" are both from Robert Finch's *Death of a Hornet and Other Cape Cod Essays* (Washington, DC: Counterpoint, 2000), 16–20; 186–189.

"Random Pleasures: Nine Quatrains" by Tu Fu is translated by Irving Yucheng Lo in *Sunflower Splendor: Three Thousand Years of Chinese Poetry*, edited by Wu-chi Liu and Irving Yucheng Lo (Bloomington: Indiana University Press, 1975), 134–136.

"The Works and Wonders of God in the Deep, Observed and Improved," is from Abiel Abbot's *Sermons to Mariners* (Boston: Samuel T. Armstrong, 1812), 9–27.

Rebecca Cox Jackson's "The Dream of Washing Quilts" is taken from her autobiographical writings, collected and edited by Jean McMahon Humez in *Gifts of Power: The Writings of Rebecca Jackson, Black Visionary, Shaker Eldress* (Amherst: The University of Massachusetts Press, 1981), 100–102.

Lisa Couturier's selection from "The City's Laughter" is taken from *The Hopes of Snakes and Other Tales from the Urban Landscape* (Boston: Beacon Press, 2005), 28–33.

Michael Downing's "Moon Over Miami" is taken from *Spring Forward: The Annual Madness of Daylight Saving Time* by Michael Downing (Washington, DC: Shoemaker and Hoard, 2005), 35–38.

"Untying the Knot" and selections from "The Present" are taken from Annie Dillard, *Pilgrim at Tinker Creek* (New York: Harper's Magazine Press, 1974), 72–82.

"To the Thawing Wind" and "A Prayer in Spring" by Robert Frost may be found in *A Boy's Will* (New York: Henry Holt, 1915), 22–23.

Part Three: Growth

Introduction: The golden-green leaves of spring are recounted in Robert Frost's "Nothing Gold Can Stay," first published in *New Hampshire* (1923) and included in *The Poetry of Robert Frost: The Collected Poems*, edited by Edward Connery Lathem (New York: Henry Holt, 1969), 222. Henry Howard's sonnet "The Soote Season" was first printed in *Songes and sonettes, written by the right honorable Lorde Henry Haward late Earle of Surrey, and other*, better known as *Tottel's Miscellany* (London: Richard Tottel, 1557), signature A2v. *Soote* means "sweet"; *flete,* "float"; and *mings,* "mingles." The text is modernized by the editors. "Listen" by Barbara Crooker was first published in *Literature and Belief* 24 (2004): 182.

The Shaker hymn "Springtime" is taken from *Original Shaker Music Published by the North Family of Mt. Lebanon, Col. Co., N.Y.* (New York: William A. Pond, 1893), 102.

Francis Bacon's "Of Gardens" was first printed in the last, enlarged edition of his essays (1625) published before his death; the text here, with slight modifications, is taken from *The Essays or, Counsels, Civil and Moral of Francis Bacon,* edited by Henry Morley (New York: A. L. Burt, 1883), 225–233.

The diary entries from Martha Ballard are taken from *A Midwife's Tale: The Life of Martha Ballard, Based on Her Diary, 1785–1812,* edited by Laurel Thatcher Ulrich (New York: Knopf, 1990), 309–314.

"The Colour of the Young Year" is taken from *Colour in My Garden* by Louise Beebe Wilder (Garden City, NY: Doubleday, 1918), 39–53.

Selections from "In Lilac Tide" are taken from *Old-Time Gardens, Newly Set Forth* by Alice Morse Earle (New York: The Macmillan Co., 1901), 132–160.

"Called Out" was written by Barbara Kingsolver with Steven Hopp and is taken from *Small Wonder* by Barbara Kingsolver (New York: HarperCollins, 2002), 88–92.

Samuel Johnson's "On Spring" was first published in the *Rambler* on April 3, 1750, the fifth issue of that journal. It is printed more accessibly in Samuel Johnson, *The Rambler,* edited by W. J. Bate and Albrecht B. Strauss in *The Yale Edition of the Works of Samuel Johnson,* vol. 3 (New Haven: Yale University Press, 1969), 25–30.

Dorothy Wordsworth's *Grasmere Journals* have been most recently transcribed from their manuscripts in *Journals of Dorothy Wordsworth,* edited by Mary Moorman (Oxford: Oxford University Press, 1971). They were first transcribed by William Knight in *The Journals of Dorothy Wordsworth* (London: Macmillan, 1897). The present text is taken from the earlier transcription, pages 105–119.

"Spring" by Donald Hall is taken from *Seasons at Eagle Pond* (New York: Ticknor & Fields, 1987), 23–40.

Part Four: Pilgrimage

Introduction: The lines by Po Chü-i are from "The Flower Fair" translated by L. Cranmer-Byng in *A Lute of Jade: Being Selections from the Classical Poets of China* (New York: E. P. Dutton, 1918), 95.

The Shaker hymn "Welcome Spring" is taken from Daniel Offord, *Shaker Music, Original Inspirational Hymns and Songs Illustrative of the Resurrection Life and Testimony of the Shakers* (New York: William A. Pond, 1884), 102.

The lines by Geoffrey Chaucer are the introduction to his "General Prologue" for the *Canterbury Tales* (lines 1–18). The present translation is by the editors.

The writer of this Japanese classic is identified in the text only as Takasue no Musume (Takasue's daughter), but she has become known as the Lady Sarashina from an allusion in one of her poems to the mountainous Sarashina district in central Japan. Our selection is taken from *The Sarashina Diary* in *Diaries of Court Ladies of Old Japan,* translated by Annie Shepley Omori and Kochi Doi (Boston: Houghton Mifflin, 1920), 46–52.

"Fear" is taken from *As Far as the Eye Can See: Reflections of an Appalachian Trail Hiker* by David Brill (Nashville, TN: Rutledge Hill Press, 1990), 21–33.

The three African American spirituals collected here are readily available in many editions, along with their transcribed music. Those wishing to read these within their larger African contexts might see the first two sections of Patricia Liggins Hill's magisterial collection, *Call and Response: The Riverside Anthology of the African American Literary Tradition* (Boston: Houghton Mifflin, 1998).

Lionel Basney's "Meditations for Lent" were first published in *The Banner* (February 1999); they are available at www.calvin.edu/academic/engl/people/basney/med_lb1.htm. Basney's environmental call is *An Earth-Careful Way of Life* (Downer's Grove, IL: InterVarsity Press, 1994).

"Adventures in New Testament Greek: *Metanoia*" by Scott Cairns was first published in *Philokalia: New and Selected Poems* (2002). "The Theology of Delight" was first published in *The Theology of Doubt* (1985). Both poems are here taken from *Philokalia: New and Selected Poems* (Lincoln, NE: Zoo Press, 2002), 15, 58.

Part Five: Dance

Introduction: The lines from William Wordsworth are from the second book of *The Excursion,* lines 118–137. The sonnet is presumed to have been written by Vivaldi himself; the translation is by Michael Meacock. The lines from James Thomson's "Spring" are taken from *The Seasons* by James Thomson (London: W. Strahan, et al., 1778), 12; "The charming agonies of love" is also from Thomson's "Spring," page 41. The notion of balance as dance was proffered by Calvin College colleagues John Hare and John Netland. Images from Hans Holbein's *Dance of Death* may be viewed at http://www.image.pe.ca/index/woodcut/holbien.html. The quotations from *Perelandra* are from the last chapter: C. S. Lewis, *Perelandra* (New York: Macmillan, 1944), 222–225; 232. The words of the prophet as found in Jeremiah 31:11–13 are taken from the Geneva translation of the Bible (1560).

The Shaker hymn "Vernal Season" is taken from Daniel Offord, *Shaker Music, Original Inspirational Hymns and Songs Illustrative of the Resurrection Life and Testimony of the Shakers* (New York: William A. Pond, 1884), 151.

"Some African Birds" and "I Will Not Let Thee Go Except Thou Bless Me" by Isak Dinesen are taken from *Out of Africa* (New York: Random House, 1937), 270–271, 278–280.

Edmund Spenser's *The Shepherd's Calendar* was first published in 1579 and appears in all standard editions of Spenser's poetry, such as J. C. Smith and E. De Selincourt's *Spenser: Poetical Works* (Oxford:

Oxford University Press, 1912). The text here is edited and modernized by the editors.

The poems by Paul Laurence Dunbar are all found in *The Complete Poems of Paul Laurence Dunbar* (New York: Dodd, Mead, 1920), 188–189, 26, 166.

The poems by Ts'en-Ts'an, Ssü-K'ung T'u, and Wang Ch'ang-Ling as translated by L. Cranmer-Byng can be found in *A Lute of Jade: Being Selections from the Classical Poets of China* (New York: E. P. Dutton, 1918), 48–49, 105, 66.

"Picture Postcards" by Elizabeth Vander Lei is original to this volume.

"The Portico" by Abram Van Engen is original to this volume.

"Social Security" is taken from Nancy Stringfellow's *Report from Grimes Greek After a Hard Winter* (Boise, ID: Limberlost Press, 1990), 11–14.

William Blake's "To Spring" is from his *Poetical Sketches,* written between 1769 and 1777. The book was printed in 1783, but never offered for sale. "The Ecchoing Green," the first "Holy Thursday," and the first "Nurse's Song" were composed for *Songs of Innocence,* published in 1789; the second "Holy Thursday" and the second "Nurse's Song" was included in the companion volume—actually printed with *Songs of Innocence*—as *Songs of Experience,* published in 1794, two years before Blake's death. The standard edition for all of Blake's writing is *The Poetry and Prose of William Blake,* edited by David Erdman and Harold Bloom (Garden City, NY: Doubleday, 1965, rev. 1981). The standard edition for Robert Burns's poems and songs is still the *Centenary Edition,* edited by W. E. Henley and T. F. Henderson, 4 vols. (Boston and New York: Houghton, Mifflin, 1896–1897). Gerard Manley Hopkins's "Spring" was penned in 1877; Robert Bridges, Hopkins's literary executor, printed it in *Poems of Gerard Manley Hopkins* (London: H. Milford, 1918).

AVAILABLE FROM BETTER BOOKSTORES. TRY YOUR BOOKSTORE FIRST.

Global Spiritual Perspectives

Spiritual Perspectives on America's Role as Superpower
by the Editors at SkyLight Paths
Are we the world's good neighbor or a global bully? From a spiritual perspective, what are America's responsibilities as the only remaining superpower? Contributors: **Dr. Beatrice Bruteau • Rev. Dr. Joan Brown Campbell • Tony Campolo • Rev. Forrest Church • Lama Surya Das • Matthew Fox • Kabir Helminski • Thich Nhat Hanh • Eboo Patel • Abbot M. Basil Pennington, ocso • Dennis Prager • Rosemary Radford Ruether • Wayne Teasdale • Rev. William McD. Tully • Rabbi Arthur Waskow • John Wilson**
5½ x 8½, 256 pp, Quality PB, ISBN 1-893361-81-0 **$16.95**

Spiritual Perspectives on Globalization, 2nd Edition
Making Sense of Economic and Cultural Upheaval
by Ira Rifkin; Foreword by Dr. David Little, Harvard Divinity School
What is globalization? Surveys the religious landscape, explaining in clear and non-judgmental language the beliefs that motivate spiritual leaders, activists, theologians, academics, and others involved on all sides of the issue. Includes a new Afterword and Discussion Guide designed for group use.
5½ x 8½, 256 pp, Quality PB, ISBN 1-59473-045-8 **$16.99**

Hinduism / Vedanta

Meditation & Its Practices: A Definitive Guide to Techniques and Traditions of Meditation in Yoga and Vedanta
by Swami Adiswarananda
The complete sourcebook for exploring Hinduism's two most time-honored traditions of meditation.
6 x 9, 504 pp, HC, ISBN 1-893361-83-7 **$34.95**

The Spiritual Quest and the Way of Yoga: The Goal, the Journey and the Milestones *by Swami Adiswarananda*
The Yoga way to attain the goal of life and overcome obstacles on the spiritual path.
6 x 9, 288 pp, HC, ISBN 1-59473-113-6 **$29.99**

Sri Ramakrishna, the Face of Silence
by Swami Nikhilananda and Dhan Gopal Mukerji
Edited with an Introduction by Swami Adiswarananda; Foreword by Dhan Gopal Mukerji II
Classic biographies present the life of Sri Ramakrishna and explain systems of Indian thought intimately connected with his life.
6 x 9, 352 pp, HC, ISBN 1-59473-115-2 **$29.99**

Sri Sarada Devi, The Holy Mother: Her Teachings and Conversations
Translated and with Notes by Swami Nikhilananda
Edited and with an Introduction by Swami Adiswarananda
Brings to life the Holy Mother's teachings on human affliction, self-control, and peace.
6 x 9, 288 pp, HC, ISBN 1-59473-070-9 **$29.99**

The Vedanta Way to Peace and Happiness
by Swami Adiswarananda
Introduces the timeless teachings of Vedanta—divinity of the individual soul, unity of all existence, and oneness with the Divine.
6 x 9, 240 pp, HC, ISBN 1-59473-034-2 **$29.99**

Or phone, fax, mail or e-mail to: SKYLIGHT PATHS Publishing
Sunset Farm Offices, Route 4 • P.O. Box 237 • Woodstock, Vermont 05091
Tel: (802) 457-4000 • Fax: (802) 457-4004 • www.skylightpaths.com
Credit card orders: (800) 962-4544 (8:30AM–5:30PM ET Monday–Friday)
Generous discounts on quantity orders. SATISFACTION GUARANTEED. Prices subject to change.

Kabbalah from Jewish Lights Publishing

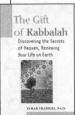

Ehyeh: A Kabbalah for Tomorrow by Dr. Arthur Green
6 x 9, 224 pp, Quality PB, ISBN 1-58023-213-2 **$16.99**; HC, ISBN 1-58023-125-X **$21.95**

The Enneagram and Kabbalah: Reading Your Soul by Rabbi Howard A. Addison
6 x 9, 176 pp, Quality PB, ISBN 1-58023-001-6 **$15.95**

Finding Joy: A Practical Spiritual Guide to Happiness by Dannel I. Schwartz with Mark Hass
6 x 9, 192 pp, Quality PB, ISBN 1-58023-009-1 **$14.95**; HC, ISBN 1-879045-53-2 **$19.95**

The Gift of Kabbalah: Discovering the Secrets of Heaven, Renewing Your Life on Earth
by Tamar Frankiel, Ph.D.
6 x 9, 256 pp, Quality PB, ISBN 1-58023-141-1 **$16.95**; HC, ISBN 1-58023-108-X **$21.95**

Zohar: Annotated & Explained
Translation and annotation by Dr. Daniel C. Matt. Foreword by Andrew Harvey
5½ x 8½, 160 pp, Quality PB, ISBN 1-893361-51-9 **$15.99**

Meditation / Prayer

Prayers to an Evolutionary God
by William Cleary; Afterword by Diarmuid O'Murchu

How is it possible to pray when God is dislocated from heaven, dispersed all around us, and more of a creative force than an all-knowing father? Inspired by the spiritual and scientific teachings of Diarmuid O'Murchu and Teilhard de Chardin, Cleary reveals that religion and science can be combined to create an expanding view of the universe—an evolutionary faith.
6 x 9, 208 pp, HC, ISBN 1-59473-006-7 **$21.99**

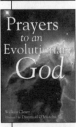

The Song of Songs: A Spiritual Commentary
by M. Basil Pennington, OCSO; Illustrations by Phillip Ratner

Join M. Basil Pennington as he ruminates on the Bible's most challenging mystical text. You will follow a path into the Songs that weaves through his inspired words and the evocative drawings of Jewish artist Phillip Ratner—a path that reveals your own humanity and leads to the deepest delight of your soul.
6 x 9, 160 pp, HC, 14 b/w illus., ISBN 1-59473-004-0 **$19.99**

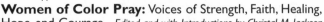

Women of Color Pray: Voices of Strength, Faith, Healing, Hope, and Courage   Edited and with Introductions by Christal M. Jackson

Through these prayers, poetry, lyrics, meditations and affirmations, you will share in the strong and undeniable connection women of color share with God. It will challenge you to explore new ways of prayerful expression.
5 x 7¼, 208 pp, Quality PB, ISBN 1-59473-077-6 **$15.99**

The Art of Public Prayer, 2nd Edition: Not for Clergy Only
by Lawrence A. Hoffman   6 x 9, 288 pp, Quality PB, ISBN 1-893361-06-3 **$18.95**

Finding Grace at the Center: The Beginning of Centering Prayer
by M. Basil Pennington, ocso, Thomas Keating, ocso, and Thomas E. Clarke, SJ
5 x 7¼, 112 pp, HC, ISBN 1-893361-69-1 **$14.95**

A Heart of Stillness: A Complete Guide to Learning the Art of Meditation
by David A. Cooper   5½ x 8½, 272 pp, Quality PB, ISBN 1-893361-03-9 **$16.95**

Meditation without Gurus: A Guide to the Heart of Practice
by Clark Strand   5½ x 8½, 192 pp, Quality PB, ISBN 1-893361-93-4 **$16.95**

Praying with Our Hands: Twenty-One Practices of Embodied Prayer from the World's Spiritual Traditions   by Jon M. Sweeney; Photographs by Jennifer J. Wilson; Foreword by Mother Tessa Bielecki; Afterword by Taitetsu Unno, PhD
8 x 8, 96 pp, 22 duotone photographs, Quality PB, ISBN 1-893361-16-0 **$16.95**

Silence, Simplicity & Solitude: A Complete Guide to Spiritual Retreat at Home
by David A. Cooper   5½ x 8½, 336 pp, Quality PB, ISBN 1-893361-04-7 **$16.95**

Three Gates to Meditation Practice: A Personal Journey into Sufism, Buddhism, and Judaism   by David A. Cooper   5½ x 8½, 240 pp, Quality PB, ISBN 1-893361-22-5 **$16.95**

Women Pray: Voices through the Ages, from Many Faiths, Cultures, and Traditions
Edited and with introductions by Monica Furlong
5 x 7¼, 256 pp, Quality PB, ISBN 1-59473-071-7 **$15.99**;
Deluxe HC with ribbon marker, ISBN 1-893361-25-X **$19.95**

Spiritual Biography—SkyLight Lives

SkyLight Lives reintroduces the lives and works of key spiritual figures of our time—people who by their teaching or example have challenged our assumptions about spirituality and have caused us to look at it in new ways.

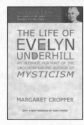 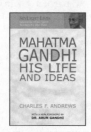  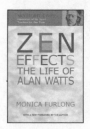

The Life of Evelyn Underhill
An Intimate Portrait of the Groundbreaking Author of *Mysticism*
by Margaret Cropper; Foreword by Dana Greene
Evelyn Underhill was a passionate writer and teacher who wrote elegantly on mysticism, worship, and devotional life. This is the story of how she made her way toward spiritual maturity, from her early days of agnosticism to the years when her influence was felt throughout the world.
6 x 9, 288 pp, 5 b/w photos, Quality PB, ISBN 1-893361-70-5 **$18.95**

Mahatma Gandhi: His Life and Ideas
by Charles F. Andrews; Foreword by Dr. Arun Gandhi
Examines from a contemporary Christian activist's point of view the religious ideas and political dynamics that influenced the birth of the peaceful resistance movement, the primary tool that Gandhi and the people of his homeland would use to gain India its freedom from British rule.
6 x 9, 336 pp, 5 b/w photos, Quality PB, ISBN 1-893361-89-6 **$18.95**

Simone Weil: A Modern Pilgrimage
by Robert Coles
The extraordinary life of the spiritual philosopher who's been called both saint and madwoman. Robert Coles' intriguing study of Weil is an insightful portrait of the beloved and controversial thinker whose life and writings influenced many (from T. S. Eliot to Adrienne Rich to Albert Camus), and continue to inspire seekers everywhere.
6 x 9, 208 pp, Quality PB, ISBN 1-893361-34-9 **$16.95**

Zen Effects: The Life of Alan Watts
by Monica Furlong
Through his widely popular books and lectures, Alan Watts (1915–1973) did more to introduce Eastern philosophy and religion to Western minds than any figure before or since. Here is the first and only full-length biography of one of the most charismatic spiritual leaders of the twentieth century.
6 x 9, 264 pp, Quality PB, ISBN 1-893361-32-2 **$16.95**

More Spiritual Biography

Bede Griffiths: An Introduction to His Interspiritual Thought
by Wayne Teasdale 6 x 9, 288 pp, Quality PB, ISBN 1-893361-77-2 **$18.95**

Inspired Lives: Exploring the Role of Faith and Spirituality in the Lives of Extraordinary People
by Joanna Laufer and Kenneth S. Lewis 6 x 9, 256 pp, Quality PB, ISBN 1-893361-33-0 **$16.95**

Spiritual Innovators: Seventy-Five Extraordinary People Who Changed the World in the Past Century *Edited by Ira Rifkin and the Editors at SkyLight Paths; Foreword by Robert Coles*
6 x 9, 304 pp, b/w photographs, Quality PB, ISBN 1-893361-50-0 **$16.95**; HC, ISBN 1-893361-43-8 **$24.95**

White Fire: A Portrait of Women Spiritual Leaders in America
by Rabbi Malka Drucker; Photographs by Gay Block
7 x 10, 320 pp, 30+ b/w photos, HC, ISBN 1-893361-64-0 **$24.95**

Spirituality

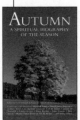

Autumn: A Spiritual Biography of the Season
Edited by Gary Schmidt and Susan M. Felch; Illustrations by Mary Azarian
Rejoice in autumn as a time of preparation and reflection. Includes Wendell Berry, David James Duncan, Robert Frost, A. Bartlett Giamatti, Kimiko Hahn, P. D. James, Julian of Norwich, Garret Keizer, Tracy Kidder, Anne Lamott, May Sarton.
6 x 9, 320 pp, 5 b/w illus., Quality PB, ISBN 1-59473-118-7 **$18.99**; HC, ISBN 1-59473-005-9 **$22.99**

Awakening the Spirit, Inspiring the Soul
30 Stories of Interspiritual Discovery in the Community of Faiths
Edited by Brother Wayne Teasdale and Martha Howard, MD; Foreword by Joan Borysenko, PhD
Thirty original spiritual mini-biographies that showcase the varied ways that people come to faith—and what that means—in today's multi-religious world.
6 x 9, 224 pp, HC, ISBN 1-59473-039-3 **$21.99**

Summer: A Spiritual Biography of the Season
Edited by Gary Schmidt and Susan M. Felch; Illustrations by Mary Azarian
"A sumptuous banquet.... These selections lift up an exquisite wholeness found within an everyday sophistication."— ★ *Publishers Weekly* starred review
Includes Anne Lamott, Luci Shaw, Ray Bradbury, Richard Selzer, Thomas Lynch, Walt Whitman, Carl Sandburg, Sherman Alexie, Madeleine L'Engle, Jamaica Kincaid.
6 x 9, 304 pp, 5 b/w illus., Hardcover, ISBN 1-59473-083-0 **$21.99**

Winter: A Spiritual Biography of the Season
Edited by Gary Schmidt and Susan M. Felch; Illustrations by Barry Moser
"This outstanding anthology features top-flight nature and spirituality writers on the fierce, inexorable season of winter.... Remarkably lively and warm, despite the icy subject." — ★ *Publishers Weekly* starred review.
Includes Will Campbell, Rachel Carson, Annie Dillard, Donald Hall, Ron Hansen, Jane Kenyon, Jamaica Kincaid, Barry Lopez, Kathleen Norris, John Updike, E. B. White.
6 x 9, 288 pp, 6 b/w illus., Deluxe PB w/flaps, ISBN 1-893361-92-6 **$18.95**; HC, ISBN 1-893361-53-5 **$21.95**

The Alphabet of Paradise: An A–Z of Spirituality for Everyday Life
by Howard Cooper 5 x 7¼, 224 pp, Quality PB, ISBN 1-893361-80-2 **$16.95**

Creating a Spiritual Retirement: A Guide to the Unseen Possibilities in Our Lives
by Molly Srode 6 x 9, 208 pp, b/w photos, Quality PB, ISBN 1-59473-050-42 **$14.99**; HC, ISBN 1-893361-75-6 **$19.95**

The Geography of Faith: Underground Conversations on Religious, Political and Social Change *by Daniel Berrigan and Robert Coles; Updated introduction and afterword by the authors* 6 x 9, 224 pp, Quality PB, ISBN 1-893361-40-3 **$16.95**

God Lives in Glass: Reflections of God for Adults through the Eyes of Children
by Robert J. Landy, PhD; Foreword by Sandy Eisenberg Sasso
7 x 6, 64 pp, HC, Full-color illus., ISBN 1-893361-30-6 **$12.95**

God Within: Our Spiritual Future—As Told by Today's New Adults *Edited by Jon M. Sweeney and the Editors at SkyLight Paths* 6 x 9, 176 pp, Quality PB, ISBN 1-893361-15-2 **$14.95**

Jewish Spirituality: A Brief Introduction for Christians *by Lawrence Kushner*
5½ x 8½, 112 pp, Quality PB, ISBN 1-58023-150-0 **$12.95** *(a Jewish Lights book)*

A Jewish Understanding of the New Testament
by Rabbi Samuel Sandmel; New preface by Rabbi David Sandmel
5½ x 8½, 384 pp, Quality PB, ISBN 1-59473-048-2 **$19.99**

Journeys of Simplicity: Traveling Light with Thomas Merton, Bashō, Edward Abbey, Annie Dillard & Others *by Philip Harnden* 5 x 7¼, 128 pp, HC, ISBN 1-893361-76-4 **$16.95**

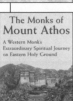

Keeping Spiritual Balance As We Grow Older: More than 65 Creative Ways to Use Purpose, Prayer, and the Power of Spirit to Build a Meaningful Retirement
by Molly and Bernie Srode 8 x 8, 224 pp, Quality PB, ISBN 1-59473-042-3 **$16.99**

The Monks of Mount Athos: A Western Monk's Extraordinary Spiritual Journey on Eastern Holy Ground *by M. Basil Pennington, ocso; Foreword by Archimandrite Dionysios*
6 x 9, 256 pp, 10+ b/w line drawings, Quality PB, ISBN 1-893361-78-0 **$18.95**

One God Clapping: The Spiritual Path of a Zen Rabbi *by Alan Lew with Sherril Jaffe*
5½ x 8½, 336 pp, Quality PB, ISBN 1-58023-115-2 **$16.95** *(a Jewish Lights book)*

Spiritual Practice

Divining the Body
Reclaim the Holiness of Your Physical Self   *by Jan Phillips*
A practical and inspiring guidebook for connecting the body and soul in spiritual practice. Leads you into a milieu of reverence, mystery and delight, helping you discover a redeemed sense of self.
8 x 8, 256 pp, Quality PB, ISBN 1-59473-080-6 **$16.99**

Finding Time for the Timeless
Spirituality in the Workweek   *by John McQuiston II*
Simple, refreshing stories that provide you with examples of how you can refocus and enrich your daily life using prayer or meditation, ritual and other forms of spiritual practice.   5½ x 6½, 208 pp, HC, ISBN 1-59473-035-0 **$17.99**

The Gospel of Thomas: A Guidebook for Spiritual Practice
by Ron Miller; Translations by Stevan Davies
An innovative guide to bring a new spiritual classic into daily life. Offers a way to translate the wisdom of the Gospel of Thomas into daily practice, manifesting in your life the same consciousness revealed in Jesus of Nazareth. Written for readers of all religious backgrounds, this guidebook will help you to apply Jesus's wisdom to your own life and to the world around you.
6 x 9, 160 pp, Quality PB, ISBN 1-59473-047-4 **$14.99**

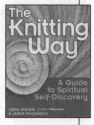

The Knitting Way: A Guide to Spiritual Self-Discovery
by Linda Skolnik and Janice MacDaniels
Through sharing stories, hands-on explorations and daily cultivation, Skolnik and MacDaniels help you see beyond the surface of a simple craft in order to discover ways in which nuances of knitting can apply to the larger scheme of life and spirituality. Includes original knitting patterns.
7 x 9, 240 pp, Quality PB, ISBN 1-59473-079-2 **$16.99**

Earth, Water, Fire, and Air: Essential Ways of Connecting to Spirit
by Cait Johnson   6 x 9, 224 pp, HC, ISBN 1-893361-65-9 **$19.95**

Forty Days to Begin a Spiritual Life
Today's Most Inspiring Teachers Help You on Your Way
Edited by Maura Shaw and the Editors at SkyLight Paths; Foreword by Dan Wakefield
7 x 9, 144 pp, Quality PB, ISBN 1-893361-48-9 **$16.95**

Labyrinths from the Outside In
Walking to Spiritual Insight—A Beginner's Guide
by Donna Schaper and Carole Ann Camp
6 x 9, 208 pp, b/w illus. and photographs, Quality PB, ISBN 1-893361-18-7 **$16.95**

Practicing the Sacred Art of Listening: A Guide to Enrich Your Relationships
and Kindle Your Spiritual Life—The Listening Center Workshop
by Kay Lindahl   8 x 8, 176 pp, Quality PB, ISBN 1-893361-85-3 **$16.95**

The Sacred Art of Bowing: Preparing to Practice
by Andi Young   5½ x 8½, 128 pp, b/w illus., Quality PB, ISBN 1-893361-82-9 **$14.95**

The Sacred Art of Chant: Preparing to Practice
by Ana Hernandez   5½ x 8½, 192 pp, Quality PB, ISBN 1-59473-036-9 **$15.99**

The Sacred Art of Fasting: Preparing to Practice
by Thomas Ryan, CSP   5½ x 8½, 192 pp, Quality PB, ISBN 1-59473-078-4 **$15.99**

The Sacred Art of Listening: Forty Reflections for Cultivating a Spiritual Practice
by Kay Lindahl; Illustrations by Amy Schnapper
8 x 8, 160 pp, Illus., Quality PB, ISBN 1-893361-44-6 **$16.99**

Sacred Speech: A Practical Guide for Keeping Spirit in Your Speech
by Rev. Donna Schaper   6 x 9, 176 pp, Quality PB, ISBN 1-59473-068-7 **$15.99**;
HC, ISBN 1-893361-74-8 **$21.95**

Spirituality

Prayer for People Who Think Too Much
A Guide to Everyday, Anywhere Prayer from the World's Faith Traditions   *by Mitch Finley*
5½ x 8½, 224 pp, Quality PB, ISBN 1-893361-21-7 **$16.99**; HC, ISBN 1-893361-00-4 **$21.95**

The Shaman's Quest: Journeys in an Ancient Spiritual Practice
by Nevill Drury; with a Basic Introduction to Shamanism by Tom Cowan
5½ x 8½, 208 pp, Quality PB, ISBN 1-893361-68-3 **$16.95**

Show Me Your Way: The Complete Guide to Exploring Interfaith Spiritual Direction
by Howard A. Addison   5½ x 8½, 240 pp, Quality PB, ISBN 1-893361-41-1 **$16.95**;
HC, ISBN 1-893361-12-8 **$21.95**

Spirituality 101: The Indispensable Guide to Keeping—or Finding—Your Spiritual Life
on Campus   *by Harriet L. Schwartz, with contributions from college students at nearly thirty campuses across the United States*   6 x 9, 272 pp, Quality PB, ISBN 1-59473-000-8 **$16.99**

Spiritually Incorrect: Finding God in All the Wrong Places
by Dan Wakefield; Illus. by Marian DelVecchio
5½ x 8½, 192 pp, b/w illus., Quality PB, ISBN 1-59473-137-3 **$15.99**; HC, ISBN 1-893361-88-8 **$21.95**

Spiritual Manifestos: Visions for Renewed Religious Life in America from Young
Spiritual Leaders of Many Faiths   *Edited by Niles Elliot Goldstein; Preface by Martin E. Marty*
6 x 9, 256 pp, HC, ISBN 1-893361-09-8 **$21.95**

A Walk with Four Spiritual Guides: Krishna, Buddha, Jesus, and Ramakrishna
by Andrew Harvey 5½ x 8½, 192 pp, 10 b/w photos & illus., Quality PB, ISBN 1-59473-138-1 **$15.99**;
HC, ISBN 1-893361-73-X **$21.95**

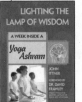

What Matters: Spiritual Nourishment for Head and Heart
by Frederick Franck 5 x 7¼, 144 pp, 50+ b/w illus., HC, ISBN 1-59473-013-X **$16.99**

Who Is My God?, 2nd Edition
An Innovative Guide to Finding Your Spiritual Identity
Created by the Editors at SkyLight Paths 6 x 9, 160 pp, Quality PB, ISBN 1-59473-014-8 **$15.99**

Spirituality—A Week Inside

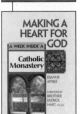

Come and Sit: A Week Inside Meditation Centers
by Marcia Z. Nelson; Foreword by Wayne Teasdale
The insider's guide to meditation in a variety of different spiritual traditions. Traveling through Buddhist, Hindu, Christian, Jewish, and Sufi traditions, this essential guide takes you to different meditation centers to meet the teachers and students and learn about the practices, demystifying the meditation experience.
6 x 9, 224 pp, b/w photographs, Quality PB, ISBN 1-893361-35-7 **$16.95**

Lighting the Lamp of Wisdom: A Week Inside a Yoga Ashram
by John Ittner; Foreword by Dr. David Frawley
This insider's guide to Hindu spiritual life takes you into a typical week of retreat inside a yoga ashram to demystify the experience and show you what to expect from your own visit. Includes a discussion of worship services, meditation and yoga classes, chanting and music, work practice, and more. 6 x 9, 192 pp, b/w photographs, Quality PB, ISBN 1-893361-52-7 **$15.95**; HC, ISBN 1-893361-37-3 **$24.95**

Making a Heart for God: A Week Inside a Catholic Monastery
by Dianne Aprile; Foreword by Brother Patrick Hart, ocso
This essential guide to experiencing life in a Catholic monastery takes you to the Abbey of Gethsemani—the Trappist monastery in Kentucky that was home to author Thomas Merton—to explore the details. "More balanced and informative than the popular *The Cloister Walk* by Kathleen Norris." —*Choice: Current Reviews for Academic Libraries*   6 x 9, 224 pp, b/w photographs, Quality PB, ISBN 1-893361-49-7 **$16.95**; HC, ISBN 1-893361-14-4 **$21.95**

Waking Up: A Week Inside a Zen Monastery
by Jack Maguire; Foreword by John Daido Loori, Roshi
An essential guide to what it's like to spend a week inside a Zen Buddhist monastery.
6 x 9, 224 pp, b/w photographs, Quality PB, ISBN 1-893361-55-1 **$16.95**;
HC, ISBN 1-893361-13-6 **$21.95**

Spiritual Poetry—The Mystic Poets

Experience these mystic poets as you never have before. Each beautiful, compact book includes: A brief introduction to the poet's time and place; a summary of the major themes of the poet's mysticism and religious tradition; essential selections from the poet's most important works; and an appreciative preface by a contemporary spiritual writer.

   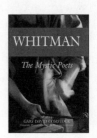

Hafiz: The Mystic Poets
Preface by Ibrahim Gamard
Hafiz is known throughout the world as Persia's greatest poet, with sales of his poems in Iran today only surpassed by those of the Qur'an itself. His probing and joyful verse speaks to people from all backgrounds who long to taste and feel divine love and experience harmony with all living things.
5 x 7¼, 144 pp, HC, ISBN 1-59473-009-1 **$16.99**

Hopkins: The Mystic Poets
Preface by Rev. Thomas Ryan, CSP
Gerard Manley Hopkins, Christian mystical poet, is beloved for his use of fresh language and startling metaphors to describe the world around him. Although his verse is lovely, beneath the surface lies a searching soul, wrestling with and yearning for God.
5 x 7¼, 112 pp, HC, ISBN 1-59473-010-5 **$16.99**

Tagore: The Mystic Poets
Preface by Swami Adiswarananda
Rabindranath Tagore is often considered the "Shakespeare" of modern India. A great mystic, Tagore was the teacher of W. B. Yeats and Robert Frost, the close friend of Albert Einstein and Mahatma Gandhi, and the winner of the Nobel Prize for Literature. This beautiful sampling of Tagore's two most important works, *The Gardener* and *Gitanjali*, offers a glimpse into his spiritual vision that has inspired people around the world.
5 x 7¼, 144 pp, HC, ISBN 1-59473-008-3 **$16.99**

Whitman: The Mystic Poets
Preface by Gary David Comstock
Walt Whitman was the most innovative and influential poet of the nineteenth century. This beautiful sampling of Whitman's most important poetry from *Leaves of Grass,* and selections from his prose writings, offers a glimpse into the spiritual side of his most radical themes— love for country, love for others, and love of Self.
5 x 7¼, 192 pp, HC, ISBN 1-59473-041-5 **$16.99**

AVAILABLE FROM BETTER BOOKSTORES.
TRY YOUR BOOKSTORE FIRST.

About SKYLIGHT PATHS Publishing

SkyLight Paths Publishing is creating a place where people of different spiritual traditions come together for challenge and inspiration, a place where we can help each other understand the mystery that lies at the heart of our existence.

Through spirituality, our religious beliefs are increasingly becoming a part of our lives—rather than *apart* from our lives. While many of us may be more interested than ever in spiritual growth, we may be less firmly planted in traditional religion. Yet, we do want to deepen our relationship to the sacred, to learn from our own as well as from other faith traditions, and to practice in new ways.

SkyLight Paths sees both believers and seekers as a community that increasingly transcends traditional boundaries of religion and denomination—people wanting to learn from each other, *walking together, finding the way.*

For your information and convenience, at the back of this book we have provided a list of other SkyLight Paths books you might find interesting and useful. They cover the following subjects:

Buddhism / Zen	Gnosticism	Mysticism
Catholicism	Hinduism /	Poetry
Children's Books	Vedanta	Prayer
Christianity	Inspiration	Religious Etiquette
Comparative	Islam / Sufism	Retirement
Religion	Judaism / Kabbalah /	Spiritual Biography
Current Events	Enneagram	Spiritual Direction
Earth-Based	Meditation	Spirituality
Spirituality	Midrash Fiction	Women's Interest
Global Spiritual	Monasticism	Worship
Perspectives		

Or phone, fax, mail or e-mail to: SKYLIGHT PATHS Publishing
Sunset Farm Offices, Route 4 • P.O. Box 237 • Woodstock, Vermont 05091
Tel: (802) 457-4000 • Fax: (802) 457-4004 • www.skylightpaths.com
Credit card orders: (800) 962-4544 (8:30AM–5:30PM ET Monday–Friday)
Generous discounts on quantity orders. SATISFACTION GUARANTEED. Prices subject to change.

**For more information about each book,
visit our website at www.skylightpaths.com**